ONE
HUNDRED
YEARS OF
STRUGGLE

WOMEN'S SUFFRAGE AND THE STRUGGLE FOR DEMOCRACY
SERIES EDITOR: VERONICA STRONG-BOAG

The story of women's struggles and victories in the pursuit of political equality is not just a matter of the past: it has the value of informing current debate about the health of democracy in our country.

This series of short, insightful books presents a history of the vote, with vivid accounts of famous and unsung suffragists and overdue explanations of why some women were banned from the ballot box until the 1940s and 1960s. More than a celebration of women's achievements in the political realm, this series provides deeper understanding of Canadian society and politics, serving as a well-timed reminder never to take political rights for granted.

Books in the series:

One Hundred Years of Struggle: The History of Women and the Vote in Canada, by Joan Sangster

Ours by Every Law of Right and Justice: Women and the Vote in the Prairie Provinces, by Sarah Carter

A Great Revolutionary Wave: Women and the Vote in British Columbia, by Lara Campbell

Our Voices Must Be Heard: Women and the Vote in Ontario, by Tarah Brookfield

To Be Equals in Our Own Country: Women and the Vote in Quebec, by Denyse Baillargeon

We Shall Persist: Women and the Vote in the Atlantic Provinces, by Heidi MacDonald

Working Tirelessly for Change: Indigenous Women and the Vote in Canada, by Lianne Leddy

JOAN SANGSTER

ONE HUNDRED YEARS OF STRUGGLE

The History of Women
and the Vote in Canada

UBCPress

VANCOUVER & TORONTO

27 26 25 24 23 22 21 20 19 18   5 4 3 2 1

Printed in Canada on FSC-certified ancient-forest-free paper
(100% post-consumer recycled) that is processed chlorine- and acid-free.

Library and Archives Canada Cataloguing in Publication

Women's suffrage and the struggle for democracy /
series editor: Veronica Strong-Boag.

Includes bibliographical references and index.
Contents: Volume 1: One hundred years of struggle :
the history of women and the vote in Canada / Joan Sangster.
Issued in print and electronic formats.
HARDCOVER : ISBN 978-0-7748-3873-3 (set). – ISBN 978-0-7748-3533-6 (v. 1)
PDF : ISBN 978-0-7748-3875-7 (set). – ISBN 978-0-7748-3535-0 (v. 1)
EPUB : ISBN 978-0-7748-3876-4 (set). – ISBN 978-0-7748-3536-7 (v. 1)
KINDLE : ISBN 978-0-7748-3537-4 (v. 1)

1. Women – Suffrage – Canada – History. 2. Suffrage – Canada – History.
3. Women – Legal status, laws, etc. – Canada – History. 4. Women –
Canada – Social conditions. 5. Suffragists – Canada – History. 6. Voting –
Canada – History. I. Strong-Boag, Veronica, 1947-, editor
II. Sangster, Joan. One hundred years of struggle

JL192.W67 2018   324.6'230971   C2017-907609-4
                                               C2017-907610-8

Canadä

UBC Press gratefully acknowledges the financial support for our publishing
program of the Government of Canada (through the Canada Book Fund),
the Canada Council for the Arts, and the British Columbia Arts Council.

Printed and bound in Canada by Friesens
Set in Gill Sans and Tundra by Artegraphica Design Co. Ltd.
Copy editor: Deborah Kerr
Proofreader: Judy Dunlop
Indexer: Judith Earnshaw
Cover and series design: Jessica Sullivan

UBC Press
The University of British Columbia
2029 West Mall
Vancouver, BC V6T 1Z2
www.ubcpress.ca

CONTENTS

SURROUNDED BY MALE CANDIDATES, suffragist Margaret Haile cut an incongruous figure when she spoke on election platforms during the 1902 Ontario provincial election. At the time, women could not vote, but Haile's decision to run for the provincial legislature was nonetheless a smart strategy. The law barred women from voting, but it did not prohibit them from *running* for office. No matter how outraged other politicians were about Haile's presence, they could not remove her name from the ballot or prevent her from speaking at election meetings. Nominated by the Canadian Socialist League as its candidate for a North Toronto riding, Haile was characterized by some commentators as a courageous advocate for women's rights, but to others she was at best a curiosity and at worst a shockingly audacious woman who abandoned her proper domestic role for the public podium.

Haile received eighty-one votes; a small group of progressive men clearly supported women's right to vote *and* to run for office. Many politicians equated her election bid with the women's suffrage movement, and prominent Toronto feminists of all political stripes supported her candidacy, but her speeches did not focus solely on rights for women. On the contrary, she saw the franchise as a means to an end, a way of challenging an unjust, inhumane, unequal society, in which the ruling elite owned, controlled, and exploited working people. What we need, she told electors in no uncertain terms, is an international socialist movement that might build a new society in which all divisions regarding sex, class, colour, creed, and nationality are eradicated.

Haile's inclusive political vision was not unusual in her day. Many suffragists had far-reaching plans for social transformation, and they sought the vote not only as a basic human right for women but also as a means of producing comprehensive change.

Still, their goals varied tremendously. Women followed diametrically different pathways to suffrage: the movement included socialists and conservatives, anti-alcohol temperance advocates and free lovers, imperialists and pacifists. Suffragists offered dissimilar rationales for why the vote mattered, both as an individual right and a social imperative. Some wanted to join the ruling class, others to abolish it. Some stressed women's innate biological and psychological distinctiveness, others emphasized the human connection and commonality between women and men. Some acted in fear of impending social decline and disorder, others in a sense of religious mission or passionate commitment to justice. Some promoted ideas that we now see as a repugnant contradiction to feminism, others glimpsed utopian visions of equality that more readily suit our views. In such diversity, feminists of the past are similar to those of the present. Far from being a politically uniform and socially cohesive group of same-thinking people, they represented a wide range of social backgrounds and ideals.

One Hundred Years of Struggle, along with the other volumes in this series, tells the story of women and the franchise in Canada, attending to the diversity of suffragists' ideals and goals as these shifted over time. Popular accounts and older academic studies, from Heritage Minutes to Catherine Cleverdon's groundbreaking *The Woman Suffrage Movement in Canada* (1950), tend to centre on famous firsts and definitive origin stories such as the Toronto Women's Literary Club or Nellie McClung's performance in the Winnipeg Mock Parliament. They focus on one organization or event, celebrate one or two leaders, categorize suffrage thinking as either maternal feminism (emanating from women's family roles) or equal rights feminism (establishing women's equality with men), or they shoehorn the movement into a "typically" Canadian politics of polite "civility," especially in contrast to the more sensational, window-breaking British suffragettes.

The political thought of Canadian suffragists was far more diverse, their activism never so tidy. The achievement of the vote is often presented as an optimistic story of the onward and upward, inevitable progress of history. In reality, multiple versions of equality, divergent strategies, and differing political visions were articulated by women and men suffragists. Moreover, the path to the ballot box included gains and losses, inclusions and exclusions, depending on where women were situated within the nation.

Over a century has passed since the audacious actions of Margaret Haile and other suffragists resulted in the extension of the vote to women. White women acquired the provincial franchise in Manitoba in 1916 and had achieved it in Saskatchewan, Alberta, British Columbia, Ontario, and Nova Scotia by 1918. New Brunswick, Prince Edward Island, and the Dominion of New-foundland followed soon after, although Quebec women did not secure the provincial vote until 1940. Ottawa passed an act in 1918 that extended the federal franchise to all British subjects, men and women, over age twenty-one, yet voting restrictions on cit-izens of Asian background and those of Indigenous ancestry were in place until 1949 and 1960, respectively.

Despite this lineage of suffrage victories, culminating in the enfranchisement of virtually all adult Canadian citizens by 1972, the vote as a symbol of democracy remains a contested concept. Feminists critique the "democratic deficit" in Canadian society, arguing that persisting economic inequalities and social prejudi-ces discourage women's political participation and skew decision making in favour of those with power and influence, thus margin-alizing many women's voices. Others are dubious about elections producing substantive social change. Recently, an old anarchist slogan from the rebellious 1960s – "Don't vote: it only encourages them" – was resurrected in popular culture. In *Revolution,* his manifesto for the twenty-first century, English comedian Russell

Brand endorses direct and participatory democracy but dismisses elections as a means of change, portraying them instead as the tired old politics of political parties jousting for power while beholden to their own self-interest, corporations, and cronyism.

Young people appear to be listening to this message, as youth voter turnout has been low in many Western countries. In Canada, only 48 percent of those aged eighteen to twenty-four voted in the 2008 federal election, and in 2011 that figure dropped to a dismal 39 percent, compared to 61 percent for all ages. The provision of campus and community centre polling stations and an energetic get-out-the-vote campaign reversed this trend in 2015; more young people, especially post-secondary students, went to the polls to vote against the Conservatives. That so many young American voters supported Bernie Sanders's campaign for the US presidential primary in 2016 also suggests their hope that the ballot might deliver substantive social change rather than the same old, same old politics.

There is solid evidence behind claims that elections are less than perfect instruments of democracy, yet Canadians have also come to see the vote as a basic human right. They, like me, would take to the streets if anyone tried to deny them this right based on gender, race, or any other form of discrimination. That contradiction between ideal and reality, between our investment in, yet disappointment with, democracy speaks to the ambiguities inherent in suffrage history. We acknowledge the vote's importance as a symbol of equality and full citizenship, as our fundamental *right* to political participation, but we recognize that it has not produced a truly equal society – far from it. The vote symbolizes inclusion but was also used as a means of exclusion; it has been manipulated by those with power, but it sometimes became an effective means of popular protest. Although it is entwined with economic power, idealists still hope it can speak truth to that power. It has been celebrated as part of Canada's history of progress, yet we should be ashamed that we denied it to racialized groups as late as 1960. Our right to cast a ballot was enshrined in our Charter of Rights and Freedoms only in 1982, yet Canadians who were in prison had to go to the Supreme Court to secure it, and citizens living outside Canada recently engaged in a new court challenge to maintain their place on the voting lists.

As a contested concept, the vote offers vital insights into Canadian social and political history. Using the knowledge accrued in nearly a half-century of feminist research into Canada's past, as well as my own ideals and sympathies, I tell the story of power, protest, and argument behind the century-long struggle for women's suffrage. The history of the vote reveals the deep fissures of inequality that transverse our society, their immense resilience, and why some groups clung adamantly to the status quo in gender relations. Opponents of women's suffrage, such as Stephen Leacock, one of the country's best-known writers and humorists, fervently believed that women should be domestic beings, that they were not capable of meaningful political debate, and that granting them the vote would seriously undermine the patriarchal (male-dominated) family and the British Empire, dragging Canada down into the mire of crass American materialism.

Yet Leacock also conceded that the movement would probably succeed. Why it did so had much to do with the energetic mobilization of the disenfranchised, who demanded their rights, made convincing arguments, developed innovative organizing tactics, and created temporary coalitions of dissimilar activists. Suffragists from differing political corners constructed alliances to win the vote, but they intended to use their new-found rights in disparate ways. Some women and men tried to employ the franchise to enhance social equality, others concentrated on lowering the barriers to women's individual success, and still others wanted to use the vote to regulate the lives of people who were deemed socially or intellectually inferior.

One Hundred Years of Struggle is an entrée to these suffrage debates, an invitation for readers to explore the topic further, as subsequent books in this series appear, and perhaps to dispute what I have presented here. Writing a national overview poses special challenges, outside of the fact that the provinces, not the federal government, determined who could vote for much of our history. One question bedevilled me: What and whom do I *leave out* of this incredibly rich, complicated story? Modern feminism did not take root in the late nineteenth century, when suffragists came of age. It germinated much earlier, within intellectual and political revolutions that raged through Europe and its colonies from the seventeenth to the nineteenth centuries, promoting new ideals of reason, secular inquiry, and human equality. The industrial revolutions of the late eighteenth and the nineteenth centuries likewise transformed class relations and women's labour inside and outside the home, and anti-colonial and anti-slavery movements questioned the "God-given," natural hierarchies of race, gender, and class that underpinned and justified nations and empires. Women may not have been the intended beneficiaries of this revolutionary thinking, but they adopted these ideals as their own. With male allies, they posed a new question: What was and should be "the condition of women"? Was their familial and social subjection natural or man-made by law and tradition? Was it just? Did women deserve an education that recognized their humanity as well as their femininity? Did their paid labour degrade and oppress them? By the late nineteenth century, the condition of women had ceased to be solely an intellectual debate: it had become multiple movements for social change. The suffragists and their various causes were only the most visible stream.

These revolutions were also global in reach. Movements to secure voting rights for women were shaped by national cultures and nation-building projects but also by the transnational circulation of ideas, people, and organizing. The agitation for women's suffrage cannot be contained strictly within Canadian borders.

Canadian suffragists were inspired especially by British, European, Antipodean (New Zealand and Australia), and American feminists; suffrage activism crossed national borders though the circulation of international suffrage newspapers, pamphlets, visiting speakers, conferences, and personal letter writing. Canadians were not powerful leaders in the international suffrage organizations, but they were in the loop politically and intellectually; they kept closely attuned to the arguments, events, and personalities of the struggle elsewhere. Their sense of international feminist solidarity was an integral part of the cultural feel of the movement, contributing to the emotional bonds that sustained women's commitment to the cause through times of hope and despair. Internationalism, of course, was not without its flaws. However idealistic, organizations such as the International Woman Suffrage Alliance were also conditioned by existing power relations and hierarchies; they found it difficult to completely shake off the national and ethnic prejudices and class divisions that pervaded world politics.

Canadian suffragists kept an eye on international events, but they collaborated most directly with women closer to home, from similar cultural, language, ethnic, and class backgrounds. Suffrage movements inevitably take on the concerns and peculiarities of their nation's history, social relations, and gender and racial ideologies. Economic crises, war, chance, contingency, and the personalities of leaders also shaped the course of each national movement. In keeping with Canada's strong regionalism, suffrage organizations were highly decentralized. Cohesive national associations were less the case in Canada than were city, regional, and provincial networks, which rose, fell, and re-emerged over decades.

There were collaborations between urban and rural, working-class and middle-class, socialist and liberal women within regions, but ideological, social, and cultural differences inevitably beleaguered the movement. Racialized women were often completely ignored. Many Indigenous women, for instance, were denied voting rights unless they were legally enfranchised under the federal Indian Act, and becoming enfranchised automatically negated their treaty rights and erased their Indian status. As a result, the very word "enfranchisement" was understood completely differently, usually quite negatively, by Indigenous women. Language also divided the movement. Quebec women reformers and suffragists concentrated their efforts in either anglophone organizations, such as the Montreal Local Council of Women, or francophone ones, primarily the Fédération nationale Saint-Jean-Baptiste. English- and French-speaking feminists made important efforts at mutual accommodation, building bi-cultural organizations, but language, religion, and culture inevitably created two solitudes of suffrage struggle in Quebec.

These fractures within the movement remind us that suffrage is not easily separated from the complex history of major social divisions in Canadian society relating to ethnicity, race, colonialism, and class. Moreover, suffrage was only one component in the larger history of feminism. The suffrage movement can be imagined as a circle of ideas and people that sits within two other social movement circles. The inner circle was comprised of individuals who campaigned specifically for the vote. They believed in women's basic humanity and equality with men, even if some saw women's roles and capabilities as inherently and intrinsically different from those of men. Some wanted to go further, freeing women from their traditional, limiting roles, expanding their intellectual and social lives as much as their political ones. I often refer to these suffragists as "feminists," although the word was first claimed during the 1910s by an elite group of British and American avant-garde radical, non-conformist, individualist women and only gained more widespread popular traction in Canada during the 1920s. Still, "feminism" seems an appropriate label: in our day, the word stands for individual autonomy and self-determination, human equality, and social justice for the oppressed, concepts that found succour in the suffrage movement.

The campaign for the vote was surrounded by a second circle of activism: the women's social reform movement. Its proponents were not focused so resolutely on women's equality, though they did endorse ideas about change that drew on women's gender-specific insights, abilities, and social worth. They were increasingly drawn to suffrage as a means to secure reforms to improve the lives of women, children, and families. Beyond the second circle was a much larger and more politically diffuse one that could be called the "women's movement" (confusing, I know, since the word is usually equated with feminism today), at that time comprised of many women's clubs, organizations, and religious, reform, and suffrage groups, all of which mobilized women on the basis of gender, all of which celebrated their special capabilities and perspectives. Their goals ranged from philanthropy that did not challenge the status quo to social reforms that did. The boundaries between these three overlapping circles of activism – suffrage, social reform, and the women's movement – were fluid, as women moved from one cause to another or embraced multiple goals. Some women's views shifted significantly over their lifetimes and as new ideas and events challenged their thinking.

We tend to know far more about middle-class suffragists, such as Nellie McClung, whose popular writing, autobiographical self-presentation, public speaking, and political involvement, including after the vote, ensured her place in history. Revisionist histories, penned under the influence of second-wave feminism, such as Carol Bacchi's *Liberation Deferred? The Ideas of the English-Canadian Suffragists, 1877–1918* (1983), were highly critical of these suffragists' motives, even questioning their feminist credentials. Although I take this critique into account, I attempt to widen the parameters of suffrage history, adding significant but lesser-known women who tackled the question of social inequality from different angles than reformers like McClung. How, for example, did race influence who could or could not vote in the nineteenth century? The story of one of Canada's pioneer advocates for women's rights, Mary Ann Shadd Cary, an African Canadian teacher and founder of a remarkable anti-slavery newspaper, the *Provincial Freeman,* contains some answers.

Shadd Cary's endorsement of women's rights as early as 1852 also underscores the importance of stretching out the chronology of suffrage history, too often pressed only into the period from the 1880s to 1918. Tracing the roots of suffrage history to the early nineteenth century raises another question: Why was property holding a key issue in nineteenth-century debates about suffrage for both men and women? Extending the focus beyond 1918 allows us to ask what happened to suffragists after many secured the vote through the federal "Act to Confer the Electoral Franchise upon Women." Why did political commentators assume that the struggle was over and done with, yet many feminists claimed it was only just beginning? Also, was the 1940 provincial enfranchisement of Quebec women evidence that they were political outliers in Canada, or should we compare their struggle to that of women in European countries such as France? Why were all Indigenous people not included in the electorate until 1960?

Exploring the diversity of feminist ideas behind suffrage is intrinsic to a more expansive definition of suffrage history. Nineteenth-century socialist debates about the "woman question" – or women's inequality – predated the emergence of many suffrage organizations. How did socialist writing about feminism shape the ideas of Francis Marion Beynon, a Prairie journalist, advocate of farm women, and suffragist whose passionate opposition to the First World War brought her into conflict with more conservative suffragists and led to her self-exile from Canada? Why do we know so little about Margret Benedictsson, an Icelandic immigrant who transplanted radical feminist ideas about the family, welfare, women's work, and "free thought" (challenging Christianity) into her editorship of the longest-running pro-suffrage newspaper in Canada, *Freyja* (Woman)?

Nellie McClung, Francis Marion Beynon, and Margret Benedicts-son all lived in Winnipeg, Manitoba. They were united on the need to face down anti-suffragists who peddled patriarchal and misogynist ideas that denigrated women as inferior and denied them the vote; they respected each other; they sometimes collaborated politically. They also came to disagree on key feminist issues. This trio of Winnipeggers symbolizes how dreams of equality have occasionally drawn feminists together in pursuit of a common goal, though the differences separating women never entirely disappear. It is these complicated relationships, inequalities, and ideological differences, along with how women interpret and negotiate them, that makes suffrage history so fascinating, vital, and pertinent to current feminist debates.

Our definitions of emancipation and the issues that we see as important are light years away from those of suffragists a century ago, who responded to feminism and anti-feminism by both using and challenging the knowledge and convictions of their time. The history of the vote, characterized by setbacks as well as advances, unforeseen consequences, and ideals both realized and co-opted, is nonetheless a sobering reminder that we should never rest on our legal laurels, which are always fragile, limited, and in need of reflective re-evaluation. Contemporary feminist concepts may help us understand power and privilege, oppression and exploitation better than earlier suffragists; however, the misuse of power and the inequality of privilege they identified remain at the heart of feminist critiques. The issues that suffragists glimpsed but could not conquer – the despotism of violence, the irrationality of wealth inequality, and the tyrannical domination of the powerful – remain just as pressing today as they were in the past, and we have much to learn from their struggles.

"It was true that neither money nor the possession of property was conclusive evidence of a person possessing brains ... but it was the best security they could get that a person having gathered around him some property would not be likely to wish to see the laws and the institutions of the country disregarded ... [Male voters should have an economic or propertied] stake-in-the country."

ATTORNEY GENERAL OF NEW BRUNSWICK, 1855

THE PRIVILEGE OF PROPERTY

Julie Papineau, wife of Louis-Joseph Papineau,
and their daughter Ézilda, 1836. Although his mother,
Rosalie, once voted, Louis-Joseph Papineau did not favour
women's suffrage. His wife and daughter represent more
affluent women of influence in colonial Canada.

ROSALIE PAPINEAU, mother of Louis-Joseph Papineau, the famed Patriot leader of the 1837 rebellion, voted in a Lower Canada (Quebec) election in 1809. Not surprisingly, she voted for her son. Yet Louis-Joseph Papineau later offered his enthusiastic support to a bill, first adopted in Lower Canada in 1834 and confirmed in the laws of the Province of Canada in 1849, that removed all women's right to vote. His wife and daughter, he believed, should be protected from the immodesty of public display in elections, guaranteed their rightful place in the privacy of the family. It was odious, he wrote, to see women "dragged up to hustings [platforms where voting took place] by their husbands, girls by their fathers, often against their will. The public interest, decency and modesty require that these scandals cease."

There is no evidence of women being dragged to the polls, and indeed some intrepid women did attempt to vote during the colonial period. Seven rural widows (one of them Laura Secord's daughter) cast ballots in 1844 in Halton, Canada West (present-day Ontario), though their votes for the conservative candidate were immediately contested. In New Brunswick and Nova Scotia, some women also endeavoured to exercise their rights as eligible property holders. The colonial constitutions of Nova Scotia and Upper and Lower Canada (1791) were somewhat ambiguous on the question of the franchise, since they listed the rights of "persons," without differentiating between men and women. That was precisely the ambiguity that Louis-Joseph Papineau and his fellow politicians sought to correct.

The few women who strove to vote were part of an already limited electorate. White, male settlers in the Canadian colonies began casting "viva voce" ballots (by raising their hands or shouting out) in the mid-eighteenth century, but differences of race, religion, profession, or class regularly excluded significant groups: at one time or another, Quakers, Roman Catholics, African Canadians, new immigrants, the poor, workers without property, "lunatics," criminals, Doukhobors, Hutterites, and Aboriginal people were all denied the ballot. Rationales for exclusion varied with the group, over time, and in each specific colony or province. Although a few individuals (such as judges) were barred because they had government-funded jobs, most were excluded because they were seen as incompetent, incapable, or even as undeserving of the vote. They were imagined as second-class citizens: akin to children, irrational, not loyal to the British Crown, illiterate, and lacking the mental capacity to make decisions, or more often, lacking the required stake in the community signified by their ownership of property.

The inclusion of groups was never a steady and sure process of ever-increasing enlightenment. In each colony, and later province, the widening of the vote was intermittent and piecemeal, with some groups included, excluded, and included again. Nor did inclusion always flow from a commitment to equality and democratic rights. Still, the denial of the franchise to women, half the population, needs particular explanation. Why, given that so few women actually tried to vote, did governments in British North America feel the need to pass legislation barring them from doing so? Did women find other means of expressing their political views?

COLONIAL AND NINETEENTH-CENTURY VOTING

Representative assemblies – the precursor to today's parliamentary institutions – were first established in Canadian colonies such as Lower Canada, Upper Canada (Ontario), Nova Scotia, New Brunswick, Prince Edward Island, and British Columbia in the eighteenth and nineteenth centuries: the first was in Nova Scotia in 1758, Ontario's in 1792, and British Columbia's in 1856. Rules on voter eligibility were borrowed from Britain. Men took an oath of allegiance to the Protestant monarchy, a requirement that automatically excluded Catholics and Jacobites (who did not support the Hanoverian rulers); state oaths compelling voters to "swear" and to be loyal to Christianity also barred Quakers and Jews respectively.

The Quebec Act (1772) exempted Catholics from such requirements, and by 1847, when Canada's colonial assemblies could finally determine their own voting rules, these religious exclusions were generally abandoned. *The Franchise and Politics in British North America,* a classic history of the franchise by John Garner, downplayed colonial-era restrictions as minor, noting that "no numerous and important segment of the population was excluded" from voting. Although the percentage of the voting male population increased significantly over time, moving toward universal manhood suffrage by 1921 (in fact, a vote for all white men), exclusions were hardly insignificant. They reveal the political ideas and economic relations that moulded the nation and how compromised the concept of citizenship was in our history. Although I focus on women and the vote, all exclusions are important, for they set the context for women's suffrage: namely, a society fractured by divisions of race, religion, and class, as well as gender. These interconnected circuits of power also shaped how, when, and why certain women secured the vote.

Political debates in the early nineteenth century, however, centred far less on barring voters than on whether representative government should be replaced by responsible government, with cabinets no longer appointed by an executive or the governor, but instead responsible to the majority in the legislature. After the rebellions of 1837 in Lower and Upper Canada, and the granting of responsible government by 1849, many men hoped that their vote would entail a more direct stake in government decisions. By the mid-nineteenth century, voting was also becoming a party affair, with ballots increasingly cast based on party platforms.

Voting rights were also connected to British efforts to establish imperial ownership of Aboriginal land and as an inducement for white settlement. In British Columbia, incorporated initially as a fur-trading post, the British instructed their appointed governor to hold an election in 1856. The idea that the majority of its residents, the First Nations, might vote was never entertained and was purposely precluded by the British definition of property qualifications. Forty white men participated (including absentee landlords, who could vote through an agent), producing an assembly with seven representatives. However absurd this exercise seemed, it spelled the future: cheap land and voting rights for white male settlers (though initially excluding the rough-and-tumble transient gold miners) were intended to ensure a white-dominated settlement geared toward the economic development of land and resources.

Voting rules were shaped by both the common law (established traditions of British law) and legislated law (through legislatures and Parliament), though Quebec was also governed by elements of the old French civil law. Only rarely were the courts dragged into interpretations of the franchise, although voting practices often skirted or contradicted any notion of democratic process. In the colonial period, administrators appointed by the British government could literally make or break an election outcome. In 1841, when the vote decided the union of Upper and Lower Canada, the governor general, Lord Sydenham, controlled so many aspects of the election – rearranging constituencies, choosing candidates, flashing the bait of government money, and firing officials – that any notion of democratic choice was ludicrous.

Voters might also be denied the opportunity to cast a ballot simply because of logistics, as was made clear by one inaccessible polling booth that served a vast rural nineteenth-century constituency with few roads. Canada's wild election practices in the nineteenth century would shock even today's jaded voter. Election dates differed from one constituency to another, allowing politicians to use success in one constituency to pressure voters elsewhere, and voting was a public affair until legislation from the mid-nineteenth century onward introduced the secret ballot. New Brunswick led the way in this regard in 1855, but before that, and even afterward (until Canadian legislation in 1874), voting lasted for days and occurred in public spaces, where your friends, neighbours, opponents, and anyone who might want to buy your vote with a few drinks could hear you name your choice. Fake voters were sometimes imported from other constituencies, even from the United States, and intimidation, hired thugs, and bribes were routine. Liquor often flowed freely. The results were skirmishes, police and army interventions, occasional riots, and even deaths: one count in the period before 1867 put the death toll at twenty.

Such deficiencies had their defenders. An Ontario politician denounced the secret ballot in 1831 as a terrible invention, a disreputable "sneaking system" that hid the identity of political participants. The open verbal casting of ballots, he suggested, was more British, more imperial, more manly. Presumably, facing down thugs and bribes was the stuff of which nineteenth-century masculinity was made. Corrupt election practices did not simply disappear after the secret ballot was introduced. Both Liberals and Conservatives bribed voters with patronage and liquor, and corruption was notoriously difficult to prove. When Sir John A. Macdonald, a consummate expert in such methods, won his Kingston riding by only thirty-seven votes in 1874, he faced a legal petition demanding that the election be voided due to corruption. Witnesses who testified for him during the subsequent trial had remarkably sudden lapses of memory, protecting him despite the decisive evidence that treating with free liquor had bought votes.

The fact that elections were public, raucous, and occasionally dangerous was a key rationale for excluding women, at least respectable, virtuous ones, who should not have to endure the swearing, intimidation, and violence that male voters encountered. Unusual incidences of women voting often became public knowledge when politicians claimed their unscrupulous opponents were manipulating the vote of the so-called weaker sex for political gain. When women voted in the highly contentious 1840 election in Amherst Township and again in Annapolis County, Nova Scotia, their participation produced a public hullaballoo. One party member scornfully commented on his opponent's use of female votes in Annapolis: "I rode down to Annapolis Town to see what was going [on] in the enemy's camp, and lo and behold, what did I find the Tories there up to? Getting all the old women and old maids, and everything in the shape of petticoats to be carried to the hustings the next and last day to vote for" their candidate. Not to be outdone, this observer rode all day and night to encourage *his* supporters to use the very same tactic of enlisting women to vote against the Tories. Women were assumed to be obedient and malleable family members rather than thinking individuals, voting as their menfolk told them to in this tit-for-tat electoral strategy.

Surviving poll books (ledgers recording who voted and for whom) identify even more significant numbers of women who voted in provincial and municipal elections in Lower Canada. In Montreal's tumultuous and violent election of 1832, women property owners made up 14 percent of the electorate, the highest percentage recorded in nineteenth-century Quebec, and likely a reflection of the strong property rights of widows under Quebec's distinct legal regime. The credentials of some single women (less so widows) were publicly challenged, but they braved these intimidating tactics at the hustings day after day, a testament to their courage and strong convictions.

Aspiring female voters attracted attention. Hostile newspapers questioned their virtue and dismissed them as "incompetents" who should be classed with non-voters such as "cripples, the elderly and infirm." In 1832, the mayor of Montreal travelled the city, making a note of every female elector, her choice, and whether she cast a ballot at a crucial moment in the contest. His assiduous collection of evidence may have been the precipitating spark that prompted the Lower Canada legislature to propose the bill that denied the franchise to all women. Other provincial legislatures such as those of Ontario and Nova Scotia acted with similar dispatch in the mid-nineteenth century to legally dis-enfranchise women lest they try to exercise their voting rights as eligible property holders. Although female voting had always been extremely limited and tenuous, by 1849 it was officially pro-scribed with laws that reaffirmed the electoral process as the preserve of men.

The Quebec law banning women voters was uncontroversial, opposed by no party or legislator. Defending this decision, Louis-Joseph Papineau explained that women's interests were encom-passed within the patriarchal family, already represented by its male head. Besides, rowdy public election rituals would morally disrupt women's proper place in the domestic privacy of the family and endanger their morality. Politicians claimed that the new laws were intended to avoid the easy manipulation of impressionable female voters, but larger social forces were at work. As Quebec historian Allan Greer argues in *Patriots and the People*, politics were being redefined, or "remasculinized," in the mid-nineteenth century, in keeping with emerging Victorian ideals of masculinity and femininity, which valued a more rigid separation of the public and private spheres for men and women. The legal expulsion of women from the public sphere may seem a contradiction to eighteenth-century Enlightenment ideals about the rational nature of man and the inherent rights of the people, or mankind, to govern themselves. The 1837 rebellion in Lower Canada came on the heels of European revolutions and uprisings, including the French Revolution, inspired in part by such Enlightenment and republican ideas. But radical Enlightenment thinkers were not egalitarian as we understand the word, perceiving all people to be equal. (After all, in the United States, a republican revolution and a new Constitution did not abolish the ownership of slaves.) On the contrary, Jean-Jacques Rousseau, a key Enlightenment philosopher, defended distinct roles for men and women: men were best suited for "the responsibilities of citizenship" and women for the domain of "family, childbirth and nurturing."

Women's assertion of their own intellectual and political equality was discordant to male advocates of revolution and reform. The efforts of even a few women to affirm their democratic rights loomed as a disturbing sign of sexual disorder, a threat to the patriarchal family, and an invitation to political corruption and debauchery. On the eve of the 1837 rebellion in Lower Canada, "Adelaide" wrote to the newspaper *La Minerve,* declaring her support for this French Canadian nationalist cause, as she believed the Patriots would protect the French civil code custom of equality in the marriage contract (as opposed to English common law). Her courageous call for equality, however, was out of step with the times. Sexual equality was not an apt description of marriage in Lower Canada, and more importantly, neither the republican Patriots nor their loyalist opponents supported women's equal political rights. Enlightenment principles of human rationality, equality, and the inherent right of the people to self-govern were applied in highly circumscribed ways, even to white men. Enlightenment ideals nonetheless remained deeply compelling for groups who lacked rights, who were shut out of the democratic process. Their claims on equality and democracy would reappear, again and again, not only during the suffrage debates but also in other social movements for racial, sexual, and economic equality in the future.

POLITICAL INFLUENCE WITHOUT THE VOTE

Women in colonial Canada may have lacked the vote, but beliefs about gender were interwoven with political debate, and women of all classes cultivated innovative strategies to influence political life. Ideals of femininity and masculinity were highly relevant to political arguments, to notions of good government, and even to the symbolic visual display of newspaper cartoons. As historians of Upper Canada Bryan Palmer and Cecilia Morgan show, political discussions were deeply imbued with recurring metaphors of gender, family, and sexuality. The young colony was structured around assumptions of patriarchal and paternal (father-headed) relationships, stretching from the family to the highest levels of government. Both rebellious Reformers, who wanted responsible government, and their Tory opponents, who did not, equated the rule of the governing elites with the rightful patriarchal dominance of men and fathers in society. Political satire often incorporated gendered images, linking men with rationality, women with irrationality. In Upper Canada, one satirical article mocks a hysterical, badly informed person as "Mrs. Slipshod" and designates the rational, independent politician as "Mr. Canada." In cartoons, countries and politicians who were perceived to be weak or passive were sometimes portrayed as women, whether old and infirm or young and seductively impressionable, whereas more assertive and aggressive nations and politicians were powerful men, towering over them.

Women also intervened directly in political struggles. Some aired their views in journals (under their own names or pseudonyms); others worked behind the scenes, lobbying kin, friends, and social connections on behalf of chosen causes; and still others took part in "common people's politics," in the fields, streets, and shared spaces that were associated with labouring and poor men and women. Two disparate examples from Prince Edward Island highlight the range of women's political activities in one colony, one woman supporting rebellion and reform, the other protecting the elite and status quo.

Prince Edward Island secured an elected assembly in 1773, and by the nineteenth century, one issue increasingly dominated its attention: absentee British landlords who held massive tracts of its real estate. The British monarchy gave large gifts of Crown land to favoured aristocrats, some of whom never set foot on the island, never fulfilled their obligations to develop the property with settlers, and therefore had difficulty paying their "quit rent" or taxes to the Crown. Tenant farmers, who could barely scrape together the money to pay their rent to such landlords, organized an Escheat movement in opposition to the absentee landlords (escheat meant having the Crown reclaim the land). Farmers organized petitions, rent strikes, and public meetings; one goal was the election of sympathetic Escheat candidates to the legislative assembly so that it might force the sale of unused land to tenant farmers.

Women were an important part of these protests, often at the forefront of local resistance. When landlords' agents arrived with law enforcement officers to collect the rent, remove farmers' property, or evict them, women defended their own homes and combined with neighbours to disrupt tax collecting and expulsions. In 1833, a visibly pregnant farmer, Isabella Macdonald, led a rebellious group against a nervous official, Constable Donald McVarish, who had come to collect the rent. The constable aimed his pistol directly at Isabella, who turned out to be

POTASH BOILING

This image captures the lives of poor, rural women such as Isabella Macdonald: incessant toil was their lot. C.W. Jefferys's iconic sketches of colonial life were printed in school texts; this one was later used by feminists to symbolize the unrecognized work of pioneer women.

just as dangerous a target as the male farmers in the crowd. Wielding a board as her weapon, she and her supporters disarmed McVarish and sent him packing. Perhaps one reason why women were in the vanguard of these community protests, suggests historian Rusty Bitterman, was the perception that their presence might dissuade middle-class law enforcement officers from making arrests, though it did not succeed in Isabella's case. She was tried in court for assault, and though found guilty, she was pardoned by the governor, given the "advanced condition" of her pregnancy.

Women were often at the fore of such popular protests across Europe and North America. They demonstrated alongside men to demand bread, wages, land, and even revolution; they also organized spontaneous collective resistance to crises such as food shortages, which spoke directly to their everyday domestic labour. In the farming context of Prince Edward Island, their spirited activism was probably shaped by their family and economic roles. Work on poorer farms was shared equally between men and women; men regularly left home to earn wages, leaving women in charge; and one-room houses prohibited any notion of a protected, domestic private sphere for women.

Isabella Macdonald fought for subsistence and survival. Charlotte Sulivan, a British absentee landlord, struggled to protect her PEI property and upper-class privilege from the Escheat movement. Like other "lady landlords," Sulivan inherited her 66,000-acre estate from male relatives. According to British law, women who brought property *into* a marriage might continue to manage it, though only if their legal marriage contract allowed this. Also, if a man died without a male heir, his widow could inherit his estate, as could his sisters and daughters, if they were unmarried. These upper-class "lady landlords," accustomed to a world in which social position and wealth gave them backroom access to power, became involved in island politics to defend their property.

The PEI legislature tried to secure British approval for a law to end absentee landlordism by having the Crown sell off disputed property, but Sulivan fought back with all the legal tools she could muster. She was a formidable, unshakeable lobbyist on her own behalf, much to the astonishment of the British Colonial Office in London. It tried to coax her into selling by appealing to her "charitable" (perhaps womanly) instincts, and when that failed, it turned to veiled threats, though that too was a losing battle. Undeterred, even after land reform legislation was approved in 1875, Sulivan instructed her lawyer to take her cause to the Supreme Court of Canada, despite the fact that it was virtually unknown for a woman to do so. She lost her case, but her political efforts, extending from private lobbying to public legal pressure, show that women who lacked voting rights nonetheless deployed whatever strategies they could to influence political life.

PROPERTY AND THE VOTE

Isabella and Charlotte, two women who were so very different in class and status, symbolize a fundamental aspect of the history of the vote: the importance of property and wealth in defining the electorate. In colonial Canada, and even after Confederation in 1867, the right to vote was linked to the ownership of property, either as land, savings, or through payment of a certain level of rent, though exact amounts differed across urban and rural areas, and until 1885, across provinces. Whatever the Enlightenment philosophers may have said in theory, in practice some men were far more equal than others. The nineteenth-century franchise was designed not to upset the apple cart of existing social relations of power and prestige, and property holding was a key means of ensuring this.

Established, affluent men were regarded as having the most important stake in the community and were thus seen as most likely to exercise a common-sense vote. The New Brunswick attorney general conceded that "neither money nor property" was irrefutable evidence that a man "possessed brains," but they were good indicators that he would not disregard the status quo as expressed in the laws of the land. The provincial vote was a "privilege for men of independence and prosperity" whose "investment in society" was exemplified by their payment of property taxes. The average salaries of labouring men were so low that they were beyond the pale of voting rights. Governments used other legal exclusions to create an affluent electorate. In nineteenth-century Nova Scotia, for instance, anyone who received public assistance was denied the vote, a means of barring the poor from political participation. This had race as well as class implications. African Canadian Loyalist settlers were initially barred from voting for the colonial-era legislative assembly, but their marginal economic status in the nineteenth century would have produced the same result. Nova Scotia briefly introduced the radical practice of universal male suffrage as a means of stamping out rampant electoral corruption, but this experiment collapsed only nine years later, in 1863, when its legislature returned to the more common property-based franchise.

During the 1837 rebellions, and later in the nineteenth century, a few radical voices called for a vote for all adult men. Quebec's Parti Rouge, loyal to egalitarian Enlightenment thought, was one of these. But defenders of the property qualification were far more powerful. The debates about the franchise during the lead-up to Confederation show that wealth, social standing, and class were fundamental to the evolution of the state. All representatives at the Quebec pre-Confederation meeting in 1865 rejected universal male suffrage. Liberals and Conservatives alike stressed property qualifications as a check on the dreadful prospect of unrestrained mob rule. Neither a strictly liberal nor a conservative order was promoted; politicians drew on philosophical ideals from both traditions to justify their emphasis on property and affluence as a prerequisite for the vote.

Sir John A. Macdonald, probably the most feted Father of Confederation, declared that "there is no inalienable right in any man to exercise the franchise." He believed that the electorate should be as restricted as possible, with the "ascendency of property" safeguarded. Macdonald is famous for his revealing quip that "minority" rights – that is, the rights of the rich – needed protecting. His French Canadian counterpart, George-Étienne Cartier, likewise warned that the "unbridled democracy" of universal suffrage lay behind the "sad spectacle of civil war" in the United States. Universal manhood suffrage, he cautioned, would usher in "mob rule": "disorder, anarchy, war and annexation" to the United States would result if this radical idea were implemented in Canada. Although the emphasis on property was elitist, it potentially gave *some* women an opening to demand suffrage rights. If possessing property were the most important mark of a citizen's stake in society, why did it matter whether a woman or a man owned it? Landowning did in fact become a foot-in-the-door for suffragists, who claimed some sporadic, small victories by the turn of the century as some municipalities gave single and widowed female property owners the right to vote for city councils and school boards.

New labour associations representing working men and women, however, voiced their opposition to such class- and property-based voting. The Knights of Labor, founded in 1869 and dedicated to organizing all workers irrespective of gender, skill, or religion, endorsed universal suffrage for both women and men instead of a male, property-based franchise. A social movement as much as a trade union, the Knights used unique methods, including grassroots community mobilization, cultural events, workplace unions, and participation in elections, to promote its distinctive vision of working-class dignity and solidarity. According to the Knights, all workers who produced the wealth of society, including women, merited social respect and equality; all should receive a fair wage for their daily labour. These appealing principles drew thousands of members into the Knights' democratically organized city and workplace assemblies across Ontario, the Prairies, and in Montreal, though racist antagonism to Chinese workers produced a narrow, white-only organization in British Columbia.

The Knights' insistence on the worth and dignity of all working people encouraged a wider debate about gender equality. One of the group's ritual pledges was to uphold "equal pay for equal work" wherever women were employed. Knights of Labor journalist Phillips Thompson used his pen to promote the idea that women had the right "to be regarded in all matters of citizenship and all relations between the government and the people as the equal of men." How could any clear-sighted labour reform movement think otherwise? he asked. Whereas the Knights expressed a chivalrous, Victorian desire to protect pure and virtuous women, its female members insisted on the dignity of working-class women's labour and their right to fair compensation and protection from sexual harassment. Katie McVicar, who began work as a teenager in a Hamilton shoe factory, was an impassioned advocate of working women's empowerment through their collective mobilization under the Knights banner. Organization was the only hope of working women, she wrote, and not just for factory operatives like herself but also for clerical and especially domestic workers, the latter the most "underpaid" and "underfed drudges" in the labour force. The Knights' enticing message for women, linking respectable femininity and working-class solidarity, resulted in the creation of at least eight all-female assemblies across Ontario, with Katie McVicar elected the first "directoress" of the Hamilton women's Excelsior Assembly.

McVicar's early death cut short her advocacy, but the Knights, in any case, faded away by the 1890s, supplanted by the Canadian Labour Congress, which was dominated by craft-based (skilled) unions, with predominantly male memberships and a more limited political vision. At its founding convention in 1883, the congress endorsed universal manhood suffrage and protested property qualifications for the municipal vote. But it did not demand the franchise for women, which demonstrates that the cause of women's equality was never straightforwardly progressive and expansive. Some skilled working-class leaders were incorporated into the Liberal and Conservative Parties, persuaded that it was in their economic interest to support John A. Macdonald in exchange for the Tories' partial legalization of trade unions in 1872 and commitment to jobs in the manufacturing sector. Skilled male workers also cultivated their identity as respectable, white, "free-born Englishmen," a self-definition that implied political equality with other men but not with women, and their unions increasingly advocated for a "male breadwinner" wage, used to support wives ensconced in the domestic sphere – an ideal shared by many working-class women.

Alliances between ruling elites and working people, however, are always subject to change. Nineteenth-century working-class leaders could repudiate the Liberals and Conservatives if they denigrated or resisted working men's demands for democratic rights. When a well-heeled Ontario Liberal legislator lobbied to alter the municipal property qualification for the franchise, giving multiple votes to men with more property, working-class men protested in horror. His rationale for abandoning the principle of one man, one vote, was simple: propertied men should assume their superior, *rightful* role in directing politics. The vote, in other words, was perceived to be one instrument in a struggle that entailed far more than casting a ballot on election day: it was a means to class power.

Issues of status, class, affluence, and social control were not limited to the colonial period and the nineteenth century. They resurface through the history of suffrage – and still do. As we shall see in the next few chapters, they were central to arguments about the 1885 franchise bill, they shaped socialists' arguments for women's suffrage, and they were integral to some suffragists' rationale for the right to vote.

Some Men foolishly deny to Woman the right to speak in public, to practice medicine, to vote. [The question is] ... has she anything to say? Does she say it with propriety? Does she mount the platform at the expense of the duties she owes her family?

MARY ANN SHADD CARY, "WOMAN'S RIGHTS,"

PROVINCIAL FREEMAN, 12 AUGUST 1854

To give the franchise to women would interfere with their proper position ... It would be a burden instead of a benefit to them. This, I believe, to be exactly the case as regards the Indian. What idea has the Indian of our constitution, our government? How is it possible for the Indian to understand our system of government so that he may be able to exercise in an intelligent manner the right to vote?

MR. FAIRBANK, CANADA,

HOUSE OF COMMONS DEBATES, 2 MAY 1885

TWO

RACE AND THE IDEA
OF RIGHTS FOR WOMEN

A feminist anti-slavery advocate,
Mary Ann Shadd Cary contemplated the question
of women's rights decades before suffrage
organizations were formed.

BORN IN 1823 to a free black family in Delaware, Mary Ann Shadd grew up immersed in abolitionist politics. Her father was a well-known anti-slavery activist, and she was educated by Quakers – often abolitionists – after the family moved to Philadelphia. She subsequently taught school in New York City for ten years, working in the poorly funded, segregated black school system before moving to Canada in 1851. Like her father, she embraced middle-class ideas about racial uplift for blacks, but rather than simply demanding that they pull themselves up by their bootstraps, she stressed their right to "education, moral refinement and economic self sufficiency." She also contended that self-organization and the political unity of her fellow African Canadians were the means of challenging the institution of slavery and white racial superiority.

Mary Ann Shadd became a formidable force in the black community of Ontario (then called Canada West): she advocated tirelessly for primary education for black students and founded her own anti-slavery newspaper in 1853, the *Provincial Freeman,* which also discussed women's rights. Although the beginnings of Canadian feminism are often attributed to organizations such as the Toronto Women's Literary Club of 1877, they were preceded not only by similar women's literary societies founded by African Canadians in southwestern Ontario but also by Shadd's courageous newspaper, which commented on women's right to work, education, and political speech in the context of abolitionism.

Race and racial identity, which are cultural constructs rather than biological realities, were central to the history of suffrage.

For example, African Canadians could officially vote in Canada if they satisfied the property requirement, but African Americans were barred from doing so in the pre–Civil War United States. Aboriginal people were sometimes specifically excluded from the franchise, and British Columbia had its own racial prohibitions, denying some citizens of Asian heritage the vote until 1949. Race-based arguments for either granting or withholding the franchise were intertwined with conceptions of gender, culture, and economic status, though they become especially visible during flashpoints of intense debate: for example, surrounding mid-nineteenth-century anti-slavery politics or during the 1885 parliamentary dispute regarding a new franchise act.

MARY ANN SHADD CARY AND AFRICAN CANADIAN POLITICS

The nineteenth-century American women's suffrage movement was closely connected to abolitionism. Before the American Civil War (1861–65), many white women who were involved in anti-slavery causes enlarged their agenda to include votes for women as well as African Americans, and some black female abolitionists warmed to feminist ideas, articulating a comprehensive vision of gender and racial equality. The public culture of African American life in the mid-nineteenth century was immersed in its own debates about the condition of women, as political activists wrestled with questions about women's proper place in the family, community, church, and other institutions. Whether they came as refugee slaves or as freewomen, African American immigrants to Canada brought these new ideas about women's responsibilities and rights with them.

Although slavery existed in colonial Canada, it did not flourish economically as it did in the United States, and in 1793, Britain halted the importation of slaves and entirely disallowed slaveholding in 1833. African Americans came to Canada as part of the United Empire Loyalist migrations that were prompted by the

American War of Independence in 1783 and, later, as refugees and opponents of slavery; black settlements were founded in Nova Scotia, as they were in Canada West, near Toronto and the southwestern vicinity of Windsor, Chatham, and Buxton. African Americans debated whether emigration to Canada or to Africa was preferable to organizing for freedom in the United States; however, the 1850 US Fugitive Slave Act, which gave slave owners total impunity to hunt down and recapture blacks whom they claimed as their own, shifted the political landscape. This arbitrary, draconian law unleashed a new torrent of anti-black violence and intensified abolitionists' despair about ending slavery, leading to renewed migrations of blacks across the 49th parallel to Canada. Mary Ann Shadd was among them.

She first moved to Toronto and then, in 1851, to the Windsor area, where she used her teaching credentials to open a school. She immediately became embroiled in the debates about black emigration, settlement, and education in Canada West. Two years after her arrival, she published a pamphlet titled *A Plea for Emigration; or Notes of Canada West* (1852), in which she extolled the merits of British North America as a new home for American blacks. True to her middle-class background, she assumed that African Canadians who embraced hard work, thrift, and independence could successfully put down new roots, but she was also aware of the limitations of her adopted country. She believed strongly in integrated, mixed-race education, not segregated or "caste" schools for black children only, but she soon realized that institutionalized racism in Canada West militated against integrated schools. On black settlements, Shadd rejected schemes that offered land solely to escaped slaves, not free blacks, and she criticized white missionary schemes that she claimed portrayed African Americans as incompetent and pathetic, begging for protective segregation from whites. Her strong views, penchant for political argument, and criticisms of other black abolitionists led her into direct conflict with other influential black leaders such as Henry and Mary Bibb, and their supporters in the American Missionary Society – leaving a complicated history of acrimony for historians to dissect.

Shadd did not limit her criticisms to abolitionist strategies and the nature of black identity. She condemned Christian churches that apologized for slavery and was increasingly forthright about the public role that women should play in the black liberation struggle. Choosing to focus on activism, she left teaching and established her own newspaper, the *Provincial Freeman*, in Windsor in 1853. She subsequently moved it to Toronto, hoping to reinvigorate the lagging anti-slavery movement there, but when the paper floundered financially, she returned to Windsor to edit it, where she drew on the aid of her extended family. Although she astutely enlisted a man, Samuel Ringgold Ward, a well-known, black anti-slavery advocate, as the nominal editor, she served as the actual editor and increasingly assumed public authorship of the paper's articles and editorials.

Shadd rightly saw herself as a feminist trailblazer, who "broke the Editorial Ice" in the hopes that other women could follow in her footsteps. Yet she was also trapped in a cruel contradiction for black women: they were both romanticized as extraordinarily strong slave-types (a Mammy stereotype) and caricatured as promiscuous and amoral. These constructed images were essential to the racist thinking that justified the oppression of all blacks and more specifically undermined black women's capabilities of publicly speaking, organizing, and just being. Some members of the black community believed that the solution was to adopt the prevailing Christian, Victorian white image of the family, which assumed that women were naturally physically weaker, though morally superior, and that men were destined for the public sphere of work and politics, women for the private sphere of domesticity. If black women stressed their domestic subordination, virtue, and morality, it was reasoned, black men might then "reclaim their status as honourable men."

Shadd sometimes played to this ideal, demanding that her opponents treat her like a lady, and the *Provincial Freeman* reprinted articles that counselled women on how to accept male chivalry, find an appropriate husband, and express their femininity. The domestic and familial role was often assumed to be their priority. Yet Shadd herself performed a decidedly male role, as public speaker and newspaper editor, and by doing so, she encountered exclusion, criticism, and disapprobation, even in her own community. The fact that she was verbally acidic, seldom apologetic, and not deferential to her superiors (men) made her a special target. She would have appreciated suffragist Nellie McClung's later advice to women: "Never explain, never retract, never apologize. Just get the thing done and let them howl." Whereas some male black leaders praised her, others refused even to allow her to grace their public platforms. At one such convention, they dismissed her with a sharp rebuke: "This is not a women's rights convention."

To be sure, Shadd used the *Freeman* to address women's rights at a time when almost no other newspapers did, including the black press. One article asked, given that women were allowed to nurse both men and women, why were only male doctors permitted to minister to female ailments? Other articles captured Shadd's dual commitment to both feminine propriety and female independence. "Our young women want a more vigorous, practical and useful Education," said the *Freeman*. Education should endow a woman with the means "to get her own living, to make out her own course in life, to [countenance] any position she chooses to occupy." Yet knowledge was also needed for her most important task: motherhood. In words that anticipated the later suffrage movement, the *Freeman* reminded readers that, through mothering, women "impress the mind of the next generation ... Cultivate the woman's mind and you cultivate the race."

In the *Freeman*, Shadd printed articles that described the lives of unusually independent women and lauded white feminist abolitionists such as Harriet Beecher Stowe, Lucy Stone, and the radical Angelika Grimke, whose impassioned letter advocating armed action against slavery was republished in the *Freeman*. It used satire to highlight the restrictiveness of Victorian ideals; one rather saucy column, titled "Men's Sphere," spoofed the pompous advice literature for ladies, which was invariably penned by men. Shadd raised the more concrete issue of legislated rights for women less often than education, but she did comment on legal reform. A front-page article titled "Women's Rights" praised the New York legislature for passing new laws giving wives some control over their own earnings and custody of their children. Another article, playfully titled "Can You Tell Where We Stand on Women's Rights?" explored differing political views in the women's movement, as well as some women's claims that they did not *want* new rights and would happily defer to "men's definition" of their roles. A key sentence reflected Shadd's own desire to cultivate a public role, using her talents to further the interests of both her race and gender: "Some Men foolishly deny to a Woman the right to speak in public, to practice medicine, to vote." Women might certainly have "God-given" roles as mothers, but the real question about a woman speaking in public was this: "Has she anything to say? Does she say it with propriety? Does she mount the platform at the expense of the duties she owes her family?"

Shadd encouraged her black female readers to emulate the public, political role she herself had assumed. When a timid "Henrietta" wrote to the paper in 1854, asking if it would accept the views of a woman, "Dolly Bangs," perhaps Shadd herself, replied with dispatch. Although Bangs sympathized with Henrietta's anxiety, she dismissed as sadly ridiculous the idea that a woman would have *to ask* if she could be heard. No human should tell a woman not to use her God-given talents. "Would it not be preposterous," Bangs concluded rhetorically, to ask the same of a man?

Shadd must have struggled with the questions she raised about women's proper roles when she too became a mother, marrying a widower with children, barber Thomas Cary in 1856, and giving birth to two children of their own. When Thomas died prematurely in 1860, she was left a young widow with children to support, but she did not abandon her causes. She closed down the *Provincial Freeman* and returned to the United States, where she worked as a recruiter for the Union army during the Civil War. With high hopes for post-war Reconstruction, she moved to Washington, taught school, and attended law school, earning her law degree at sixty.

After leaving Canada West, Shadd continued to advocate for both African American and women's rights. Unlike many black women, she supported the National Woman Suffrage Association in the United States and took part in an 1874 feminist campaign of civil disobedience, when sixty-three women attempted to register as voters. She also testified before the House Judiciary Committee in favour of black voter rights, arguing that these should not be limited to men. Few black women joined her. White women's suffrage organizations increasingly employed racist arguments to support their demand for white women's enfranchisement, destroying any hope of the collaborative alliances once promoted by abolitionists. Black women's groups and newspapers in the late nineteenth century did, however, take up Shadd's attempt to produce an integrated analysis of race and gender oppression. Her unique efforts to advocate for both African Canadian and women's equality, and to link these struggles through black women's empowerment, were innovative and courageous in mid-nineteenth-century Canada. As her biographer Jane Rhodes aptly observes in *Mary Ann Shadd Cary*, she "spent her life fighting at the margins."

A DEFINING MOMENT: THE 1885 FRANCHISE ACT
In 1883, twenty-three years after Mary Ann Shadd Cary closed the doors of the *Provincial Freeman*, and sixteen years after the British colonies in Canada came together in Confederation, a Toronto suffrage group sent its first petition requesting the vote to Prime

Minister John A. Macdonald. The idea was in the air, nationally and internationally: two western US states had enfranchised women, serious discussion about legislation was under way in New Zealand, and a few Canadian municipalities had given propertied, single women a say in local matters. In 1885, two years after receiving the petition, Macdonald presented a bill to the House, which proposed common, federally defined voting criteria for the entire country and the extension of the franchise to a limited number of women and Aboriginals.

Conservative members of Parliament sat in sulky silence as they listened to Macdonald's scheme for enfranchising widows and single women – the latter called spinsters at the time – who had the requisite property qualifications. Few welcomed the idea, but some Liberals were just as unhappy. The Liberals in general wanted voter eligibility to be set by the provinces, whereas Conservatives felt that this task should fall to the federal government. Debate about enfranchising single women, however, did not divide automatically on party lines. Conservatives who favoured this reform saw the all-important distinction between the propertied and the non-propertied as more critical than gender ideology. Some Liberals supported the idea, though for different reasons: votes for women was an inevitable step in the natural march of progress; women might aid the temperance cause; and they would help to purify politics. Liberal reformer John Charlton, known for his efforts to legislate against male seduction of innocent young women, enthused that new female voters would usher in important social and moral reforms. A few MPs even questioned, in the vein of a truly expansive Enlightenment, how the vote could be given to "one half the human race but not to the other half."

Far more MPs found the idea unsettling. They feared that admitting spinster voters might be the thin edge of the wedge, opening the door to the calamity of full female suffrage, or even worse, Indigenous and Asian women showing up at the polls. One MP asked whether "squaws" and Chinese women who owned property could vote if the franchise bill were passed. If John Charlton thought the women's vote would bring virtue to Parliament, others felt that virtue belonged in the home – and should stay there. Some men had no desire to see purity and temperance intrude in the House of Commons. Opponents argued that suffrage was a slippery slope that would destabilize the family, endanger the marriage relation, and invert the God-given order of society. A Quebec MP prophesied "indescribable trouble and social disorder," and invoked the fearful memory of ungodly female insurgents in the French Revolution. Finally, they warned that the vote would masculinize women; indeed, suffragists secretly wanted to *be* men, to "wear the pantaloons." Feminists were destined never to hear the end of that argument. Given the vociferous objections, especially from Quebec MPs, Macdonald backed away from his proposal, originally floated as more of an experiment than a resolutely held principle.

Debate over an expanded Aboriginal vote was far lengthier and more heated and acrimonious. At the time, most provinces prohibited Indigenous people from voting. Ontario law excluded any person of "Indian origin or partly Indian blood" who resided on a reserve and received monies from the government (such as treaty payments). Manitoba had a similar law, though it did not necessarily exclude the Metis. British Columbia simply banned "Indians" and anyone of "Chinese origin," whereas Indians in Nova Scotia were excluded in 1854 when the legislature adopted a more comprehensive manhood suffrage, but included in 1863 when it reverted to a more limited property-based franchise. The inclusion was illusory at best: most Aboriginal people were disqualified because they did not hold the required *individual* property (as "fee simple"), but rather held property collectively on reserves (as "lease holders").

Some Indigenous leaders in Ontario (such as Peter Jones, an Ojibway minister and chief) supported inclusion in the franchise, but others (such as Six Nations leaders) did not, seeing it as an infringement on their autonomous nationhood. Reasons varied but one common fear expressed by Indigenous people was the loss of their treaty rights. The federal Indian Act allowed them to become "enfranchised" as British subjects and vote, but *only* if they gave up their Indian status, their right to live on reserves, collect treaty payments, and endow their children with Indian rights. Indian wives had no choice in the matter: if their husbands became British subjects and lost their status, they and their children did too.

Euro-Canadian patriarchal thinking shaped the creation of the nineteenth-century Indian Act, the same ideas that motivated Louis-Joseph Papineau to remove women's voting rights in Lower Canada. Rather than allowing Indigenous peoples to preserve their own forms of family organization, the Canadian state imposed Indian Act regulations that were designed to encourage a male-dominated, patriarchal family, a project in line with vigorous efforts by Christian churches to convert Aboriginal people. White women who married status Indians secured rights as Indians; Indian women who married white men lost theirs (a discriminatory clause that was not altered until 1985).

In pursuit of his cherished political goal of a truly conservative property-based franchise for the entire nation, Macdonald initially proposed that the vote be extended, with no loss of Indian status, to Aboriginal men who owned individual property and had made improvements on it. This plan married his fundamental belief in assimilation with his conservative values: he believed that the "Indian problem" would be solved if Indigenous people adopted the superior values of white civilization, exemplified by their accumulation of property. If they insisted on remaining in their traditional territory, laying claim to the communal use of the land, Macdonald's alternative solution – in the Prairie West at least – was to starve them into submission, forcing them into reserves so that white settlement could triumph.

Intersecting arguments about property, culture, gender, and race shaped parliamentarians' responses to Macdonald's proposal.

Both Liberals and Conservatives saw the assimilated, property-owning Indian as a sign of progress, unlike the "ancient, tribal" Indian, whose eligibility for treaty payments made him a dependent ward of the state. Like women, Aboriginal people were equated with incapable minors or children. Liberal MP Wilson Mills insisted that they were "dealt with by the government precisely as children are dealt with, as wards of the government, incapable of managing their own affairs." Liberals suspected that Macdonald's political motive was to create a pliant group that would be loyal to his Tory government, since childlike Indians would vote for those who looked after and "fed them," surely an ironic apprehension, given Macdonald's resolve *not* to feed starving Prairie Indians who were seen as an obstacle to white settlement. Aboriginal men were portrayed as noble primitives because of their ability to survive in the wilderness but also as symbols of a doomed way of life. White men, on the other hand, were modern, rational, educationally and intellectually advanced. There was a world of difference, MPs claimed, between Indian men who lived like "nomads" and those who owned property, "managed their own affairs," and supported their own families, all signs of manly (white) independence. Some women, whose own claim on the vote had recently been brushed aside, registered similar objections. One wrote to her MP, asking how men could question the ability of upright "women of property to exercise the franchise," contrasting them to the "vilest and most ignorant Indian and Hottentot [Indigenous person]."

Liberals and Conservatives alike rarely rose above the colonial mindset that placed Indigenous peoples lower down on the scale of social and political development. They were not seen as having the education, ability, experience, or inclination to engage in politics, and entrusting them with the vote would "degrade" British parliamentary traditions. MPs spoke hopefully of a future in which they would be "trained up" to equal whites. Macdonald wanted them to "become independent like white subjects ... to civilize [themselves] by slow degrees." Some alternative voices advocated the vote as restitution for Indigenous people's loss of land or called for their humane treatment, including one MP from northern Ontario who stated that the many educated Indians in his area who paid taxes would vote responsibly.

Most MPs, however, dismissed these arguments. The debate came on the heels of the Northwest Rebellion of 1885, a desperate protest of Prairie Indigenous and Metis people against oppression, starvation, and land loss. MPs registered exaggerated fears about their disloyalty: warriors, one MP warned in exceptional hyperbole, would be heading "from a scalping party to the polls." In the House of Commons, MPs referred to Indigenous people as uncivilized, yet newspapers were even more sensational, whipping up racist fears of the dire consequences if ignorant "barbarians" were given the ballot: the Globe shrieked that "Indian murderers" would be allowed to vote but the "patriotic volunteers" sent to quell the 1885 rebellion would not. Such views were not uncommon. Prominent nineteenth-century Canadian historians such as François-Xavier Garneau thought that Indigenous people were "habitually addicted to the cruelty of war" and prone to "enslave their wives" before "enlightened Europeans" arrived.

MPs similarly claimed that Aboriginal men's "brutal" mistreatment and exploitation of women was evidence of their "inherent savagery." "Better to give the squaw a vote than Indians," said one MP in jest, after claiming that oppressed Aboriginal wives supported their "lazy" men. Another raised the spectre of "orgies" at potlatch ceremonies in British Columbia, banned only the year before, as a sign of sexual and familial disorder in Aboriginal cultures. Allowing First Nations women to vote was especially worrying, given their portrayal as pathetic, submissive, and easily manipulated by both white and Indigenous men alike. MPs also speculated on what was better or worse: women, Indians, or Chinese people voting. A few rational voices asserted that race should not determine the vote, but the majority opposed granting it to

Chinese men, who, they stated, were not even *potential* British subjects, but rather perpetual aliens. Race and gender were intertwined in the indignant arguments of MPs who queried why Indigenous people should vote, when "noble [white] young men" and "our intelligent women" could not. One Quebec MP claimed that awarding the franchise to Aboriginal men while withholding it from white labourers would be an outrage, though he did not propose universal suffrage so that working-class men without property *could* vote.

When the 1885 Franchise Act finally passed, it gave Ottawa control over the right to vote, but instead of producing a uniform electorate across the country, it diversified it even more. The act enlarged a limited Aboriginal vote, but only after Macdonald reassured white settlers beyond Lake Superior, where the majority of Indigenous people actually lived, that *those* Aboriginal people would not be allowed to vote. British Columbia, determined to become a white man's country, had exerted special pressure to ensure the exclusion of both "Asiatics" and Indians.

Voting rights were again the subject of debate in 1898, when the Liberal government revised the franchise, returning it to provincially set rules. Race but not gender lay at the centre of these discussions. The Liberal Party had already refused Indigenous people the vote in the Northwest Territories (later Saskatchewan and Alberta), but its 1898 federal law complicated the issue by forbidding the exclusion of individuals who "belonged to any class of persons." Japanese and Chinese people, deemed a class of persons, might vote again federally, though not necessarily provincially. By contrast, Indians, not considered a class of persons, were now disqualified by provincial regulations. Ontario, for instance, reverted to more stringent rules, requiring Indigenous men not only to give up their Indian status, but also to hold *more* property than white men in order to vote.

The 1885 and 1898 contests between the Conservatives and Liberals regarding qualifications for the vote have been interpreted as evidence of each party's partisan quest for votes and their differing opinions on federal versus provincial power. True enough. Yet other considerations were at stake, revealing some shared assumptions. The ruling elites assumed that capitalism, private property, and the individual accumulation of wealth drove economic progress, and that Aboriginal life, stressing communal landholding and the redistribution of wealth, was a deterrent to sound development. Both Liberals and Conservatives envisioned a state that would rule, regulate, and legislate to protect values they held dear, relating to white settlement, economic development, morality, gender roles, and the family. On this count, they shared a common faith in white men, and perhaps assimilated Aboriginal men, who had an economic stake in the community, as best suited to direct the nation. These values, reflecting shared cultural assumptions about state formation, resulted not only in the exclusion of Asians and women, but also of most Aboriginal Canadians, who supposedly could not fathom the moral and political basis of civilization.

ANCIENT RIGHTS AND WOMEN'S RIGHTS

Few politicians in the 1880s and 1890s looked beyond stereotypes to explore how Indigenous people governed themselves and how these practices correlated to Euro-Canadian definitions of democracy. It was taken for granted that British institutions were superior and that Aboriginal methods of governance were backward, primitive, barely formulated. "Our institutions are entirely repugnant to [the Indian's] ideas of right and wrong," said one MP with great assurance in the 1885 debate. The stereotype – later promulgated in Hollywood films – was that Indian chiefs dictated orders to their underlings.

Nor did the nineteenth-century women's suffrage movement in Canada question whether First Nations forms of governance incorporated the gender equality they sought, even though some American suffragists did. The latter lauded the matriarchal and egalitarian nature of Iroquois, or Haudenosaunee, governance and

"DECLINED WITH THANKS."

"Enfranchised" Indian—I DON'T WANT THIS BOX; TAKE IT BACK. IT BRINGS ME INTO CONTACT WITH WHITE-MAN POLITICS, AND DEMORALIZES ME.

This cartoon, published in *Grip,* a Toronto weekly magazine, on 2 July 1887, satirizes political corruption by citing a petition from members of the Grand River Reserve (Six Nations), which asked "Parliament to relieve them of the ballot, thrust upon them by a paternal government." The cartoon foreshadows later First Nations debates about enfranchisement.

the high value that Iroquois society placed on women. Matilda Gage, a resident of upstate New York, had learned first-hand about her Oneida and Onondaga neighbours, and like fellow suffragist Elizabeth Cady Stanton, she took inspiration from anthropological writings of the time that detailed Iroquois women's influential role in the clan organization of the longhouse. In speeches, Stanton claimed that Iroquois women "ruled the house" in large part because property and children were traced through the "female line," and she contrasted the reasonable "Indian style divorce" to the irrational situation of American women who

found themselves trapped in miserable marriages by legal prohibitions against divorce. Iroquois women, she suggested, rarely
experienced domestic violence because wives were never under
the control of the husband, and female leaders would simply
ask the violent man to leave the longhouse.

Gage likewise saw Indigenous matriarchies of the past as a
"viable alternative to American white patriarchy." As president
of the National Woman Suffrage Association, she wrote articles
for a New York newspaper on Haudenosaunee governance,
claiming that "the division of power between the sexes in this
Indian republic was nearly equal," with the family structure "demonstrating women's superiority in power." Gage too traced
Indigenous women's power to their key role in agricultural production and matrilineal control over the family and the longhouse. Although she understood that Western concepts of voting
were not part of these traditions, she highlighted the consulta-
tive, democratic nature of Iroquois decision making: "each sex had
its own council," but women took a prominent role in choosing –
and potentially deposing – chiefs.

It is no coincidence that Gage and Stanton were extremely
critical of Western Christianity and its links to patriarchy, far
more so than other suffragists. In *Women, Church and State,* Gage
drew a positive picture of pre-Christian matriarchal societies,
with their natural equality of condition, and contrasted this to
the Christian doctrine of women's inherent sinfulness and inferiority. The state, she continued, followed the church's lead, rendering
women, through law, an inferior piece of property, unprotected
from violence. Able to see beyond the widely accepted religious
tenets of her own society, Gage was open to cross-cultural comparisons that questioned the designation of Indigenous women
as pagan and primitive.

Gage and Stanton were not entirely alone in their views. Some
abolitionist suffragists who were concerned with the natural
rights of humankind also wrote positively about Indigenous

culture, as they sought historical antecedents on which to ground their own rights claims. Yet suffragist thinking about Indigenous peoples was always shot through with contradiction. Stanton lauded Haudenosaunee culture, but she prioritized votes for white women *over* the vote for African Americans, and Gage saw Haudenosaunee matriarchy as a noble remnant of the past but believed that Indigenous women were now "dependent and confined to reservations," needing the helping maternal hand of their better-educated white sisters.

COLONIALISM, RACE, AND EARLY CANADIAN FEMINISM

Gage's esteem for Haudenosaunee social organization did not resonate with most nineteenth-century Canadian feminists, despite the presence of Haudenosaunee peoples in central Canada and occasional press coverage of their efforts to maintain their own governing councils of hereditary or life chiefs, who were selected by the clan mothers. At the St. Regis (Akwesasne) Reserve in Ontario, the Department of Indian Affairs was so determined in 1898 to impose its version of superior, Western-style elections on "pagan" Indians that it employed brute force: police were brought onto the reserve, an Indigenous protester killed, and the hereditary chiefs imprisoned, even made to pay for their own legal defence. Petitions to the government earlier that same year from the Haudenosaunee women of the Akwesasne and Caughnawaga Reserves had been contemptuously brushed aside. Appealing in the name of another mother, Queen Victoria, the women implored the government to recognize their own version of democracy: the ancient rights of clan mothers to appoint and depose life chiefs, based on assessments of their moral and political behaviour.

Praise for Haudenosaunee women's role in governance was also voiced by prominent Mohawk English poet Pauline Johnson. Her chapter on Iroquois women in the National Council of Women of Canada's encyclopedic *Women of Canada* portrayed their accomplishments as equalling those of white women, though she

PETITION OF WOMEN OF CAUGHNAWAGA
TO CLIFFORD SIFTON, MINISTER OF THE
INTERIOR AND SUPERINTENDENT GENERAL
OF INDIAN AFFAIRS, 1898

We are simply women, but it is in the confidence of our noble and gracious mother, the Queen of England, who, being a woman, and recalling to remind you that your mother was also a woman ... Kindly hear our words of petition, and do not despise the words and voice of a woman ... Since the change of our chiefs into councilors ours sorrows manifolded, we have lost many advantages, it has caused many family dispute, brother against brother. It has separated them, and it has caused an ill feeling which is yet burning.

PETITION OF THE CLAN MOTHERS
OF ST. REGIS TO THE GOVERNOR GENERAL, 1898

We have considered the elective system as not being intended for us Indians and we would therefore return to our old method of selecting our life chiefs according to our Constitution of Iroquois Government. As your Excellency must know, the ancient custom of creating life chiefs is that they are selected according to the different clans ... [by] clan mothers ... But if any misdemeanor shall offend their clans, these women first hold council with the women of their own clan, and if they find his offense of sufficient strength to warrant his resignation, these women will call upon the men members of their clan and they meet and select another member to represent them.

suggested that Iroquois cultural "superiority" was lacking in other Indigenous women, her "less fortunate sisters." Like Gage, she stressed the matrilineal nature of Iroquois society and reminded white feminists that "not all civilized races honour their women as highly as do the stern old chiefs, warriors and braves of the Six Nations Indians." Johnson, however, was the sole Indigenous author in this collection. Her personal politics registered far less than her cultural success as an author-performer, which led some whites to suggest that Indigenous people were better treated in Canada than in the United States.

Since the 1970s, feminist anthropologists and historians have resurrected these debates about the egalitarian nature of Aboriginal cultures, asking how colonialism fundamentally altered the significant roles of Indigenous women in their own political and social affairs. In "Women in Huron and Ojibwa Societies," Marlene Brant Castellano, Mohawk academic and research director for the 1996 Royal Commission on Aboriginal Peoples, stresses the importance of recognizing the diversity of Indigenous women's changing gender roles across Canada, rather than asserting a blanket "myth of female dominated matriarchy." Yet both Indigenous knowledge and cross-cultural studies show how wrong Canadian MPs were when they claimed in 1885 that all Indigenous women suffered sexual subordination and patriarchal oppression in their own cultures. Quite the contrary was often true.

It is curious that Canadian suffragists did not cite examples of Indigenous cultures to justify their movement. Perhaps timing is a partial explanation: a better organized suffrage movement emerged in Canada after the 1880s, just as white settlement, Aboriginal dispossession, and racism intensified in the aftermath of the 1885 rebellion. Although few white women could legally claim homesteads of their own, they nonetheless benefitted from the overall dispossession of Indigenous land. Many female settlers shared and promoted the Canadian state's vision of a new

Poet and entertainer Emily Pauline Johnson (1861–1913), also known as Tekahionwake (Double Wampum), was the daughter of a Six Nations Mohawk chief and a white, English mother. Exposed to both a Western education and the traditions of her Mohawk ancestors, she incorporated her hybrid identity, as Haudenosaunee and British, into her writing and cultural performances. Johnson championed a more inclusive nationality, with enhanced dignity and respect for Indigenous peoples, and reminded white feminists of the esteemed role that Haudenosaunee women played in their communities. Her fictional story, "A Red Girl's Reasoning," was a powerful indictment of the racism experienced by Aboriginal women.

nation of superior, white, British rural settlements inevitably replacing backward Indian tribes. Moreover, few Canadian suffragists offered such a daring and searing public critique of Christianity as did Matilda Gage.

Nor did Canada's late-nineteenth-century suffragists recognize and build on Mary Ann Shadd Cary's pathbreaking writing, which attacked multiple levels of gender and race discrimination, oppression, and marginalization. She challenged male superiority – white and black – just as she opposed slavery and racism. She denounced segregationist whites who denied black children equal education, just as she criticized black women who were too timid to stand up for their rights. Canadian suffragists, however, had little grounding in abolitionist traditions; rather, they were more attuned to other intellectual and political ideals, both liberal and socialist, as rationales for gender equality.

There is just a little humbug about our anti-suffrage friends' argument when they say that their reverence for women [as Angels of the Home] inspires their desire to keep them out of the hurly-burly of politics ... These men are self deceived ... Would they let an angel woman scrub the floor and sit idly by while an angel girl who is underfed does dreary and disgusting work for a miserable wage and long hours? Would they look with complacency on poverty and compel girls to sell their bodies on the streets for bread?

HELENA GUTTERIDGE, *BC FEDERATIONIST*,

21 NOVEMBER 1913

Together men and women have made the world as it relates to humanity, and together they must go on producing the world conditions under which men and women are to live. How can it be right that only half of the responsible population of the earth shall have any part in making of the rules which equally concern all the world?

Women have a right to be individuals, neither sex slaves nor pampered poodles.

We have a right to say whether we will do this or that work ... and be paid an equal wage ...

We have a right to demand that home life be taken off the list of non-reproductive work ...

How men even half-trained in democracy can refuse to acknowledge not only the justice but the inevitableness of such demands is astonishing.

"WHAT WOMEN DEMAND," REPRINTED FROM

THE AUSTRALIAN WORKER IN *CANADIAN FORWARD*,

10 MARCH 1917

THREE

SUFFRAGE AS A
SOCIALIST ISSUE

A British immigrant, Helena Gutteridge
stood at the crossroads of many causes: suffrage, socialism,
the labour movement, rights for working women, and, later, when
she sat on Vancouver City Council during the 1930s, the rights
of the unemployed.

KNIGHTS OF LABOR AUTHOR, journalist, and crusader for the socially disenfranchised, Phillips Thompson was a staunch ally of women's suffrage. In 1886, a year after Parliament rejected votes for women, Thompson resurrected the suffrage debate in the Knights' newspaper, the *Palladium of Labor*, urging progressive labour men to support "equal citizenship" for women. To deny them the vote, he wrote with characteristic candour, was just as "stupid and unreasonable" as the arbitrary distinctions made between men according to "race, creed, birth or property" and just as unfair as the past exclusion of working men from political life by the wealthy few. He denounced the popular notion that women were the property of their husbands or fathers, calling this a form of "petty class rule" and a "survival of savagery" from the prehistoric past. Nor did Thompson accept for a minute the idea of a natural, God-given order of male dominance: after all, very similar arguments about race had propped up the pernicious system of slavery.

Women suffragists encountered adamant, hostile resistance from many men, but they also benefitted from the political, social, and emotional support of allies like Thompson, usually reformers who were involved in other progressive, socialist, labour, and religious organizations. Thompson's support for feminism was inextricably linked to his socialism. He saw the class system as fundamentally immoral and inequitable: capitalist social relations not only devalued women's labour but also put the working-class home in jeopardy. Economic and social democracy required the political participation of all working people. Politics shaped women's "happiness as much as men's," he reminded *Palladium* readers, and their responsibility for home and children was reason enough to enfranchise them, as they would bring their "protective" impulses to bear on social reform and public policy.

Thompson was addressing what socialists commonly referred to as "the woman question." Much like the condition of women question, it was initially posed by writers as multiple questions about the changing nature of women's work, education, politics, and literary pursuits. By the late nineteenth century, socialists used the term as shorthand for one perplexing problem: What was the origin of women's oppression, and how might it be eradicated? Given the importance of that query, one might wonder why socialist and labour women are often relegated to the fringes of suffrage histories. Granted, they are not easily slotted into one political group. Socialist suffragists entertained a critique of capitalism and were just as likely to be involved in socialist parties as in suffrage organizations; labour suffragists often made trade unions or local labour parties, modelled on the British Independent Labour Party, their priority. At times, their activism and strategies also overlapped. Together, they created an energetic suffragist constituency that stressed the alleviation of class as well as gender inequality and focused especially on the daily social needs of working-class women. Moreover, their ideas also influenced other suffragists: feminist intellectuals such as Dr. Emily Stowe or Prairie newspaperwoman Francis Marion Beynon drew eclectically on both socialist and liberal thought of their day.

Socialist feminists' double loyalty to two causes, however, sometimes means that they are forgotten as feminist foremothers. Yet their politics, their attempts to understand intersecting inequalities, and sometimes their anguish over their own divided loyalties make them interesting and relevant to us today. Socialist feminism, which began to take shape in the late nineteenth century, became a continuing stream of activism and theory after the First World War, surfacing in various parties, causes, and pressure groups throughout the twentieth century and into this one.

THE WOMAN QUESTION OR THE PARTY QUESTION?

Internationally, socialism arose as multiple political movements in the early to mid-nineteenth century, responding to changes in capitalism, working-class mobilizations, disappointment with liberal revolutions, and radically new social theories of human emancipation, including Marxism. Canadian socialist groups emerged later than those in Europe and the United States, and were relatively small (due largely to our small population), regionally based, and somewhat isolated from international socialist organizations. Nonetheless, the conditions that produced socialism beyond Canadian borders were evident here too: exploitative employment relations, wealth inequality, cyclical unemployment, child labour, and rampant poverty.

By the 1880s, Canadian socialists were taking up debates about women's equality that had long preoccupied European socialists, though they often disagreed with each other as much as they clashed with more liberal, middle-class suffrage associations. Exploring both the common elements of left-wing thought and socialists' internal differences is important: they reveal dynamic debates, ideological diversity, and the influential imprint of inspiring, individual thinkers as well as the power of collective party politics. Many socialist and labour women placed their hopes *in* parties as the most important vehicle for social change, and what we might perceive as doctrinal wrangling between socialist parties was more than intellectual word play to them. Debate was seen as the midwife to a correct analysis of, and solution for, women's inequality.

Socialists usually agreed on the general precept that women's oppression was connected to capitalism and class inequality, though some also attributed it – as did Thompson – to outdated ideas of male superiority and dominance. They drew on a range of foundational texts and ideas, shared across international borders, to understand the relationship between class and gender, and how socialists might strive for a more egalitarian, ideal future. Utopian socialism, imported from Europe and the United States, promised one way forward, stressing an optimistic faith in the possibilities of every human's intellectual, personal, and social transformation – without resorting to the violence of revolution. Women's equality was part and parcel of utopian socialists' vision of a world built on co-operation, love, truth, and universality, which they tried to create by actually *practising* socialism in separate egalitarian communities. Often shaped by charismatic leaders, these experiments were intended as feasible evidence of people's ability to live in harmony in co-operative commonwealths that eradicated all hierarchical and oppressive personal, familial, and economic relationships.

Matti Kurikka, a prominent Finnish socialist writer, established Canada's best-known utopian socialist community in 1901 on Malcolm Island, just off the coast of mainland British Columbia. Finnish Canadian immigrants encouraged him to help them construct their model community, which they named Sointula (Place of Harmony). Given to the Finns by the provincial government to encourage white settlement, the island was supposed to provide "refuge for all Finnish socialists," and like similar utopian communities in the United States, it incorporated collaborative labour, pooled profits, and communal living. Shared kitchens and domestic labour, free schooling for all children, and equal remuneration of men and women were part of a socialist feminist vision of co-operation and equality. Kurikka, deeply influenced by leading Finnish socialist suffragist writer Minna Cath, also introduced her ideas about marriage and sexuality to Sointula. He believed that women not only needed equal legal rights and suffrage, but also freedom from the traditional marriage contracts that affirmed their subordination to men. Kurikka's advocacy of female sexual freedom, without the ties of legal marriage, soon earned Sointula the reputation as a scandalous bastion of promiscuous free love.

Kurikka's ideas were shared by some other "sex radicals" of the time. They saw marriage as a form of legal bondage that suppressed women's free expression of sexual desire and felt that love, marriage, and motherhood should not be forcibly linked, but allowed to flourish separately. Women would be equal only when they had attained both legal rights and the freedom to reject patriarchal marriage, a form of material and sexual slavery. Outraged Christian clergy denounced Sointula's free love philosophy, but the colony also faced problems of economic sustainability and some internal dissension, including women who were not entirely convinced of the benefits of free love. In 1905, Kurikka left Sointula with half of its settlers, set up a new, short-lived utopian community in British Columbia's Fraser Valley, returned to Finland, and then moved to the more welcoming bohemian environment of New York City. However, the idea that marriage was an aspect of female subordination and that church and state had no place in the unions of couples remained a lasting element of Finnish socialism in Canada.

Utopian socialism shared some intellectual overlap with Christian, or ethical, socialism, which also promoted a new vision of women's equality. Both utopian and ethical socialism extolled the Christian ideal of "doing unto others as you would have them do unto you"; both shared the optimistic belief that men and women could be inspired by a new moral vision of co-operation; and both rejected the competitive and exploitative nature of capitalism. Nineteenth-century ethical socialists often cited Edward Bellamy's famous utopian novel of 1888, *Looking Backward,* as their inspiration. In Bellamy's imaginary utopia, a nineteenth-century man time travels to 2000, where he discovers a rational, co-operative, egalitarian society, the mirror opposite of his own. Bellamy's literary argument for the possibility of socialist transformation sparked hundreds of Bellamyite study clubs

Theosophy emerged in the late nineteenth century as an alternative spiritual perspective. It promoted religious equality, optimistic idealism, and an inclusive humanity. Its founding document called for the "Universal Brotherhood of Humanity" without any distinction of race, creed, caste, or colour; the study of all world religions; and the search for the unexplained in the universe. Theosophist societies rejected Christian church doctrine but maintained an interest in spiritual exploration and, in doing so, opened the door to radicals also intrigued by the occult and spiritualism. Feminists Emily Stowe, Flora MacDonald Denison, and Augusta Stowe-Gullen – along with many artists, writers and progressive reformers – were attracted to theosophy's message of tolerance, equality, and hope.

across North America. Other Canadian reform groups popularized similar moral, ethical solutions to the ills of modern industrial society: the Single Tax Clubs (attacking landed wealth), temperance organizations (decrying alcohol), and theosophy (a spiritual perspective that rejected organized religion and favoured human equality). Ethical socialists sometimes embraced all these causes. Phillips Thompson, for instance, was a suffragist, single taxer, theosophist, and a member of the Canadian Socialist League.

Formed in 1899, the Canadian Socialist League (CSL) stressed co-operation, education, and political agitation as the peaceful pathway to social transformation. Sixty-two CSL locals across Canada established a set of principles that included female enfranchisement, and the CSL newspaper, *Citizen and Country,* tried to recruit members from women's reform groups such as the Woman's Christian Temperance Union (WCTU). For ethical socialists, suffrage was the right of all citizens, male or female, but also a potent means for women to translate their domestic and maternal concerns into a politics of social improvement. A women's column in *Citizen and Country*, penned by Sarah Wrigley, was titled "The Kingdom of the Home." As Linda Kealey shows, that name encapsulated socialists' hope that "home and family" might become the rudder for a reformed nation in which the values of "love and collective responsibility" would impel social transformation.

Socialist women, already accustomed to communicating a radical anti-capitalist message to the public, were often courageous in pushing the bounds of respectable femininity to promote feminist ideas. In 1902, the CSL nominated Margaret Haile as its provincial candidate for a North Toronto riding. Since Haile could not legally vote, she was soundly denounced by some politicians, but they could not prevent her from running or speaking at election meetings. Like Matti Kurikka, she symbolizes the transnational essence of suffrage agitation. An American immigrant, she had considerable organizing experience in the Socialist Party of America, and like many socialists, she believed that women's struggle for equality transcended national borders. Known as an impressive writer and speaker, she took a public stand for women's rights during the Ontario election, which earned her eighty-one sympathetic male votes. Her candidacy was portrayed in "Election Day," a 2015 episode of the popular CBC TV series *Murdoch Mysteries,* with Haile and other "suffragettes" fiercely blockading the door to a polling booth to ensure that her name was not removed from the ballot. The suggestion that Canadian suffragists acted like the militant British suffragettes was more fiction than fact, but most striking is the portrayal of Haile as a feminist, though *not* a socialist. Yet her election speeches made it crystal clear that she saw capitalism as the enemy: the 1 percent, not the male percent, was the focus of her critique.

The CSL also thrived in British Columbia, a hotbed of socialist ideas, parties, and debates, in which women's suffrage figured prominently. In 1901, the BC chapter of the CSL combined with other socialists to establish a new party, which evolved into the Socialist Party of Canada (SPC). By 1910, it was the largest expression of organized socialism in the country, with at least three thousand members. Moving away from ethical socialism, the SPC endorsed the materialist socialism (termed "scientific" at the time) of Karl Marx, Frederick Engels, and their many interpreters. Marxists saw capitalism as inherently exploitative, extracting surplus value from workers (in what we might call an inevitable form of wage theft). Thus, the economic interests of the working classes were diametrically opposed to those who owned and managed private property. Optimistically, Marxists believed that history transitioned through economic epochs, creating new social relations and opening up the possibilities of change, especially through working-class mobilization.

A historical analysis of private property was also the cornerstone of the Marxist answer to the woman question. The SPC drew heavily on Frederick Engels's famous book, *The Origins of the Family, Private Property and State*, which argued that the centuries-old oppression of women was linked to the emergence of private property and capitalism, as women's subordination in the patriarchal, monogamous family became the means to ensure male inheritance of property. Engels based his theory upon the same anthropological evidence about egalitarian Iroquois societies that influenced American suffragists such as Matilda Gage, who claimed that matriarchal, egalitarian societies predated modern patriarchal ones. Engels's theory was translated into a message that the SPC heartily embraced: if women's equality were to be achieved, capitalism must first be abolished.

Yet some SPCers recognized that female suffrage might be more easily accomplished than the complete overthrow of capitalism. James Hawthornthwaite, an elected SPC member of the

BC legislature, tabled women's suffrage bills in 1906 and 1909, even though he cautioned that enfranchisement could never bring *real* freedom to women since it was not a cure for economic evils. His ambivalence was echoed by SPCers, who saw parliamentary reform in general as partial, piecemeal, and inadequate, lulling the working class into thinking that capitalism could simply be tinkered with rather than eradicated. Some SPC leaders – both male and female – rejected suffrage as a bourgeois issue, promoted by middle-class women who were naively unaware that the vote could never address the capitalist origins of inequality. From these naysayers also came contemptuous dismissals of women as conservative, backward, and isolated in the minutia of domesticity. Suffrage was sometimes ridiculed by the socialist paper the *Western Clarion,* as one dismissive writer did in 1909: "We are not interested in Votes for Women, the Right to Work and the rest of the nonsense that is heralded as immediate demands. We have only one immediate demand and that is the abolition of capitalism. We proletarians have not time to waste on Votes for Women."

Yet feminists who had socialist inclinations still gravitated toward the SPC. The party's first vice-president, Bertha Merrill Burns, wrote a regular column, "We Women," in the *Canadian Socialist* (later the *Western Clarion*) that combined advice on working-class life, marriage, and childrearing with a feminist interpretation of socialism. Letters from her readers often agreed that women's emancipation would come only when socialism triumphed. Prostitution, one correspondent stated, would be abolished only when capitalism was destroyed and impoverished women were no longer required to sell themselves for survival. Writing under the pseudonym of Dorothy Drew, Burns courageously raised touchy and controversial issues, such as the need for sex education for children and equal pay for women, while she reiterated conventional wisdom about women's innate mother love and concern for children. In her unique blend of feminist, ethical, and Marxist socialism, she attempted to

A REMINDER
MRS. VANCOUVER: Remember, you men are hired to *clean* this city,
not merely to move its filth from one spot to another.

Prostitution and *A Reminder,* two 1913 cartoons printed
in the *Western Clarion* and the *Vancouver Sun,* respectively.
As these cartoons show, views of prostitution differed. For
the *Western Clarion,* a socialist newspaper, prostitution was
the direct effect of labour under capitalism. For the more
conservative *Vancouver Sun,* it was a moral scourge that
needed to be eliminated by BC politicians.

nurture working-class women's class consciousness, promote suffrage as a question of human justice, and bring women *into* the political world of sisterhood and socialism. Suffrage, she might have said in shorthand, *was* a socialist issue.

Other female SPC leaders, such as Ruth Lestor, disagreed. Although she did not consistently describe women as hopelessly backward and reactionary, she thought the vote would do little to defeat the true enemy of humanity: the "follies and slavery of capitalism." Socialist parties, not unlike social democratic ones today, housed an eclectic mix of radicals, looking for political company in their critique of capitalism, so internal differences on the suffrage issue were predictable. Socialist feminists sought an organized community of comrades, working together for the greater good, and they had few other left-wing party options at the time. Moreover, most did believe that the collective project of socialism, not the limited equality of opportunity associated with liberalism, was the true solution to women's oppression, so they used the party to cautiously educate their male comrades. When party leaders expressed ambivalence or contempt about suffrage, socialist feminists answered back with suggestions that men should look after the home for a change, so that women could attend socialist meetings and join the struggle. Other women asked their male comrades how they could advocate the emancipation of only *half* of humanity. "Our work is to arouse the workers to revolt," Edith Wrigley, daughter-in-law of Sarah Wrigley, reminded male socialists, so "let us arouse the workers, not one sex; let us have more equality and democracy in our work."

One of the most unconventional and complicated SPCers was Dora Forster Kerr, a socialist feminist advocate of birth control and marriage reform, both radical causes associated with free love. Despite her differences with the SPC, she remained a socialist. And despite her differences with middle-class women's suffrage groups, she organized joint meetings with them. Kerr believed in female enfranchisement not as an end, but as a means to emancipation: it would not "remove all injustice," she conceded in a piece in *Cotton's Weekly* in 1909, "but it is the first step towards justice." Women also desperately needed the vote if they were to challenge the legal shackles of marriage and motherhood, exemplified by laws that prevented them from claiming legal custody of their children. Kerr's blend of socialist, feminist, and sexual liberation (and problematically, some eugenicist) ideas was not easily packaged into a socialist party platform: like many socialist women, she sometimes felt divided loyalties. As she confided in a private letter to Toronto feminist Flora MacDonald Denison, she truly wished she could say that all the "sex bias and unfairness" came from men, but she found just as much to deplore among elite female reformers whose "retrograde ignorance and fanaticism" was expressed through their inhumane support for the flogging of male prisoners and their efforts to impose their version of moral purity on others.

Heated SPC disagreements over whether the struggle against capitalism or against women's inequality should take priority may seem unsophisticated to our ears, but they reflected dilemmas that plagued socialism internationally. Socialist and anarchist writers from abroad toured and lectured across Canada, airing these debates. Anarchist Emma Goldman, for instance, publicly disparaged suffrage as a misdirected middle-class movement that would not free working-class women from economic or sexual oppression, even though she was committed to women's economic independence, sexual freedom, and access to birth control. In Britain, socialist feminists campaigned for universal adult suffrage, but they often opposed a limited extension of voting rights to more affluent female property holders or rent payers: class trumped sex in their strategies. In the United States, where suffrage for all white men was common but race was a universally divisive issue, the Socialist Party of America endorsed suffrage for white women and set up a Women's National Committee to support the cause through women's papers, organizing campaigns, and speakers. Suffrage, in other words, was tied to many other forms of inequality and power struggles; differing national contexts and cultures produced divergent forms of cooperation, tension, or hostility between socialists and feminists.

The Socialist Party of Canada was somewhat isolated from these debates because it never joined the large Socialist International (SI), which represented most European and American socialist parties. Internationally, a resurgent wave of socialist feminist organizing in the late nineteenth and early twentieth centuries, both within parties and parallel to them, contributed immeasurably to the growing vigour of the suffrage movement. The SI, prodded by German socialist leader Clara Zetkin, sponsored an International Conference on Socialist Women in 1907, and the nine hundred delegates endorsed a resolution that it was the "duty of Socialist Parties of all countries to agitate most energetically for the introduction of universal women's suffrage." Some national parties redoubled their efforts to campaign for a socialist vision of suffrage, but the SPC was not represented at the conference, and its isolation reinforced its narrow view of all reforms as capitulation to bourgeois politics. This stance earned the party the nickname "impossibilist" – a label that contained a grain of truth.

The SPC ambivalence to reforms inspired a breakaway socialist party in 1909, the Social Democratic Party, which advertised its support for women's suffrage as a point of distinction with the rival SPC: "Social Democrats," it reassured women, "do not sneer at woman suffrage." Finnish immigrants in the new party were especially strong advocates of the franchise for women, as Finland had granted it in 1906; women émigrés brought progressive values and their experience in Finnish politics with them. The party's organizing campaigns, including separate study groups in which Finnish women read socialist classics, debated current issues, and sewed for the cause, provided a lively forum for discussion of women's rights. A social order in which women lacked full control

over their own wages and custody of their children had to be challenged: if women had the vote, the party insisted, they would
change these outrageous legal strictures. Universal suffrage for
men and women was also a matter of human justice since there
should be "equality of the sexes in every department of life." The
Social Democratic Party's rationale for female enfranchisement
nonetheless leaned heavily on ideas about class solidarity and
economic justice. Women socialists should join men in the
battle to rid society of the "parasitical [owning] classes," and because they witnessed first-hand the suffering that capitalism
caused, they would probably use their vote to abolish child labour,
protect the working-class family, and combat prostitution. When
it came to the latter issue, socialists from varying parties spoke in
unison, criticizing any commentary that blamed prostitution on
the low morals or personal weaknesses of working-class women.

Like many liberal and middle-class feminists, socialists often
situated women's labour at the core of their arguments for the
vote: as industrialization drew more women into paid work and
altered their domestic labour, they needed a political say in social
issues. Some socialist feminists also supported temperance
legislation, even though the Woman's Christian Temperance
Union (WCTU) was predominantly a middle-class movement.
Mary Cotton Wisdom, editor of the women's page in the socialist
newspaper *Cotton's Weekly* (founded by her brother), believed that
male drunkenness contributed to poverty and domestic violence.
Temperance was the answer. If women wanted to protect their
families, they should help clean up the corrupt political system
that was ruled by the overly powerful liquor business interests.
Unlike some WCTUers, however, Wisdom was not solely preoccupied with temperance. Her newspaper column was an eclectic mélange of household hints, recipes, discussion of women's
issues, and feminist politics. Her rage at the oppressive legal and
social situation of women sometimes echoed the views of British
suffragettes, who had moved away from their labour roots by

Mary Cotton Wisdom wrote fiery columns on
women's rights for the socialist paper *Cotton's Weekly*.
After the First World War, she edged back politically
to her middle-class, liberal roots.

1909 to embrace a more radical feminist critique of male domination and patriarchy. Wisdom defended the militant tactics of
the suffragettes in her column, dismissing the "mush heads" in
the press who fretted over their destruction of property. After all,
she pointed out, the so-called violence of window smashing
was nothing compared to the "violence of a government that
governs without the consent of the governed."

After declaring emphatically that "we are going to insist on
women having the vote," Wisdom foretold exactly what feminists

would do with it: "When that day arrives, we will see to it that some of the infamous man-made laws now in force are abolished in short order ... We are heartily sick of being governed, ruled, judged, sentenced, imprisoned and even hanged by men and man-made laws." Wisdom had a radical feminist critique of a judicial system that "punished women" yet "let men go free" for exactly the same crime, but she also drew on the socialist theories of Engels. Women's subordination, their "low status" in marriage, she wrote, had a "materialist" basis in property relations, so the only way to liberate women from legal "concubinage" was to provide them with complete "economic freedom." Wisdom's eclectic column encompassed feminist conviction, social reform rhetoric, and socialist doctrine. Her views did not exactly match the official platform of any one socialist party, but they mirrored the broader intellectual ferment of the times: an international context of intense socialist writing and organization, bold new forms of feminist agitation, and an urgent sense of the need for immediate attention to widespread social ills.

LABOUR SUFFRAGISTS

The ideas of many labour suffragists displayed the same hybridity. Mary Cotton Wisdom's concerns overlapped with those of labour suffragists, some of whom were also sympathetic to socialism. In *Cotton's Weekly,* she called for wage justice for the deplorably exploited working woman, whether she was a "sales girl, tobacco factory worker or female hobo" without a job, sentiments echoed by labour suffragists, a diverse group of women who were active in labour churches, parties, newspapers, unions, and study groups. Their definitions of equality were shaped by the day-to-day experiences of working-class women: their confinement to low-wage, precarious work and homemakers' struggle to feed their families on insecure wages at a time when pensions, medical insurance, and unemployment benefits did not exist. They sometimes collaborated with middle-class social reformers, but, cognizant of their different class interests, they also staked out their own distinct ideological territory. For example, whereas many middle-class women's reform organizations talked about the problem of finding responsible servants, labour suffragists claimed that long hours, poor working conditions, and demanding employers were the real problems.

From the late nineteenth century onward, the labour movement became increasingly involved in suffrage debates: it endorsed suffragist organizations, joined them in lobby delegations, promoted suffrage petitions, and established women's columns in labour newspapers. City and provincial labour parties promoted themselves as the voice of working people, endorsing an egalitarian democracy free of manipulation by the moneyed interests, a fair deal for all citizens, and a parliamentary road to social and economic reform. The female franchise was added to their election platforms, both a means and an end to their vision of steady working-class improvement. Most trade union federations eventually added female suffrage to their platforms, though they sometimes lagged behind socialist and labour parties. After the Knights of Labor declined in the early 1890s, few women were unionized, and most trade unions were ambivalent about their paid work, viewing them as mothers-in-the-making rather than as lifelong wage earners. Male unionists, however, defended better conditions for single working women and by the First World War had endorsed universal suffrage for men and women, rejecting stringent property qualifications for voters that would favour the more affluent voter.

Moreover, the ideal of a male breadwinner was endorsed by some women labour suffragists who campaigned for the vote by invoking the maternal, domestic duties of working-class housewives. Suffragist, socialist, and labour movement activist May Darwin began her political life in the Toronto Union Label League, an organization that mobilized homemakers, based on their role in budgeting and buying daily necessities for the family.

Like working-class women in the United States Label Leagues, where the idea originated, Darwin believed that the energies of housewives could be harnessed to aid trade union struggles for decent wages by having women purchase union-made goods. She also represented the fluid boundaries between socialist and labour feminism. She chaired the Trades and Labour Council's educational committee and wrote a column for its paper, the *Toronto Tribune*, mixing commentary on domesticity, motherhood, and femininity with invocations of class solidarity and the need for socialism. She was also a member of the Canadian Socialist League, and her speeches stressed the indispensable connections between women's emancipation and socialism. Optimistically, she predicted that women might become the socialist vanguard since they suffered most from "the competitive system," and they would so clearly benefit from socialism's emphasis on "the equality of the sexes."

Yet Darwin exists on the fringes of suffrage histories, in part because of her multiple loyalties to class, gender, and socialism, in part because she sometimes wrote under a pen name in short-lived labour papers. Other rank-and-file labour suffragists are even less visible, though they spoke up during periods of working-class mobilization and crisis. In British Columbia, the wives of Nanaimo coal miners imprisoned during a 1913 strike organized a meeting of five hundred supporters: they passed a pro-suffrage resolution that linked the need for female enfranchisement to the working-class struggle against employers and a repressive state.

We know May Darwin largely through her columns in the *Toronto Tribune*. The print media were especially critical means of reaching working-class women, who did not always have the means or the time to attend election debates and public meetings. Labour newspapers such as the *Winnipeg Voice* also brought together coverage of union, labour party, and suffrage activists. Long before the better-known suffrage group associated with

Nellie McClung, the Winnipeg Political Equality League (PEL), the *Voice* published feminist-inspired columns, editorials, and articles. In 1895, three women from the newly formed Equal Suffrage Club, including Amelia Yeomans, a local physician, and Mary Hislop, the wife of a Winnipeg trade unionist and labour alderman Charles Hislop delivered speeches to the Trades and Labour Council on women's suffrage: the *Voice* printed them all. A mix of professional and working-class women, the Equal Suffrage Club appealed to universal principles of social justice and a fair deal for all citizens. Although some club members pointed to women's special maternal insights and their capacity for moral uplift in politics, they concurrently stressed women's basic human right to equality. Their message was also tailored to labour movement concerns. Once enfranchised, they stressed, working-class women and men could press for laws that would regulate oppressive and dangerous working conditions and introduce welfare measures to aid their families. Labour men also entered the debate. When one anti-suffragist expressed his reservations in a letter to the *Voice*, Charles Hislop quickly chastised him for his backward views. Equal rights for women, he lectured, would result in better "human relationships" for everyone, shaped by "justice instead of injustice."

During its eighteen-year run, the *Voice* printed news of both the international suffrage movement and the Equal Suffrage Club, and it sponsored a lively women's column by Ada Muir, suffragist and advocate of free vocational education for women. When professional and middle-class women later created the Winnipeg PEL, they also looked to the labour movement for endorsement, sharing public platforms with labour candidates in hopes of electing pro-suffrage men. This alliance was strategic for both sides. Although labour men worried that middle-class suffragists did not necessarily appreciate the needs of working-class women, combining for a common cause did have its benefits. However, coalitions built on a single issue can be fragile, as this one was. Letters to the *Voice* wondered whether middle-class suffragists really understood the pressing need to unionize female workers, and as victory for suffrage neared during the First World War, such skepticism intensified. One labour critic warned in 1915 that the ballot would not be a magic bullet, suddenly creating economic and social equality, and he asked if allies like Nellie McClung stood firmly on the side of labour or if they were truly Liberals and Conservatives at heart. An answer came during the Winnipeg General Strike of 1919, when McClung sided with employers and the state against the labour movement.

Like the *Voice,* labour papers across the country promoted the female franchise. Those with a designated women's columnist often showcased suffrage especially well. In British Columbia, where a vibrant socialist-suffragist milieu had existed since the late nineteenth century, Helena Gutteridge, a British working-class immigrant, became a leading advocate for women's rights in the Vancouver Trades and Labour Council and as a columnist for the *B.C. Federationist,* a labour paper. Gutteridge arrived in Vancouver in 1911, armed with knowledge of unions from her work in the London tailoring industry and political experience from her participation in the militant suffragette movement. Her *Federationist* columns took particular aim at the exploitation of working women in a capitalist economy. Sweatshops and unhealthy factory conditions provoked her passionate denunciation, as did bosses who profited from the employment of women in low-wage job ghettos. Unlike many other female trade unionists, she was not afraid to criticize working-class men's apathy about the plight of super-exploited working women: "The history of women in industry ... is the story of struggle against not only the capitalist class who have exploited them mercilessly, but also against the men of their own class who said because they were women they must not expect to be looked on as co-workers or receive the same pay." Anti-suffrage men, including religious leaders, earned her sharp rebuke. After hearing an anti-suffrage

priest rhapsodize about the virtues of "feminine helplessness,"
she exploded in disgust: "Does the Reverend Father walk around
Vancouver with his eyes closed? Perhaps [he] will devise some
means of keeping the bodies and souls of women together without food, and their bodies warm without clothes or shelter that
they may remain feminine and charming."

Strategically, Gutteridge was a multi-tasker, always working
on more than one political front. She joined Vancouver's main suffrage organization, the Pioneer Political Equality League (PPEL),
but was also critical of its establishment-minded, middle-class
leaders, such as Helen Gregory MacGill (later a judge), who were
politically aligned with the Conservatives and Liberals. The PPEL,
in any case, was never very welcoming to this assertive working-
class woman with her "cockney" accent. After her suffragette experience in London, Gutteridge was deeply suspicious of mainstream political parties, which had routinely betrayed their promises to British suffragists. Nevertheless, understanding the need
for coalition politics, she worked with the PPEL and helped to
draw all the geographically, socially, and ideologically diverse BC
suffrage organizations into one umbrella group, the United
Suffrage Societies.

However, still critical of suffragists' failure to recruit working-
class women, she established a new group in 1913, the Suffrage
League, which met at night at the Labour Temple – a space and
meeting time frowned upon by some middle-class suffragists as
"uncomely" – to accommodate the schedule of women wage earners. Taking her cue from British socialist suffragette Sylvia
Pankhurst, who founded a separate East London Federation and
newspaper for working-class women, Gutteridge launched the
Pioneer Woman, but the paper faltered in the face of financial con-
straints, and no copies survive. The league also delivered suffrage
speeches on street corners, a British suffragette tactic that middle-
class suffragists in Canada avoided. Seeking out the support of
the masses through soapboxing in public spaces also had a long

working-class and socialist pedigree. It was the choice of activists who lacked comfortable homes, could not afford to rent halls, and did not feel comfortable meeting in churches – precisely the working-class women whom Gutteridge hoped to recruit.

When the First World War began in 1914, the economy, already in recession, spiralled downward, intensifying the economic vulnerability of wage-earning women. Gutteridge and fellow suffragist Laura Jamieson responded quickly, setting up the Women's Employment League to help women deal with the shock of unemployment. As a self-supporting wage earner, Gutteridge identified with their plight: without family to fall back on, she knew that unemployment meant no money for rent or food, no means of support, and the fearful prospect of homeless destitution. Although middle-class feminists certainly sympathized with the difficulties of working women, Gutteridge understood the relationship between suffrage and labour rather differently. As her biographer Irene Howard points out in *The Struggle for Social Justice in British Columbia*, her middle-class allies wanted to help working-class women, much like social workers did. Gutteridge was less inclined toward charitable approaches, more committed to empowering working women so they might use their political clout to challenge their exploitation and transform the economic system.

Gutteridge, like Dora Forster Kerr or May Darwin, balanced multiple political commitments to the labour movement, feminism, and socialism, searching for strategies that addressed gender and class inequality, sometimes wrestling with conflicting loyalties. By the time she established the labour-oriented Suffrage League, there were countless varieties of suffrage groups across Canada. "Votes for Women" had become the burning question of the hour. Motivated by intellectual ideals, horror at the social condition of women, desire for regulatory reform, and sometimes utopian visions of human freedom, women and their male allies were mobilizing around the demand for suffrage.

As educated citizens and moral and loving women, we desire to be placed in the position to impress directly our thoughts on our nation. The invidious distinction of sex is an arbitrary and artificial one, having no foundation in reason or common sense. Motherhood should leave the woman free to choose her vocation as does her brother man.

EMILY STOWE, 1889

FOUR

MAKING SUFFRAGISTS

Augusta Stowe-Gullen in her graduation robes, Faculty of
Medicine, Victoria University [University of Toronto], 1883. Dr.
Emily Stowe and other suffragists fought to have women
admitted to medical schools in Canada. Stowe's daughter,
Augusta, benefitted from their success.

WHEN DR. EMILY STOWE founded the Toronto Women's Suffrage Association in 1883, any woman who came out publically as a suffragist was taking an audacious step, risking ridicule. Not only did Stowe maintain a lifelong commitment to obtaining the vote, but her daughter, Dr. Augusta Stowe-Gullen, joined her in the struggle. How do we explain their combined fifty years of dogged commitment to the feminist movement?

Emily Stowe's Quaker upbringing, which supported progressive ideas about female equality, was one factor, as were her cumulative life experiences. By sixteen, she was working as a rural Ontario schoolteacher, and at twenty-eight she became the first female principal in the province. With three children and a seriously ill husband to support, she decided on a new career: medicine. No Canadian medical schools admitted women, so Stowe trained at a Quaker-sponsored medical school in New York City, where she was exposed to the American suffrage movement and its leaders, including her mentor, Susan B. Anthony. Reunited with her family in Toronto, Stowe set up a medical practice that was devoted to the needs of women and children, and she also joined a milieu of unconventional radical thinkers who debated ideas about social reform, ethical socialism, land reform, and many other political panaceas of the day. Encouraged by this heady mix of radical thought, inspired by American suffragists, and shaped by her own experience of discrimination, Stowe put her feminist ideas into practice. She established the Toronto Women's Literary Club in 1877, a nineteenth-century version of the book club, whose members, denied a university education but hungry for knowledge, devoured literature, philosophy, politics, and poetry. Their intellectual explorations led them collectively to feminism, and in 1883 they transformed their literary group into the Toronto Women's Suffrage Association.

Stowe's political circle in Toronto included Knights of Labor journalist Phillips Thompson, with whom she and Augusta Stowe-Gullen helped to found the humanistic, free-thinking Toronto Theosophical Society in 1891 as an antidote to "Churchianity." Not all daughters follow in their mother's political footsteps, but Augusta was positively influenced by Emily's ideas and friends, the emerging social reform environment, and her own encounters with discrimination. Thanks to the indefatigable lobbying of her mother and other reformers, Augusta became the first woman allowed to train as a doctor at the University of Toronto, but she never forgot the anger and hostility directed toward her by the male medical students – save for her future husband, Dr. John Gullen, an unusually progressive student who supported her feminism.

Understandably, both mother and daughter put immense weight on women's right to an education and their intellectual worth as equal citizens. They applauded women's maternal role but built motherhood into their justification for the vote. Presenting a suffrage brief before the Ontario legislature in 1889, Stowe argued, "as educated citizens and moral and loving women, we desire to be placed in the position to impress directly our thoughts on our nation. The invidious distinction of sex is an arbitrary and artificial one, having no foundation in reason or common sense. Motherhood should leave the woman free to choose her vocation as does her brother man." Over twenty years later, Augusta Stowe-Gullen was still calling for the right of women to "be self-supporting and independent," to earn a living as did men, and to throw off "old-time prejudices and superstitions" about their roles.

Emily Stowe's biography is often the opening paragraph in popular histories of feminism in Canada. She is an appealing figure because of her articulate commitment to equality and the professional advancement of women, though her more unconventional ideas, criticisms of the church, and opposition to class privilege are sometimes forgotten. As a mother-and-daughter political team, Stowe and Stowe-Gullen were not unique in suffrage history, but they were unusual. What can we extract from their experience and ideas that explains the rise of the movement? What inspired suffragists to put themselves in the limelight of derision, how did they organize, and how expansive or limited was their vision of equality?

SHARED STRATEGIES FOR CHANGE

Like Mary Ann Shadd Cary and Helena Gutteridge, Emily Stowe represented the transnational character of nineteenth-century feminism: new and compelling ideas about organizing for equality could not be contained within nation-states, as people, political convictions, and organizations moved across multiple national borders. Yet suffragists often developed distinctly national and regional strategies and modes of organizing. Unlike their American sisters, Canadian suffragists did not create one or two national groups, focusing instead on local and provincial bodies. Canada was a sparsely populated and vast country, with strong regional newspapers, cultural and linguistic divisions, and differing local economies and political cultures: all these militated against a centralized movement. To recount the institutional history of Canada's many local suffrage associations would thus become a parade of numerous groups sporting an alphabet soup of acronyms. A few examples might better illustrate the most common tactics of suffrage organizing.

Take Stowe's Women's Literary Club. Reading and discussion opened its members' eyes to discrimination. This led to lobbying for incremental reforms, with some success. Queen's and Toronto

Universities established separate medical colleges for women in 1886, and provincial legislation opened up the possibility of municipal voting rights for widows and unmarried female property holders. Three women, including Augusta Stowe-Gullen, were elected to the Toronto School Board in 1892, and national suffrage meetings were planned. But the Toronto Women's Suffrage Association went into a temporary tailspin of inactivity during the late 1880s (attributed by Stowe to men taking over), only to be reinvigorated early in the new century by a visit and public speech by American suffragist Anna Howard Shaw. In 1903, it assumed a more grandiose national name, the Dominion Women's Enfranchisement Association, and Augusta Stowe-Gullen, Dr. Margaret Gordon, and journalist Flora MacDonald Denison endeavoured to resurrect it. After another name change to the Canadian Suffrage Association (CSA), they recruited international speakers from the United States and Britain, used Denison's newspaper column in the *Toronto World* to reach the reading public, and sent speakers to the Maritimes to establish other locals. By 1912, the CSA was augmented by new converts from respectable mainstream social reform organizations, but it was also internally divided on questions of tactics and personnel issues. As a consequence, a parallel Toronto suffrage group, the Equal Franchise League, was established by social reform women associated with the National Council of Women of Canada.

What links this story to other suffrage organizing across Canada? The original impetus often came from intellectual, educated, or working women who had to battle for other rights as well, such as access to educational institutions. Although women were the founders and mainstay of suffrage groups, they were joined by sympathetic male allies, and both men and women drew inspiration from international suffrage leaders, publications, and philosophical writing. The groups rose and fell over time, moulded by local personalities, buoyed by minor victories, but sometimes silenced by organizational setbacks or exhaustion. What perhaps made the CSA different was its presumption that Ontario women should lead the way, spreading the suffrage message throughout the country, an attitude not always welcomed in regions that saw power as already too concentrated in central Canada.

Many suffragists across Canada employed similar tactics, the most common of which was the lobbying of political leaders. This might also vary according to class and ideology, as socialist and labour women had less faith in the elites; instead, they favoured mobilizing the masses to elect their *own* representatives to government. There was some merit to their reasoning: once labour and socialist party men were elected to provincial legislatures, they often put forward private member's bills that supported the female franchise. Many suffragists of all political persuasions nevertheless pleaded with those in power to share it. The stream of suffrage petitions inundating legislators was astounding, though without result. Confronted with a ten-thousand-signature petition, Premier Walter Scott of Saskatchewan told suffragists he saw no "evidence" that women really wanted the vote. A cartoon showing a woman as puppy-dog supplicant, begging the premier for the vote, ridiculed his paternalism and was followed by a flood of indignant letters telling Scott exactly why women deserved the franchise.

In New Brunswick, suffragists similarly collected signatures on petitions, extending an established provincial tradition of women petitioning for legislators' attention, whether it was an African Canadian woman looking for freedom or teachers asking that they be paid the salaries owed to them by recalcitrant school boards. Next door in Nova Scotia, temperance suffragists flooded their politicians with thirty-four petitions between 1892 and 1895. Signing such a public document could be a courageous act if it entailed disobeying family members and transgressing local social norms. A rural schoolteacher and rank-and-file suffragist later recounted her family's dismissal of her "crazy" politics

In this cartoon, which appeared in the *Grain Growers' Guide*
on 26 February 1913, Premier Walter Scott of Saskatchewan
makes women beg for the vote. A Prairie farm newspaper,
the *Grain Growers' Guide*, supported women's suffrage from
the paper's inception.

as she traipsed over dusty farm roads, trying to collect petition
signatures.

The petition strategy was employed with thorough precision
by Dr. Margaret Gordon in Ontario. First, she convinced Toronto
City Council to extend voting rights enjoyed by propertied single
women to married women. When that passed, she wrote to 850
town and city councils across the province, asking that similar
referendums be held. Thirty-three successful referendums and
160 resolutions of support later, she had made her point, not

because radicalism prevailed across Ontario, but probably because female property owners – those with John A. Macdonald's stake in society – were more easily welcomed into the local voting elite than their less well-off sisters.

Women also met directly with politicians to present briefs arguing for the vote and for other legal, civil, and educational rights. Emily Stowe's 1889 presentation at the Ontario legislature was echoed in provincial legislatures across the country, as women made demands, recommendations, and varying rationales for enfranchisement, many of which are captured in a 1912 manifesto of Newfoundland suffragists: no taxation without representation, democracy requires full citizenship for all, women's special maternal and domestic knowledge is required in public life, and social justice and reform will proceed more rapidly once women have the vote. Even when suffragists (invariably) failed, debate and newspaper coverage of their efforts kept the issue in the public eye.

DIVERGING TACTICS

International influences had an impact on suffrage organizing, but these did not always emanate from Britain and the United States, and they might take on distinctly regional forms that catered to specific ethnic groups. Icelandic immigrants, concentrated in Winnipeg and rural Manitoba, formed their own groups and relied on their own feminist newspaper, *Freyja* (Woman), which was founded in 1898 and edited by Margret Benedictsson. Born in Iceland, Benedictsson was orphaned at a young age and worked on farms before emigrating to North Dakota, where she laboured as a domestic, upgraded her education, and with her husband Sigfus Benedictsson, became involved in the free thought movement, which countered religious belief with scientific, rational thought (she even named their two children after famous free thinkers).

SOME ARGUMENTS IN FAVOUR OF VOTES FOR WOMEN, BY ARMINE GOSLING, NEWFOUNDLAND

Because – people who have to obey laws should have a voice in making them.

Because – laws dealing with the welfare of children should be regarded from the woman's point of view as well as the man's. Questions concerning the home are now continually being legislated upon, and women have knowledge and experience which could be brought to bear helpfully on domestic legislation.

Because – men no matter how well-meaning they may be, never have made, and never can make suitable and just laws for women.

Because – no class, or race, or sex can have its interests properly attended to in legislation of a country, unless is it represented by direct suffrage.

Because – a very large number of representative women all over the world are asking for it.

After moving to Winnipeg, Margret and Sigfus launched *Freyja:* the lively women's paper became an organizing linchpin for Icelandic Canadian suffragists, publishing news and stories from Iceland, the United States, and Canada. Compared to many English-language suffragists, Benedictsson was a radical. She was critical of organized religion, sympathetic to divorce (which she also secured for herself), called for welfare for poor women,

Women from Iceland and Finland, such as Margret Benedictsson, brought their suffrage ideals with them when they immigrated to Canada. Edited and published in Icelandic by Benedictsson, *Freyja* was the longest-running pro-suffrage women's paper in Canada.

and lauded women's equal partnership in education, the family, the professions, and even in domestic labour, the latter an unusual stance for the time. Like socialist feminist Dora Forster Kerr, she held unconventional views about the importance of egalitarian marriages; occasionally, *Freyja* printed daring articles on marital and sexual freedom, drawn from the American anarchist magazine *Lucifer*.

Benedictsson believed that, strategically, suffragists needed on-the-ground organizing to accompany the newspaper. "UNITY," as she wrote emphatically in *Freyja*, "is POWER." She helped to transform Icelandic Canadian women's clubs that were dedicated to charitable pursuits into suffrage groups and founded the Icelandic Suffrage Association of America in Winnipeg in 1911. Knowing the history of suffrage organizing in Iceland (where married women had gained local voting rights by 1908) and in Manitoba, she bristled at the superiority of English-speaking, middle-class suffragists who subsequently formed the Manitoba Political Equality League. These Canadian women, she wrote, might "learn a little lesson from us in some matters." Benedictsson was unhappy with Anglo women who assumed the public mantle of suffrage leadership without ever acknowledging the previous work of Icelandic feminists: "These highly esteemed ladies have considered it below their dignity to see the co-operation of the Icelandic nationality ... These English ladies no doubt expect little appreciation of a matter like this from a foreign nationality which has come from a remote and poor country."

Benedictsson's radical views and her direct lobbying for the vote were different from the strategies used in Nova Scotia, where suffrage discussions flourished within women's temperance organizing. In Halifax, the initial effort in 1895 to address women's lack of legal rights came from a trio of educated, middle-class individuals: imperial traveller and writer Anna Leonowens (whose memoirs inspired *The King and I*); Dr. Grace Ritchie, a professor at Dalhousie (with a Cornell doctorate); and her sister, Mary Ritchie, both solidly middle-class daughters of a local judge. They held meetings in women's homes, delivering presentations on women's uncontroversial "home duties" and also their more controversial claims for equal "civic and state rights." Despite a visit by Flora MacDonald Denison of the CSA, a suffrage organization faltered and did not re-emerge until 1913. Instead, suffragists focused on other reforms, especially the Woman's Christian Temperance Union (WCTU), and it was temperance activism that spurred sympathetic male legislators to present no fewer than six women's suffrage bills to the Nova Scotia legislature between

1891 and 1897. The 1893 bill almost passed. After two successful readings, it was foiled only at the last minute by an adamantly anti-suffragist attorney general, who shuffled it off to an obscure parliamentary committee, where legislation went to die.

Just as Nova Scotia temperance advocates broached the issue of the vote by organizing within the WCTU, some Quebec women addressed women's rights very tangentially through cultural and intellectual debates about their proper social role. Francophone suffrage sympathizers initially skirted the issue of the vote, fearing that demands for political equality were precipitous, unpopular, and perhaps even unnecessary, but activists nonetheless created reform organizations that posed questions about women's education, intellectual development, and the vulnerability of women from the "impoverished" classes. This incipient feminism invoked women's special maternal knowledge as a rationale for their social engagement outside the home. As Québécoise writer and social reformer Joséphine Dandurand insisted, women had a duty to serve both the family and humanity.

Another late-nineteenth-century Quebec journalist, Robertine Barry, also used her pen to question women's status, without calling directly for political rights. A single, self-supporting author, she wrote for liberal or "rouge" newspapers such as *La Patrie* and established her own publication under a pseudonym, *Le Journal de Françoise.* Suffrage did not figure in her agenda. Rather, she encouraged women to take up social issues, continue their education, express themselves intellectually, and assert their right to support themselves through paid employment. Even these goals earned her a sharp rebuke from anti-feminist male newspaper editors such as Jules-Paul Tardivel, who condemned her as a dangerous woman, far too enamoured of Enlightenment ideas.

Unlike Barry, Joséphine Dandurand was active in both the anglophone and francophone women's movements; her unusual ability to negotiate two cultural worlds was facilitated by her elite upbringing, education, and exceptional linguistic talents. More often, however, women's organizing reflected the two solitudes in Quebec. In 1907, the Fédération nationale Saint-Jean-Baptiste (FNSJB) was created as an alternative to the English-speaking Local Council of Women (allied with the National Council of Women of Canada, or NCWC, also referred to as the National Council of Women), in part because of francophone women's discomfort with the Anglo imperialism of the National Council, but also because they preferred their own French-language group, advertising distinct Catholic social values. In 1911, the FNSJB affiliated with the international organization Union Mondiale des Organisations Catholiques Féminines, its Catholic character protecting it from the wrath of the church, which was adamantly opposed to suffrage.

The strategies and aims of the FNSJB bore some similarity to those of the Anglo women's movement. In its magazine, *La bonne parole*, FNSJB leader Marie Gérin-Lajoie noted that philanthropy and reforms intended to improve both the life of the "family and the nation" were at the top of its agenda. Animated by the spirit of Christianity, the FNSJB promoted women's moral development and their vocation and work as wives and mothers. At the same time, cultural differences modified French and English goals. Whereas francophone women supported efforts to curb excessive drinking by working-class men, anglophone temperance women were more likely to demand legislation that entirely banned the sale of alcohol. The FNSJB also developed tactics to mollify the church's antipathy to anything remotely feminist. Gérin-Lajoie and her allies tried to set up a classical college for French Catholic girls so they might enjoy an education like that of their brothers. When the church voiced its opposition to higher education for girls, the women threatened to open a secular school for their daughters. Horrified by this prospect, the Catholic hierarchy relented and acceded to the creation of a new Catholic college, L'École supérieure pour jeunes filles. The FNSJB may not have publicly endorsed suffrage, but it was slowly fostering an incipient, distinct Quebec feminism.

As these examples show, founders of suffrage organizations varied in both their politics and their methods. Not all suffrage groups were set up by and for professional and middle-class women, and not all middle-class women were affluent. The unmarried female teacher or rural daughter who cared for aging parents may have defined herself as respectably middle class, but she knew only too well what it meant to exist on the precarious economic margins. Class background or aspiration shaped one's outlook, but it did not dictate whether one became a suffrage supporter. Angered by injustice, middle-class women occasionally threw in their lot with labour and socialist women. In New Brunswick, suffragist Ella Hatheway definitely belonged to the property-owning class, as her husband was a prominent manufacturer. Yet her suffrage work facilitated her sympathy for the labour movement, and she gravitated intellectually toward utopian and British Fabian socialism, which favoured gradual reform and a planned economy to eliminate poverty. Hatheway championed the case for suffrage to the national Trades and Labour Congress in 1914, and she tried valiantly to induce fellow suffragists in the New Brunswick Women's Enfranchisement Association to read what she considered inspiring works about utopian socialism, only to encounter stiff resistance and "sniggering derision" from its more conservative members.

Hatheway's disappointing experience reflected the changing character of suffrage organizing by the early twentieth century, as more affluent middle- and upper-middle-class women became increasingly visible and dominant in the movement. Since the late nineteenth century, women had sought volunteer avenues to contribute good works to society, not only through charity, churches, and clubs, but also through reform causes. The women's movement and social reform led them to suffrage. Middle-class women's prominence had much to do with their

Fredericton suffragist Ella Hatheway was an anomaly.
a member of the property-owning class yet sympathetic to
labour and social democracy. A labour history exhibit centre
in Saint John, New Brunswick, is named after Ella and
Frank Hatheway.

education, access to news coverage, social and professional networks, and knowledge of institutional power, not to mention
their class-based confidence. But also important was *their time*.
In 1910, the largest paid occupation for Canadian working-class
women was domestic labour. Many middle-class women hired
servants to help care for their houses and children, as few labour-
saving devices were available and housework was time consum-
ing. Their ability to pursue politics and their dominant suffrage
presence was premised on other women doing their domestic
labour.

PATHWAYS TO SUFFRAGE

Whether women adopted direct or indirect tactics, whether they spoke out publicly or worked in more surreptitious ways, we still need to ask why they became suffragists. What ideas inspired them? Whom did they see as their closest allies: fellow socialists, temperance reformers, progressive social gospel churches, farmers, men of the ruling class? The range of choices says much about the ideological diversity of the movement. Although it may have begun in the mid-nineteenth century with a small group of women who challenged the limits of male-defined democracy, it had broadened into a more complex social movement by the First World War (1914–18), fuelled by multiple and even divergent political assumptions. Historical debates are often preoccupied with precisely this question: What were the intellectual influences and social experiences that turned women into feminists?

One current of thought – socialist feminism – has already been explored. Another closely related pathway to suffrage was agrarian feminism, a set of ideas that stressed human co-operation, grassroots democracy, and the economic virtues of the family farm. Rural women's groups on the Prairies became exceptionally strong advocates for the vote. After persuading the Saskatchewan Grain Growers' Association to support the female franchise, Violet McNaughton, editor of a women's page in the *Western Producer,* and farmer Zoe Haight built a new organization, the Women Grain Growers' Association (usually called the Women Grain Growers or WGG), into a strong pro-suffrage body.

McNaughton saw the vote both as women's "inalienable right as human beings" and as a means to a practical end: the improvement of farm women's lives. For the WGG, it became inseparable from parallel campaigns to lighten the load of women's agricultural work, provide the equitable distribution of marital property, and improve social supports to farm families. Rooted in an appreciation of farm women's indispensable work during this stage of white settlement, agrarian feminism promoted the democratic

Violet McNaughton hauling water on her farm. Suffragist and editor of the women's page of the *Western Producer,* McNaughton promoted agrarian feminism, which sought recognition for women's essential labour on family farms.

participation of both men and women in political life and advocated for economic reforms that would sustain small producers on the land. These Western farm women believed that many of their economic woes sprang from the region's subservience to corporate, capitalist Eastern business interests, necessitating a united front with their men. They also supported government-instituted welfare and social programs, such as the creation of rural hospitals as a means to alleviate the hardships faced by farm families.

McNaughton believed that farm men and women had shared economic interests – much like labour women's sense of shared aims with labour men – but she also promoted cross-class collaboration, facilitating a WGG partnership with urban Saskatchewan Political Equality Leagues. Together, they created a stronger province-wide suffrage organization, the Political Franchise Board. Finding some shared feminist ideals between the "busy

dirt-poor farm women" and "urban women with different politics," and building "ground work for women's common action,"
her biographer Georgina Taylor notes, was at the core of her political being and ultimately essential to the success of suffrage in
the province. Although socialism and agrarian feminism were important routes to suffrage, liberal ideas celebrating individual liberty, rights, and freedoms were extremely important influences,
not the least because they fit well with the dominant ideals of the
time. Liberal writings that emphasized the individual's right to
education and opportunity became repeated justifications for
feminism. This liberal stream of thought drew on the legacy of
Enlightenment thinkers Mary Wollstonecraft and John Stuart
Mill, whose famous expositions on the condition of women (*A Vin-
dication of the Rights of Woman,* 1792, and *The Subjection of Women,*
1869) were intellectual bedrocks of modern feminism. The link
between women's struggle to gain access to higher education and
professional work – universities, medicine, law, journalism – and
their conversion to suffrage was always strong. The ideals supporting one struggle became stepping stones to another one.

The language of citizen democracy – in which all citizens
should have a say in their governance – was also employed by
many suffragists, including liberal, agrarian, and socialist feminists, though for liberals, the emphasis was on the right of the
individual, not on class or group rights, to public involvement.
Suffragists who were willing to accept limited voting rights for female property holders – the more affluent – fit more comfortably
into this liberal, individualist tradition. Yet some progressive
nineteenth-century self-named "new liberals" were not absolute
individualists. They also aspired to communal values of civic responsibility, public duty, religious tolerance, and improvement of
the nation. These ideals inspired Canada's most elite suffragist,
Ishbel Marjoribanks, Countess of Aberdeen, the wife of the governor general and founder of the National Council of Women of
Canada.

Liberal ideals of individual freedom might be invoked alongside reform arguments stressing women's moral, virtuous character: seemingly divergent concepts often intersected in varying
permutations. The chief inspector of the Toronto School Board,
James Hughes, for instance, invoked both women's individual
rights and social responsibilities in his pro-suffrage writing. The
husband of Adeline Hughes, a feminist pioneer of kindergarten
education, he also epitomizes the important political and emotional role of male allies: they supported women suffragists close
to them, wrote pamphlets, gave speeches, and presented bills
to the legislature. Along with other Toronto supporters, Hughes
established a Men's League for Women's Suffrage to advertise
their public endorsement of the cause. In a decidedly patriarchal
and masculine culture, their backing was invaluable, emphasizing the rational and righteous nature of the movement, just
as Phillips Thompson's endorsements had done in the earlier
Knights of Labor press.

Inspired by Christian and liberal thought, Hughes stressed
women's individuality, education, intellect, and potential as
moral citizens: they were the equals of men, though with different social roles. His book *Equal Suffrage* opened with the familiar
ethnocentric, middle-class lament that uneducated lower-class
men could vote, whereas educated women could not, but his arguments rested primarily on the need to liberate women's talents,
abilities, and insights for the good of society. "Woman does not demand rights," he asserted, "she simply claims freedom to be and
do what enlightened conscience reveals to her as duty ... Being
a woman does not destroy her individuality, nor relieve her of responsibility for duty, as she conceives it for herself, not as some
man, nor as all men conceive it for her." University of Alberta
classics professor W.H. Alexander, the first president of the
Edmonton Equal Franchise League, used a similar mixture of liberal and moral arguments in his speeches. Although gender difference was exhibited in men's "executive ability" and women's

"intuitive perception," he believed that, together, these "would make an ideal combination in the government of the country."

Socialist, co-operative, and liberal ideals were all important influences on suffrage, but many women joined the movement not after reading John Stuart Mill (few did), but because they found discrimination against women morally reprehensible. Feminists such as Emily Stowe, for instance, were horrified by women's loss of legal rights when they married, a manifestation of couverture, the long-standing premise in British law that a married woman's legal identity was completely subsumed under that of her husband. As a result, wives could not control their own property or sometimes even claim their wages. Stowe and other feminists campaigned for provincial Married Women's Property Bills to correct this injustice, hoping to encourage women's economic independence and challenge the patriarchal assumptions of the law.

Legal reforms to allow married women to hold property, have custody of their children, and keep their own wages motivated feminists in almost every province, but some causes that animated suffragists, such as dower law, were highly regional. Dower laws entitled a widow to a share of her deceased husband's property. In the eastern provinces, women had either common law or legislated law entitlement to some share of their deceased husband's estate, but in the Prairie West, they had no dower rights. Discussion of this injustice pervaded farm newspapers such as the *Grain Growers' Guide.* Women found it unacceptable that they might spend their entire lives contributing to the farm yet be turned out from their home as paupers with no means of support when they became widows. Alberta suffragists likened their status to legal bondage: they could not own property and had no claim on the proceeds of their own labour. A husband could sell the family farm without even asking his wife.

In the West, feminists also objected to the federal Homestead Act (1872), which entitled white settlers to claim free land that they

had cleared. The law reflected both widespread colonial acceptance of settler displacement of the First Nations and patriarchal
assumptions, since white women (save for widows with numerous young children) were denied homesteads. When some western US states offered homesteading rights to unmarried women,
Canadian women's *lack* of rights to land was criticized even more
sharply. If a woman was unusually affluent, she might purchase
real estate, and some white women did benefit from the land distribution practices associated with Indigenous dispossession.
At the time, however, feminists were concerned only with white
women's exclusion from free homesteads. The discrimination
women faced in claiming either land or the fruits of their agricultural labour on family farms was a very powerful lesson that
they did not forget.

Nor were these the only lessons. Suffragists were often made
in struggles over discrimination and exclusion, as women came
up against what they were *not* allowed to do, by law, convention,
or force: attend university, become doctors, control their own
bodies, earn equal pay, claim custody of their children, avoid marital violence, choose work over marriage, keep their own wages,
or simply assert their individuality. Feminists, as Australian historian Marilyn Lake puts it in *Getting Equal*, "began to demand
self possession." Whether it was due to personal experience or
witnessing discrimination, women became dissatisfied, outraged,
and determined to change society.

NATION BUILDING, RACE, AND EMPIRE

When suffragists claimed new rights, they often failed to appreciate that their battle *for* inclusion was premised on the exclusion of other women. None of the leading advocates for women's
access to homesteads took the rights of Indigenous women into
account. It is true that Indigenous nations had their own cultural
definitions regarding the land: white settlers thought in terms
of individual, private property ownership, whereas Indigenous

peoples were committed to collective, community land use. White women's demands to be considered equal settler pioneers were premised on the dispossession of Indigenous people. Racial boundaries between Indigenous and newcomer peoples hardened during the late nineteenth century, especially after the 1885 rebellion and subsequent intensified white settlement. Settlers and the state facilitated the segregation of the First Nations on marginal reserves, actively undermining their farming, even though the state claimed that it was enabling the civilization of Indigenous peoples through agricultural work.

Most suffragists believed that Indigenous people needed Christianization and education: they were deemed culturally apart, excised *from* the settler nation. Aboriginal communities were portrayed in much public discourse as backward and primitive, needing moral uplifting. Christian missionary literature of the time cast western Aboriginal women as oppressed "drudges, wretched, overly sexualized," though always redeemable through Christianity. White feminists were especially outraged at sensationalized reports of polygamy and the sale of "young [Indigenous] maidens" as wives, practices that only "Christian civilization" could correct. Although these examples come from Prairie history, similar forms of racist marginalization and segregation of Indigenous peoples occurred across the country, at different times and with different regional characteristics.

A few unusual suffragists, such as Albertan Henrietta Muir Edwards, who lived on a Prairie reserve, wrote more positively about Aboriginal women, and she later argued for their equal treatment under the law. Social reformers sometimes included Aboriginal women in their efforts to protect the downtrodden and disadvantaged. The women's reform magazine *Women's Century,* for instance, reported with outrage that the Criminal Code penalties for men who forced "Indian women" into prostitution were less than those for trafficking white women and should thus be altered. However, white women's efforts at Christianization and protection represented paternalism, not equal sisterhood. Suffragists knew little of the significant labour and important political roles of Indigenous women in their own communities, so much so that they often used Indigenous women as symbols of *especially* denigrated womanhood. In *The Champion*, a BC suffragist paper, feminists triumphantly quoted an interview with Norwegian explorer Roald Amundsen, who equated anti-feminist men with ignorant "primitives." As he explained, they were known for their bad "treatment of their women," making them the same as "Esquimaux [Inuit] men," who regarded women as "so many trained dogs to be used for their pleasure and service."

Suffragists saw themselves and their male allies as enlightened nation builders, creating a more robust democracy, a more rational society, an egalitarian citizenship. But what was the image of nation they promoted? Many were influenced by transnational ideas about race, imperialism, and the need to maintain a colour line. In late-nineteenth-century Britain, America, Canada, and Australia, ideas, research, publications, people, emotions, and actual "technologies" of racial segregation increasingly delineated differences between white and non-white people. Multi-racial democracies were seen as deeply problematic, even unworkable. This entrenchment of the colour line, argued African American writer W.E.B. Du Bois, was a defensive white reaction to the enhanced mobility and political organization of people of colour and the colonized. By the 1880s, many white suffragists in the United States had switched from earlier demands for natural rights to calls for a "nationalist gender alliance" of white men and women – against blacks.

Ideas about white, Anglo-Saxon superiority were transnational, but they were promulgated through specific national methods, such as literacy voting tests, prohibition of racial intermarriage, segregation, exclusion, deportations, passports, and the "remaking" of immigrant cultures. The Indian reserve system, the exclusion of Asian and black immigrants, and the "Canadianization" of non-Anglo newcomers were all expressions of Canada's colour line. Middle-class women's reform groups (though they were not necessarily all suffragists) routinely expressed their concerns about the dilution of Canada's white population, particularly in response to South Asian and Asian immigration.

Still, Canada's membership in the British Empire might complicate these discussions of race. A controversy over whether South Asian men who had emigrated to Canada could be joined by their families situated female reformers on both sides of the debate. Opponents of immigration, especially in British Columbia, an epicentre of anti-Asian prejudice, claimed that South Asians created unassimilable enclaves and that their family values were antithetical to civilized ways. Foreigners' supposed practice of polygamy was invoked as a manufactured scare tactic, not unlike the negative depiction of Muslim families and their "barbaric cultural practices" propagated by twenty-first-century conservatives in Canada. Dissenting women reformers argued in contrast that South Asian men had a right to be reunited with their families in Canada and should be treated as fellow members of the British Empire. They suggested that exclusion was contrary to the ideals of "human brotherhood, democracy and Christianity." Better that "justice, humanity and imperial cooperation" should inform Canada's response to these "peaceful and law abiding" citizens. Both sides were inclined to see Canada as predominantly British and white, with racial groups in separate communities, but those who supported family reunification invoked the rights of minorities and Canada's duty to fellow members of the empire. And like the South Asian press, they emphasized *men's* familial rights, not the individual rights of women.

Suffragists' views on race were also complicated by their belief in the power of feminist internationalism. In publications such as

Women's Century and *The Champion*, Canadians claimed attachment to an international feminist sisterhood that included all women, irrespective of religion, political party, or race, a rhetorical point they often claimed about their own organizations. The National Council of Women of Canada celebrated its inclusive, non-partisan, and non-denominational character. The latter innovation was claimed as especially bold and progressive, given how divisive religion (equated with differences between the Catholic French and the Protestant English) had been in Canada. Suffragists also routinely expressed support for the struggles of women of colour for equal rights in colonized countries, particularly their demands for access to schooling – though one suspects they saw Western-inspired education as a means of elevating the colonized. Ideals of shared international sisterhood were always asserted, but they remained ambiguous and precarious, easily overwhelmed by the more powerful belief in white, Euro-Canadian superiority.

The colour line was also imprecise. There was some overlap between reformers' presentation of Aboriginal women as oppressed drudges in primitive communities and their negative construction of backward, "peasant" immigrants, such as the Ukrainians, from southern and eastern Europe. White, but non-Anglo immigrant women were described in pejorative, racialized language and experienced linguistic and social marginalization. Suffragists and social reformers alike often saw them as targets of assimilation, rather than sisters in struggle. Although the emigration of southern and eastern Europeans was encouraged by the state to fill Canada's labour needs and settle the West, they were considered less-than-preferred newcomers. They needed to be Canadianized, which really meant they should be assimilated to superior British ways. The ethnocentric views of social reformers inevitably spilled over into the suffrage movement, especially as social reform increasingly became a well-trodden pathway to suffrage activism.

SOCIAL REFORM

By the early twentieth century, increased immigration, intensified industrialization, and rapidly expanding cities highlighted problems of poverty, overcrowding, and ill health, creating parallel fears (though often exaggerated) of family breakdown, crime, and disorder. This worrying landscape produced a social reform movement of considerable force and widespread influence.

Social reform had multiple meanings, currents, and ambitions. Some reformers were secular and scientific in orientation, advocating more efficient, orderly, healthy cities, achieved through expert study and government regulation. Others emerged from Catholic feminism (in Quebec) or the social gospel tradition that was incubated largely in the Methodist and Presbyterian Churches (later the United Church of Canada). Social gospellers believed that Christians should construct a more humane, caring society in the here-and-now, rather than waiting for redemption of their souls in the hereafter. Whatever the driving inspiration, reform was often wrapped up in nation-building rhetoric that stressed the imperative of creating healthy cities, stable families, and sound moral values as the foundation for a regenerated Canada.

The social conscience of women reformers was often aroused by the difficult living conditions of working-class women and children. The FNSJB's twenty-two locals and *La bonne parole,* for instance, promoted a maternalist reform agenda intended to alleviate poor women's problems: legislation to prohibit them from working in factories at night, health reforms to decrease the province's high infant mortality rate, and regulations to prevent the immoral downfall of working-class girls, whom they thought were endangered more by sexual temptations of the dancehall than by their precariously low wages. Whereas the FNSJB campaigned for pure, safe milk and mothers' clinics, the Anglo-Canadian YWCA set up affordable, communal housing and healthy recreation (no dancing, drinking, or sexual dallying with men) for

Amelia Bloomer (1818–94) was an American suffragist, writer, and dress reformer who criticized the confining corsets, countless petticoats, and tight dresses that defined nineteenth-century women's fashion. Constricting clothing prevented women from being physically active; some doctors warned that it also damaged women's internal organs. Bloomer designed a solution: large, balloon-like pantaloons that allowed women more freedom of movement. In Toronto, feminist and school board trustee Augusta Stowe-Gullen not only defended the right of women teachers to wear the much-ridiculed costume but also wore bloomers when riding her bicycle around the city.

young, urban working women. Still other reformers campaigned to protect working women's bodies for future maternity (by providing chairs to sit on at work) or to abolish the unhealthy, confining corsets and dress, leading to the much-ridiculed feminist bloomer costume.

Social purity reformers advocated premarital celibacy for both men and women and demanded the elimination of the sexual double standard, venereal disease, and prostitution. Prostitution, sometimes equated with human trafficking and known as the white slave trade, remained a testy issue dividing socialist and liberal suffragists, the former insisting that sex work was a sign of women's economic oppression, the latter stressing its moral connotations.

Whatever the reform goal – and there were many – women believed they should use their aptitude for nurturing, their maternal insights, their feminine skills and experiences to create a more rational, just, and *caring* society that protected the most vulnerable – women and children. The vote was the means to achieve this. Nellie McClung personified this maternalist strain of reform. In her writing, mothering was both an undervalued social virtue and the most important contribution women made to society. Often presented in highly idealized terms, women's maternal, caring capacities, whether learned or innate, made them "guardians of the home" but also badly needed house-keepers of the nation, imperilled by too much masculinity and too little maternalism.

Maternalist arguments were commonly invoked, but they were expressed in divergent idioms, with differing social goals in mind, according to the class, culture, and philosophy of suf-fragists. Socialist, working-class activists such as May Darwin and Mary Cotton Wisdom linked women's domestic roles to suf-frage politics, but their view of maternalism differed from that of middle- and upper-class women. Conservative, middle-class women writing in the west coast *Woman's Weekly*, for example, called for "public mothering" to eliminate social evils such as "dis-ease, bad habits, legal entanglements and poverty," but their aim was a "cleaner, safer," efficient, and stable social order, *not* the abo-lition or levelling of classes that socialist women proscribed. Maternalism assumed a distinctly Catholic character in the FNSJB, which reaffirmed the church's proscribed separate but complementary spheres of men and women. Following this logic, Marie Gérin-Lajoie advocated for suffrage based on women's natural, maternal responsibility to create a more moral society. Publicly, she disavowed the liberal Anglo theories of equality that were antithetical to the church. A self-taught expert on law, Gérin-Lajoie argued for the right of women to practise law, but cautioned that this applied only to the special cases of self-supporting women, not to the majority of women, whose primary occupation was in the home.

Maternalist arguments may also have been strategically invoked in hopes of calming anti-suffragist claims that feminists would destroy the family. Moreover, maternalism and equal rights rationales were not always distinct: they were used simultaneously. In *The Canadian Woman and Her Work,* a 1912 Canadian Suffrage Association pamphlet issued to promote the cause, author Jean Blewett veered from one argument to the other within a few pages. On the one hand, she stressed women's role as the "children bearers" of the nation, but on the other, she emphasized the need for true democracy, "justice and tolerance." How do we know which argument was more important to suffragists and to their later success?

Similar questions are pertinent to suffragists' support for reforms that we would now see as puritanical, racist, or just plain wrong-headed. The most important pathway to suffrage was the Woman's Christian Temperance Union (WCTU). Founded in 1874 by American socialist feminist Frances Willard, the WCTU believed that alcohol consumption resulted in irreparable social harm, especially violence and poverty for women and children, and that the liquor businesses exerted inordinate and corrupt power in political life. The WCTU's influential temperance campaign was international, claiming to unite the moral authority of women of all classes, races, and nationalities in pursuit of political rights and social reform. Canadian suffrage cartoons often featured women armed with brooms as the new moral housekeepers of the nation – the first thing they would sweep away were the liquor interests.

In Newfoundland, which was a British colony, then a dominion until 1949, the first suffrage campaigns of the 1890s were led by elite members of the WCTU, who argued that temperance protected the home against poverty and male violence, both equated with the lower classes. Newfoundland's temperance publication, the *Water Lily* (ridiculed as the *Dandelion Flower* by opponents),

CLEANING UP THE "DIRTY MESS"

Cleaning Up the "Dirty Mess," Manitoba Free Press, 9 July 1915,
and *Everybody Votes but Mother, Grain Growers' Guide,* 1 July 1914.
Female reformers were often portrayed in cartoons with brooms,
cleaning up partisan politics and corruption, especially the liquor
interests. Many reformers also had ethnocentric views of non-
white immigrants, as the second cartoon indicates.

doubled as the suffrage paper. St. John's temperance women politely petitioned the legislature for municipal voting rights so that women could cast ballots on local options to ban alcohol sales, but male politicians refused, claiming voting would "unsex" the fairer sex. They also suspected that the local vote would be the thin edge of the wedge for suffragists who had forgotten their true place in the home and would subsequently demand further voting rights. At the other end of the country, suffrage was publicly discussed in Victoria in 1871, when American suffragist Susan B. Anthony lectured in the city, but it was Frances Willard's 1882 lectures about the WCTU that truly galvanized local women. Seventeen-year-old Maria Gordon Grant attended Anthony's lecture with her Methodist parents, who encouraged her interest in suffrage. After Willard's visit, she helped establish the Victoria WCTU, linking its work to the reform and suffrage movements. Grant became the first president of the Victoria Political Equality League, which announced its formation by stressing (in the language of 1970s' feminists) that the personal was *always* political: individual cases of injustice could be dealt with only as social problems, cured with new laws that women helped to create.

Although historians agree that temperance created suffragists, the immense appeal of the WCTU remains controversial. One interpretation emphasizes temperance as a feminist means of organizing against family violence, equated with alcohol abuse. Even the francophone FNSJB claimed that its efforts to curtail the number of taverns would reduce the *"abus de force,"* a code for wife battering. Other historians stress temperance as a controlling, middle-class effort to regulate the morals of immigrant and working families. The *Western Woman's Weekly,* for instance, equated temperance with the need to assimilate and Canadianize foreigners, who were easily "manipulated by the liquor interests" and whose loyalty to Canadian values was dubious. Both rationales were probably at play, overlapping and existing simultaneously. WCTU locals varied politically across urban and rural areas, according to the brand of Christianity they endorsed and changing external ideas. This was a cause that women could tailor to fit their local and individual goals.

Suffragists' investment in the project of moral regulation led some to advocate for eugenics, though not French Canadians, who accepted the Catholic Church's antipathy to manipulation of human reproduction, even if better breeding was the goal. English Canadian suffragists' support for eugenic controls on the sexuality and reproductive capabilities of the "feeble minded and mentally defective" mirrored many medical and scientific theories of the time and reflected British ideas of white racial hierarchy that prevailed across the empire. However, eugenics was also linked to panic-stricken predictions of race suicide, usually voiced by elite men who feared that educated, white, Anglo, Protestant women (including feminists) were not reproducing as rapidly as "undesirable" populations. Socialist feminists especially were suspicious of this anxiety over race suicide. If women were not reproducing, they countered, it was because capitalism and poverty took such a toll on working-class families, which should be allowed to make their own decisions about family size.

Our own understandable horror of eugenics has encouraged feminists to rewrite suffrage history, providing highly critical views of leaders such as Nellie McClung, who supported eugenics, including legislation to prevent the "unfit" from having children. Yet eugenics was not everything to all suffragists. It also produced debate. Flora MacDonald Denison was skeptical about it, putting more emphasis on the environment than on genes, a logical corollary of her feminist belief that social, not biological, limitations hampered women's advancement. Some feminist advocates of mothers' allowances similarly claimed that mental deficiencies were fostered by physical conditions such as poverty; they could be eliminated with better nourishment and care of children. United Farmers of Alberta MLA Irene Parlby accepted the scientific arguments for eugenics and supported her own government's sterilization legislation, but she also spoke often of reproduction as an individual responsibility. Ideas also shifted over time. BC suffragist Laura Jamieson moved from sympathy as a Juvenile Court judge to later repudiation of eugenics as a member of the Co-operative Commonwealth Federation and a birth control advocate. Emily Murphy, in contrast, was a consistently outspoken eugenicist, who advocated legally forced sterilization to protect society from the "wanton" sexual reproduction of the infirm, criminals, and those who were a financial burden on society. To Murphy, these individuals were inevitably racialized, poor, and working class. In the *Western Woman's Weekly,* she asserted that the "majority" of prostitutes were "feeble-minded," quoting a doctor who labelled the prostitute a "helpless feeble-wit selling her body because she has no brains to sell."

Suffragist eugenicists claimed that their entry into public life was evidence of positive nation building. They would create a healthy, vigorous Canada, thus contradicting elite men's warnings of the impending race suicide caused by feminists. However, their assumed stature as the preferred "future mothers of future generations" came with a hefty price for other mothers – those depicted as eugenically unfit, poor, undesirable, needing state regulation or care. More than anything else, this complicated relationship between regulatory reform and suffrage has incited historical debate. On the one hand, suffrage was bound up with religious superiority, regulation of the marginalized and the poor, middle- and upper-class privilege, and paternalistic ideas about helping others. Yet suffragist reformers also believed that their political program would free women from violence, exploitative work conditions, and the poverty associated with working-class motherhood. Images of Canada's early feminists now range wildly from principled equality-seekers to "upper class women who promoted Canada as a racially superior society of wealthy, educated,

The so-called New Woman emerged in British and American middle-class journals and fiction during the last two decades of the nineteenth century. She was a symbol, an aspiration, an invention, and sometimes a focus for critique and ridicule. The New Woman set herself apart from previous generations, questioned tradition, and aspired to new forms of independence and freedom, whether in education, work, or sexual expression. The term sometimes assumed a woman's repudiation of her presumed natural role as wife and mother. Associated primarily with more affluent, educated women – who had the resources to be independent – the New Woman might be a crusader for women's rights or she might simply want to live out her own individual quest for freedom and choice.

Anglo-Saxons" – the latter quote from an article in the not-very-progressive *Calgary Sun*!

Such simplistic conclusions ignore the remarkably diverse social causes that led women to suffrage: dower law, drink, degeneration, destitution, denial of education. The rationales for enfranchisement also varied, including equality, freedom, socialism, individualism, emancipation, maternalism, social control, ethnocentrism, and efficiency. It is difficult to pin down a singular ideological origin for the suffrage movement. Moreover, debate was ongoing over how restricted or universal women's rights should be. When some Edmonton reformers argued in 1913 that only educated and literate women, not the "foreign" element, should be enfranchised, their blatant efforts to eliminate the immigrant vote were publicly demolished in a debate by University of Alberta professor and feminist, Geneva Misener. Her insistence on a universal franchise prevailed over nativist arguments in the Edmonton suffrage organization.

The dominant political rationales for suffrage also shifted as feminism was redefined over the years. As the vote and social reform became inextricably linked by the second decade of the twentieth century, more conservative regulatory goals became embedded in the suffrage movement. Some feminists, highly attuned to the political climate, tempered their demand for human rights with calls for social housekeeping. The New Woman of the late nineteenth century, who campaigned against great odds and male antipathy for access to the professions, university education, and some of the social freedoms enjoyed by men, may have become less threatening and more accommodating as she joined the middle class in the early twentieth century.

In Canada, as in the United States, natural rights arguments were increasingly accompanied or supplanted by imperialist and nation-building rhetoric. The 1910 endorsement of suffrage by the NCWC, a reform umbrella group for Canadian women's organizations founded by Ishbel Marjoribanks, symbolized a mainstreaming of suffrage. Flora MacDonald Denison was rather cynical about its endorsement, sniffing dismissively that it was the "policy of the Council to endorse measures after it's the popular thing to do." Yet anti-suffragist opposition always threatened. If the female franchise was so popular, so mainstream, why did those in power reject it for almost half a century?

The great majority of the women of to-day find themselves without any means of support of their own. I refer of course to the civilised white woman. The gay savage in her jungle, attired in a cocoanut leaf, armed with a club and adorned with the neck of a soda-water bottle, is all right ... Then there rose up in our own time ... the Awful Woman with the Spectacles, and the doctrine that she preached was Woman's Rights ... In reality she was no new thing at all, and had her lineal descent in history from age to age. The Middle Ages called her a witch and burnt her. The ancient law of England named her a scold and ducked her in a pond. But the men of the modern age, living indoors and losing something of their ruder fibre, grew afraid of her. The Awful Woman – meddlesome, vociferous, intrusive – came into her own.

STEPHEN LEACOCK, "THE WOMAN QUESTION," 1916

FIVE

THE
ANTI-SUFFRAGISTS

Suffragists were typically portrayed as unattractive
and unfeminine. According to this cartoon by A.G. Racey,
which appeared in the *Montreal Daily Star* in July 1911, they also
wanted to physically punish men. Anti-suffragist Goldwin Smith
claimed that men who were accused of abusing their wives
had trouble getting a fair hearing in court.

STEPHEN LEACOCK is one of Canada's best-known humour writers of the early twentieth century. His name has become a symbol for excellent comedic writing: there is a Leacock literary award for the best Canadian humour writing and a summer writers' festival at the Leacock Museum in Orillia; his witty rendition of turn-of-the-century small town life, *Sunshine Sketches of a Little Town,* has been dramatized for television. When he was not writing "sunshine sketches," Leacock was a professor of political economy at McGill University, a position that gave him a prominent platform as a public intellectual. He seems an appealing Canadian icon; even the standard picture of him suggests an endearing grandfather with a twinkle in his eye.

There was one social issue that Leacock did not find amusing: women's suffrage. His writing ridiculed suffragists and social reformers alike as bossy and controlling awful women or women with spectacles (spectacles being a symbol of female unattractiveness). They were mocked for their self-indulgent and delusional moralism, their futile desire to uplift society with temperance and other silly reforms. When he was not lampooning feminists, he dismissed them as intellectually inferior, unwelcome intruders in political life. How do we explain this educated, intellectual man's deep antipathy to suffrage? Was there a range of anti-suffrage views in Canada that we need to take into account?

However out of step anti-suffragist ideas seem today, they had considerable influence in the nineteenth and early twentieth centuries. Anti-suffragists (or antis) were well-connected members of Canada's French and English elite, who enjoyed assured access to universities, newspapers, magazines, and public platforms. As elected members of provincial legislatures, antis routinely defeated woman suffrage bills. The anti-suffrage ideas of anglophone spokesmen such as Leacock and francophone leaders like Henri Bourassa both reflected and constructed anti-feminist feeling. Although less organized than suffragists, the anti-suffragists and their writing had a decided dampening effect on the struggle for the vote.

After all, if suffrage had become mainstream by 1910, as Flora MacDonald Denison claimed, why was it still out of reach? If women's incursion into the public sphere was more acceptable, why were suffragists ridiculed as unfeminine, unnatural, irrational Amazons who either hated men or wanted to be men? Why did *Saturday Night* magazine's 1 January 1916 review of Nellie McClung's moderate reform book, *In Times Like These,* dismiss it as "bitter propaganda" and "hysterical bunkum"? The perspectives of the antis are an essential part of suffrage history. They help us understand why more than forty years of struggle, organizing, speaking, lobbying, and writing elapsed before white, female Canadian citizens began to achieve their goals. For racialized citizens, it took decades longer.

ARGUING AGAINST SUFFRAGE

In English Canada, a small group of male "establishment" intellectuals set the tone for anti-suffrage ideology. As university professors and educated writers, they commanded academic expertise and considerable cultural capital. As well as Leacock, there was Goldwin Smith, an Oxford historian, former member of the British Parliament, and distinguished writer who relocated to Toronto after leaving Cornell University in a huff when it went co-ed. After Smith's death in 1910, Toronto newspapers hailed a new intellectual leader for the anti side: Sir Andrew Macphail, scientist, writer, editor of McGill's *University Magazine,* and first professor of the history of medicine at McGill University.

James Hughes's 1895 pro-suffrage book *Equal Suffrage* laid out more than forty standard objections raised by these antis, ranging from the vague "voting is unwomanly," to the illogical "bad women will vote" (don't bad men? he asked), to the biological claim that women's brains are smaller (no official at the polling booth measures men's heads, he quipped), to the militaristic "women cannot join the army." Although anti arguments were numerous, varied, and occasionally contradictory, they often clustered around five themes about gender relations: innate sex differences and separate spheres; maternity, domesticity, and the family; the protection of tradition and order (and, for Anglos, the British Empire); war and military might; and culture and religion (especially Catholicism, for francophones). Not far under the surface also lay a suspicion of democracy for the masses and a fear of socialism. Hughes's rebuttals of the antis also hinted at why suffrage terrified some men. Not only were suffragists challenging men's commanding authority over the family, they were also demanding the redefinition of masculinity. Instead of associating masculinity with force and competitiveness, they idealized men of virtue, compassion, and restraint. They also advocated a single (pure) standard of sexual behaviour and egalitarian, or "companionate," marriages.

Anti-feminism in the late nineteenth and early twentieth centuries was rooted in notions of innate and natural gender differences that were grounded in biology and psychology, an essential premise shared by some suffragists too. Antis could cite ample scientific writing to support their belief in unchangeable biological differences; many medical and psychiatric experts argued that women's reproductive systems and their psychologies shaped personalities that were more sentimental and emotional, and less rational and inductive, than men's. At one extreme, biology made women more prone to nervous diseases, even insanity. Andrew Macphail believed in the law of natural selection and the natural order of existing familial, domestic relations: both were based in women's biological role as reproducers of the race. Unmarried women who involved themselves in reform, he wrote, were simply "atoning for their failures" – they had become "masculine types" because they were "deficient in the instinct for husband getting."

The corollary of biological gender difference was immutably different social roles for men and women. One of the antis' most compelling arguments was that men and women inhabited separate spheres in society. This assertion arose from a certain observed reality about the gender divisions in work and social life, which were then interpreted as necessary and inevitable. Since women's natural functions were childbearing and childrearing, their social roles dictated domestic maternalism, but for the antis this should occur primarily in the private world of the family. Unlike suffragists, who claimed that their maternal expertise necessitated political involvement, antis felt that natural female attributes would be corrupted by such participation, and indeed, that women were not equipped to intellectually or socially withstand the rough-and-tumble rigours of public life. Goldwin Smith, who had once endorsed John Stuart Mill's call for women's enfranchisement but reversed himself later in life, claimed that the women he knew and "regarded as the best representatives of their sex" (including his wealthy wife), did not want the vote. This unimpressive "my friends don't want it" logic was accompanied by a biological rationale: because of their bodily weakness, intellectual softness, and men's natural domination over them, women could not properly exercise political rights. Women were pure and virtuous precisely *because* they had been confined to the home, which meant that their "angelic" dispositions would not fare well in the political sphere. Thrown into its corrupting influence, their angelic virtues would evaporate.

All the male antis, both French and English, endorsed a version of the separate spheres argument. Leacock bluntly stated that women were morally inferior to men, unable to think creatively, lead others, or even follow orders. There was no need to legislate against their admission to professions since they would fail anyway. Smith was slightly more generous regarding their intellect. Women were not inferior in morality, he wrote, but "perfect equality" could not reign between two beings whose worlds had to be "complementary" but resolutely separate. For the antis, God, biology, tradition, and natural laws (some larger force) dictated that men and women must pursue different goals and roles; indeed, Macphail argued that women's duty was to live in subordination to this essential ideal. He did not object to individual women in some professional occupations, but women as a group demanding professional or equality rights was beyond the pale. Macphail did not take into account the many women who trudged down Montreal streets to work for twelve hours in factories. Like other antis, he had a myopic sense of class privilege, which was an integral part of his politics.

Protecting separate spheres meant protecting the institution of the family, which was a cornerstone of a stable Christian society. On this latter point, the antis also found some common ground with many suffragists. However, they promoted an anti-modern, corporate vision of society in which individual rights of family members took second place to the family unit as a whole, with its male head the person who should interact with the state. Women should exercise their indirect influence within and through the family, as helpmates of men and guardians of children's morality. The antis repeatedly extolled women's role in moulding future generations, including male politicians, and many claimed that the home was women's desired place. As Leacock remarked with some disdain, "they did fairly well out of it."

Thus, antis took middle-class affluence as a given and often incorporated sentimental images of inherently gentle, modest women and gallant gentlemen, an idealized old order of family life. Leacock painted a dire picture of this idealized family under threat by the emergence of a modern, industrial, and alienating society. His opposition to suffrage was always closely linked to his dislike of the materialistic American values that were supposedly infusing and ruining Canadian society. In the modern family, one no longer found a mother's kind touch and homemade pies, but rather a resentment of children and, heaven forbid, caterers at Christmas: "The home has passed, or at least is passing out of existence. In place of it is the 'apartment' ... where children are an intrusion, where hospitality is done through a caterer, and where Christmas is the 25th of December."

To safeguard the family, antis maintained, advanced states had developed traditions and laws that protected women and children. In a world where women very rationally feared violence and economic destitution, protection appealed to anti-suffrage women as well as to men. Contradicting one of the suffragists' strongest claims, that women needed direct access to the state to have their interests addressed, the antis countered that they already had privileged protection because "father rule" was coupled with male chivalry toward the weaker members of society. Smith thought it was simply a myth that women encountered violence and beatings; jury lenience toward women meant that it was men who "had difficulty getting justice." Suffragists often retorted that they would prefer equality to chivalry, since the latter proved sadly wanting in reality. Their cynicism was substantiated by the antis' claim that, if women won the vote and chivalry were destroyed, men's natural inclinations would be unleashed, and women would experience the basest, most cruel treatment. In other words, some antis pessimistically believed that men were governed by an innate, brute, and uncontrollable masculinity, only tenuously held in check by patriarchal social mores. Leacock disguised his misogyny on this count with humour, noting the fate of troublesome medieval women who challenged their place: they were burned at the stake or drowned in ponds.

These broad-stroke generalizations depict anti ideas, but we need to remember that the group was not homogeneous. For

Anglo imperialists such as Macphail and Leacock, suffrage was also an affront to the noble enterprise of the British Empire. They celebrated the incorporation of Canada into an imperialist project that included global military protection for countries of the empire and the civilization of "lesser" non-white races and cultures within its boundaries. British imperialism also set Canada apart from the disagreeable materialistic, modernizing melting pot of the United States. Many Anglo Canadian antis repeated rhetoric from British anti-suffrage publications, warning that the empire must be ruled only by men and maintained "through the proper ordering of the domestic microcosm" – namely, the patriarchal family.

Imperialist antis from Britain toured the lecture circuit in Canada, just as Emmeline Pankhurst did for the suffragists, though with less sensational newspaper coverage. When British anti Ralph Bond gave a speech to the Canadian Club in Victoria, he emphasized imperialist arguments: first, universal suffrage caused "political divisions," including the "dangerous doctrine of socialism," that threatened social unity in times of military crisis, and second, it challenged the notion that "imperial rule" was to be directed by men. As historian Sheila Powell notes of such speeches, they made the point that men alone should speak for the empire, backed by military force. The military argument also equated military service with political rights. Since women could not serve their country as armed combatants, they could not make the ultimate sacrifice needed of full citizenship (and pacifist groups such as the Mennonites and Doukhobors were sometimes also denied the vote). Women's very nature – emotional, sentimental – militated against rational decision making about war and foreign relations. Whereas Goldwin Smith claimed that women were likely to march men off to war without thinking twice, others asserted that they would be too hesitant to do so. Either way, they were not fit to rule.

The imperialist proclivities of Anglo antis were also shaped by social Darwinist ideas of an evolving natural social hierarchy and fears of impending race suicide: white, middle-class women's activism would lead to their abandonment of childbearing, allowing the less intelligent and less progressive races to reproduce with abandon, overwhelming whites. Macphail believed that scientifically ordained laws dictated a ladder of social evolution, with the better-organized societies and higher races naturally assuming more power and prestige. The reform initiatives proposed by women were unwelcome and unrealistic precisely because they were foolishly attempting to counter this natural dynamic, another reason he heaped contempt on female "busybody" reformers and their futile, "silly labours."

Anti politics were always about more than maintaining the gender status quo: race, ethnic, and class privilege was also at stake. These connected spheres of power also defined what made white men "natural" rulers. A conservative who believed in an inevitable social hierarchy, Macphail was exasperated with meddling female reformers for foolishly thinking that poverty was a social issue, when in fact the poor were destined for their roles because they lacked individual virtue and initiative. Equality in general was a fiction to Macphail; every society needed an "aristocracy of some kind." Leacock's certainty about women's inferiority was matched only by his certainly about the superiority of the white "Aryan civilization of the West," in contrast to the "uncivilized" peoples in the Orient and global South. Similar assumptions of racial superiority were scattered throughout much anti writing; it declared that the civilized West put women on a pedestal, unlike the "Hottentot" races that oppressed them in harems, slave states, and "savage" families. "Race" was also defined with characteristic nineteenth-century looseness. Jews topped Goldwin Smith's list of undesirable members of the nation. Known throughout the English-speaking world for his virulent, fanatical anti-Semitic writing, he ominously commented that the "removal" of the Jews from Europe would eliminate a "danger to western civilization."

Although many white, middle-class suffragists shared the imperialist faith in a more highly civilized white race, their ideas on race ranged more broadly, and some tried to expose the anti-feminist implications of fears about race suicide. Antis were generally more pessimistic about an unbridgeable chasm between the more advanced northern European cultures and their less evolved southern and eastern European counterparts, a highly contentious issue at the time, as both groups were settling Canada in large numbers. Suffragists, though also ethnocentric, invested more hope in evolutionary social change, the Canadian-ization of immigrants, and the eventual triumph of an integrated humanity. Indeed, when some suffragists spoke of the "mother of the race," they qualified this only by gender, noting that "one half of the human race (women) cannot be subject to the other 50% (men)." Suffragists writing in *The Champion* who were dedicated to internationalism declared that social problems were the responsibility of all "mothers of the race, whether they be black, or brown, white or yellow." Moreover, many socialist suffragists were highly critical of the antis' imperialist rhetoric as they had a well-developed critique of imperialism as the inevitable outcome of capitalism.

Anti- and pro-suffrage forces did share some strategies as well as rhetoric. Each group used pamphleteering, newspapers, and intellectual magazines to make their point, imported high-profile speakers from abroad, and drew strength from like-minded international allies. Since British and American antis were better organized and funded through their elite social networks, their publications and lecture tours bolstered the efforts of the Canadian antis. Anti- and pro-suffragists *both* claimed that their side represented true Christian teachings. Anti pamphleteer James

McGrigor Allan wrote that the female franchise was "wrong in principle and practice" because the Bible offered literal proof that God never intended women to vote. The whole "tenor and spirit" of the "good book," he insisted, "is repugnant to Sexual Equality. From Genesis to Revelations," it asserts the imperative of "women's fidelity and obedience to her husband."

Suffragists shot back with their own interpretation of Christianity. The Canadian Suffrage Association published a pamphlet by the Reverend R.J. Hutcheon, contradicting anti views of immutable separate spheres. Drawing on feminist writer Charlotte Perkins Gilman, he suggested that the civilized Christian world should aspire not to segregated masculinity and femininity, but to more "humanity" since "in the every-day world of human achievement there is practically no great difference between the sexes." Indeed, the world had suffered from too much masculinity, as seen in history books celebrating "wars and conquests to suit the combative impulses of men."

ANTI-FEMINISM AND QUEBEC

Although anti- and pro-suffrage forces both claimed Christian righteousness, they often represented different religious traditions. Antis were typically associated with churches (such as Anglican or Catholic) that stressed the traditional order of the family and the central role of the clergy in religious life, whereas suffragists emerged from dissenting religious traditions such as Quakerism or other Protestant denominations that allowed their members to interpret and act upon the scriptures as individuals. The most decisive religious difference, however, was between French Catholic and English Protestant antis.

For French Canadian antis such as Henri Bourassa, a member of Parliament, Jules-Paul Tardivel, editor of *La Vérité*, and Monsignor Louis-Adolphe Paquet, a clerical author, suffrage was a fundamental threat to a Catholic Quebec. Anti-feminism took a more aggressive turn after 1912 in Quebec as the suffrage movement became more visible, though ironically, the women's movement separated into French and English organizations at precisely this point. Catholic leaders were anxious to keep their flock from association with the "perversity" of suffrage: Paquet equated feminism with women's unnatural "false ambition," their imitation of men, and their "jealousy of men's successes." The triumph of feminism would be fatal to women and the traditional family, bringing the "speedy decay of one and ruin of the other." The church, he thundered in print, rightly "denounces and disapproves" of feminism as a "deviation from the Christian spirit."

Both Paquet and Bourassa granted women some role in the public sphere, applying their "leisure" time to "religious works and beneficial services," views that revealed their own class privilege. However, women's minds, suited only for "home care and children," could not be involved in "public policy, or calculations of government interest," topics reserved solely for "male intelligence." A highly influential spokesperson because of his popular defence of Quebec cultural and political rights, Bourassa also echoed many English anti-suffrage arguments: women were biologically and psychologically destined for the separate sphere of motherhood; society called for their protection as emotional, nurturing beings; their exposure to politics would be corrupting; and suffrage was dangerously akin to the evil of socialism.

For many prominent French Canadian antis, however, feminism was also a foreign import to Quebec, a Trojan horse bringing Protestant, individualist, materialistic, Anglo-Saxon values. After all, Bourassa reasoned, in countries where feminism was strong, one found the antithesis of Catholic family values: "female drunks, unmarried mothers, divorcees, and angel makers [abortionists]." Paquet agreed, linking feminism's roots to the Reformation, free inquiry, rampant individualism, and other Protestant evils. Suffrage, Bourassa prophesied, would lead to an assault on women's morality, domesticity, and submissiveness,

To label a woman a bluestocking was no compliment. In late eighteenth-century London, educated and literate men and women would gather for intellectual discussions in literary societies, similar to the political salons in France. Women who participated became known as bluestockings after the blue woolen (as opposed to black silk) stockings they supposedly wore. The term "bluestocking" became a synonym for aspiring, pretentious women intellectuals, and by the nineteenth century it was also equated with feminists. The famous French radical Honoré Daumier mocked les bas-bleu in a series of cartoons, depicting them as pretentious, self-aggrandizing, overbearing, pedantic and, of course, ugly. Similar depictions became staples of anti-suffrage cartoons across Europe and North America.

and ultimately to childlessness, destroying the "mother-woman" and creating in her place, "women-men," nothing less than "les monstres!" Since the Catholic family was a pillar of "la survivance" of the French Canadian nation, it too was imperilled. French Catholic antis accepted separate women's education that was suited to their proper (domestic) station in life, though not the horror of co-education. Dismissing "bluestockings" who sought a college education, newspaper editor Jules-Paul Tardivel warned that "women who want to be men are just monkeys."

What was really at issue was women's God-given natural place sustaining a distinct Catholic, French community in Canada. The powerful Archbishop Bruchesi of Montreal cautioned his parishioners that feminism would bring in its wake "a battle of the sexes," selfishness, and immoral liberal licence, all undermining family and nation. In the face of such powerful opposition, argues historian Marie-Aimée Cliche in "Droits égaux ou influence accrue?," many feminists tried to clothe their ideas in Catholic rhetoric about a positive Christian feminism that sanctioned women's public good works on behalf of the family, while denying any association with a "bad" individualist, liberal, equal rights feminism. Their concession to the power of the church led to constructive reform alliances with female Catholic orders, but it also meant that some French Canadian feminists came to accept the dogma of their God-given feminine nature, abandoned the struggle for the vote, and set back the clock on the fight for equality.

WOMEN ANTI-SUFFRAGISTS

We must be careful about overgeneralization. Not all French Canadian politicians were anti-suffrage; nor were anti-feminist ideas restricted solely to men. In the influential newspaper *Le Devoir,* "Fadette," the pseudonym of Henriette Dessaulles, Bourassa's cousin, used her women's column to argue against feminism: she urged women not to set themselves up as the rivals of men, but to embrace their separate sphere and familial role. Although earlier French Canadian columnists such as Robertine Barry represented an incipient feminism, a more concerted anti-feminism had become apparent in Quebec journalism by 1913. In English Canada too, anti-suffragist women used the print media to claim public space. The *Hamilton Herald* sponsored a regular feature titled "Anti-suffrage Notes," written by Clementina Fessenden, widow of a local Anglican minister. Using her column and her unrelenting letter-writing skills, she reached across the country in an effort to build a network of antis, circulating British imperialist anti-suffrage leaflets to anyone who was vaguely sympathetic.

An ardent imperialist and founder of the Hamilton chapter of the Imperial Order Daughters of the Empire (IODE), Fessenden put forward arguments suffused with Christian admonitions to preserve the divinely ordained sanctity of the family. It would be safe only if men's political role in the public sphere was separate from women's domestic role as Christian mother and helpmate. Fessenden's opposition to suffrage was biblically inspired, emotional, sentimental, and intense, writes historian Sheila Powell in "The Opposition to Woman Suffrage in Ontario." She believed in the "near divinity" of motherhood and forecast dire consequences if women were pressed into public roles for which they were neither prepared nor competent. She took special aim, though, at "poor" women, whom she claimed were already ignorant and neglectful of their children. Who would want these people to have the vote?

Fessenden's contempt for the "lower orders" resembled Macphail's anti-feminism, but unlike male antis, she promoted women's reform work outside the home and even suggested that women might vote in municipal elections, where questions of war and imperialism did not intrude. The ideas and style of argument used by female antis diverged in small but significant ways from those of male antis. Women often pleaded or reasoned with their suffragist opponents rather than contemptuously ridiculing them, as male antis did. Fessenden's writing also provides insight into the allure of anti-feminism for women. Not only was her imperialist faith in middle-class, white superiority appealing to some women, but she also emphasized the social value of their domestic role, recognizing the considerable labour and love they devoted to the family. In a society where women were economically vulnerable, Fessenden reassured her readers that the traditional family would offer them protection. No mother, she agreed, should have to face the "cruel uncertainties" of paid wage labour outside the home, surely a reassuring ideal to mothers who were already working inside it.

As Fessenden's one-woman crusade faded, other women banded together in a formal anti-suffrage body. Founded in Toronto in 1913, the Association Opposed to Woman Suffrage in

Canada (AOWSC) was a pale imitation of British and American anti groups, but it shared many of their characteristics. As in the United States, organized anti women had a clear sense of their gendered class interests and were intent on protecting them. They were also well aware that their opposition was a powerful resource for anti-suffrage politicians, who could point to them as proof that women did not really want the vote.

The AOWSC membership was dominated by wealthy upper-class women who were connected to each other through shared kinship and social networks, as they engaged in an endless round of teas, clubs, balls, and other events requiring a fashion budget. Some were "lady" this or that; others were married to prestigious lawyers, owners, and directors of major corporations and banks. A few professionals, such as teachers, were thrown in for good measure, but most AOWSC members came from the upper class. Thus, the class interests that they defended differed from those of middle-class suffragists, who were interested in providing better educational opportunities for their own advancement and creating a caring, professional welfare state.

Although the AOWSC repeated the common anti argument about women's place in the home, its members were not home-bound. With the luxury of servants, they were active in women's clubs and charities that helped the less fortunate (though not usually in organizations that advocated significant legislative change). Through their philanthropic, society, and personal activities, they were involved in the hidden work of constructing and reproducing their own class. They exerted social power indirectly, and like many antis, they shared a suspicion of full-fledged democracy, with voting rights for the great unwashed masses – be they men or women. Like other antis, they feared that suffrage was the gateway drug to socialism, a dreaded blight on society. Their fears reflected their own links to capitalist profit making. The first president of the AOWSC, Sarah Warren, took over as chair of the board of directors of her husband's corporation when he died and remained at the helm for decades (a job that seemed to contradict the maxim that women belonged in the home). In 1933, the University of Toronto rewarded her good works with an honorary degree.

THE CONSEQUENCES OF ANTI-SUFFRAGE THOUGHT

Suffragists sensed that the class and gender interests of these female antis clashed with their own desire for the vote, and suffrage cartoons often caricatured them as upper-class do-nothings who led a life of excessive leisure and cared nothing about poverty, child labour, or other social ills. The rich woman, happily insulated from social reality, was a favourite target in Nellie McClung's novels, personified by Mrs. Francis in *Sowing Seeds in Danny*, who plays Lady Bountiful to her servants, offering useless mothering advice (taken from a male doctor's advice manual) to working women whose basic material needs she does not comprehend. A more sinister version in *Painted Fires* is Eva St. John, a wealthy opium addict who sends her trusty Finnish maid, Helmi, to pick up her contraband, resulting in Helmi's arrest and incarceration. *The Champion* likewise reprinted poems that asked affluent women why they did nothing in the face of suffering:

> Solitude, quiet and sleep.
> Is it given to me today
> When I march in the ranks with those who fight
> To keep the wolf at bay? ...
> To the factory, shop and mill
> The feet of the working women go
> While their leisure sisters still
> Boast of the home they have never earned
> Of the ease we can never share
> And bid us go back to the depths again.

If we concentrate only on well-known, upper-class antis, however, we miss the more widespread suffusion of anti-feminist ideas through society, especially in newspapers and the political arena. In 1910, for instance, Fessenden initiated a letter-writing controversy in the *Toronto Globe* over suffrage. Letters flooded in, with about a third repeating the stock anti logic: suffragists were unfeminine and unnatural; the female franchise would destroy home life; women were ignorant about politics; and they were inclined toward emotion and hysteria. Anti newspaper editors and journalists throughout Canada also attempted to sway public opinion. In Halifax, the attorney general and editor of the *Acadian Recorder,* James Wilberforce Longley, used both his political office and his newspaper to promote his claims that suffrage would spell the end of the family. Under women's moral guidance, he believed, the home was a social bulwark against the corrupt, competitive outside world, and yet women were not morally fit for politics: they were "intellectually unable to use the ballot." Newspaper ownership was often tethered closely to partisan politics, providing antis with a ready-made public pulpit. In Newfoundland, the *Evening Standard* denounced suffragists in 1893 as inane, hysterical, and unwomanly. Twenty-seven years later, Liberal party leader and *Daily Star* owner Richard Squires discredited them as city snobs, "leading ladies" out of touch with "true born Newfoundland women."

The most effective and concrete expression of anti opinion was that of elected representatives in legislatures across the country. They had the power to stop suffrage bills in their tracks – and they did. In New Brunswick, for example, Liberal premier William Blair adamantly opposed an 1894 suffrage bill, claiming that women would be the most injured by suffrage. Though he faced split party opinion on the issue, Blair asserted that forcing women into the public sphere violated the "law of nature," which had made them "not the equal but complement of man." His fellow anti legislators applauded his words, claiming that women were already well represented by men, would lose all gentleness if pushed into the political fray, and should concentrate on their highest duty of motherhood. Even the argument that James Hughes had thoroughly ridiculed in *Equal Suffrage* was dragged out: wherever the female franchise had been granted, it was well known that "not the best class of women voted." One wonders how they knew.

Probably the most popular scare tactic used by anti legislators was the "destruction of the family" argument. If women voted, they "would neglect their homes," said BC premier Sir Richard McBride; hence, he would never support a franchise bill. "Antideluvian," responded a group of exasperated BC suffragists in *The Champion* upon hearing this. Whether it was Premier McBride in British Columbia, Roblin in Manitoba, Hearst in Ontario, or Taschereau in Quebec, anti premiers, their cabinet ministers, and legislators echoed the claims of elite antis about sex differences, separate spheres, the natural order, and military might, as they routinely defeated bills introduced by pro-suffrage men. Dozens upon dozens of such initiatives were vanquished between the 1880s and the First World War, probably the most concrete evidence of the power of anti arguments in protecting the gender, race, and class status quo. No doubt, politicians also foresaw an unimaginably disturbing domino effect. Once women had the vote, they would run for office, enact temperance, and insist on puritanical social reforms to clean up society, just as they promised. Suffragists, much like modern feminists, were imagined as dictatorial, humourless spoilers of men's fun.

Bossy and unattractive Amazonian women were often visually manifest in anti-feminist drawings and cartoons, as well as in Leacock's satire. The grim-faced, aggressive, unfeminine feminist was displayed in countless anti-suffrage cartoons. Extra-large women ordered about smaller, cowering, enfeebled men: "Are

Even the *Toronto World,* which published Flora MacDonald
Denison's feminist column, portrayed suffragists as domineering
women, bent on emasculating men. In this cartoon, published on
6 November 1909, an oversized, overbearing, and bespectacled
battleaxe has come to clean up Premier James Whitney's
ramshackle kitchen.

you not afraid the vote will make you masculine?" asks a pathetic-
ally emaciated man of an arrogant-looking woman twice his size
in a 1913 *Montreal Herald* cartoon. "It has not seemed to make you
so dearest," the frightening Amazon replies to this non-man.
The satirical reform magazine *Grip,* though on board with the female franchise, drew suffragists as overly earnest, schoolmarmish
characters. Even more derogatory images in North American publications portrayed them as unattractive, despondent failures who
could not find husbands, as the cartoon of lonely dress reformer

Amelia Bloomer glancing sadly at a happy couple indicated. Suffragists were caricatured as spoilt babies, childish naives, or perhaps most derogatory, crowing hens. How were they to counter such pervasively negative and disparaging depictions? The answer was to create their own cartoons, their own print media, their own culture.

A page brought in the word [to Parliament] that a delegation of men were waiting to be heard. Even the Opposition laughed. A delegation of men seemed to be an old and never-failing joke ... The delegation presented its case through the leader, who urged that men be given the right to vote and sit in Parliament ... [T]he Woman Premier ... gave the audience a friendly smile and then turned to the delegation ...

"Gentlemen of the delegation," she said, when she could be heard. "I am glad to see you – come anytime, and ask for anything you like. You are just as welcome this time as you were last time ... and I congratulate this delegation on your splendid, gentlemanly manners ..."

[Word for word, the woman premier imitated the Manitoba premier's own speech while the theatre responded with laughter.]

The delegation was flattered, complimented, patted on the head, as she dilated on their manly beauty and charm. "But my dear young friends," the Premier was saying, "I am convinced you do not know what you are asking me to do"; her tone was didactic now; she was a patient Sunday School teacher laboring with a class of erring boys ... "You do not know what you ask. You have not thought of it, of course, with the natural thoughtlessness of your sex. You ask for something that may disrupt the whole course of civilization."

NELLIE MCCLUNG'S FICTIONAL ACCOUNT OF THE
WINNIPEG MOCK PARLIAMENT, *PURPLE SPRINGS*, 1921

SIX

FEMINIST COUNTERCULTURES

By courtesy of "The Vote"

The cover of the August 1912 issue
of *The Champion*, which was based on a British original,
reflected the self-image of suffragist reformers: their role
was to uplift and aid less fortunate working-
class women and children.

TORONTONIANS PACKED the pagoda pavilion at Allen Gardens in February 1896 to witness a major social and intellectual happening: a Woman's Mock Parliament. Well-heeled attendees had secured tickets ahead of time to hear the latest arguments on this avant-garde issue. After some dignified classical music and an earnest statement of support by the Men's Enfranchisement Association, the feature attraction unfolded: suffragists' collectively written, dramatic rendition of a typical day in Ontario's female-dominated legislature. No less than fifty-two amateur actresses filed onto the stage to portray members of the legislature, though in skirts not suits.

The play began with the usual parliamentary practice of question period. Why, one legislator demanded, would the government not ban men working as teachers once they married? After agreeing that matrimony should end a man's teaching career, the MLAs debated political corruption, picking up on recent scandals in the news. "Why were there dead voters on the polling lists?" asked a curious MLA. Then new legislation was tabled, including laws to prevent men from wearing long stockings and knickerbockers while bicycling, and a ten o'clock curfew for men who were on the street unaccompanied by their wives. The pièce de résistance was a debate on suffrage for men, pro and con, with the usual anti-suffrage arguments turned on their heads. Instead of claiming that the Bible asserted male superiority, one legislator argued that, since Eve was created *after* Adam, woman was "certainly superior to man." Judging by the audience response and attendance, this sardonic send-up of male-dominated politics was an immense success.

Satirical theatre was a highly popular and distinctly Canadian form of suffrage spectacle, with at least twelve (probably more) Mock Parliaments (or Women's Parliaments) performed across the country between 1893 and 1915. These extravaganzas, which attracted large audiences, served as fundraisers and vehicles for educational propaganda, though they were also great entertainment. They varied in form and messaging, but they usually combined irony, parody, and satire, often using role reversal as critique. Women posed as legislators, debating and controlling men's rights, regulating their dress and social lives, routinely dismissing their pleas for equal rights with disdain.

Mock Parliaments were an integral element of the counter-culture that suffragists created to sustain their cause, their spirits, and their resolve. By the early twentieth century, they had constructed an oppositional movement culture around their demands. They penned women's columns in newspapers, published their own magazines, and wrote and distributed pamphlets. They also transcended these familiar strategies, producing theatre, novels, short stories, poems, film, posters, cartoons, parades, and banners, all of which helped to bolster feminists' intellectual and emotional resolve. This oppositional ethos elicited a sense of collaborative purpose – a deep and abiding *feeling* for suffrage. Feminists today write about the importance of "affect" for social movements: the way in which organizing spurs both intellectual growth and emotional, even passionate, feelings. The process of organizing, writes Rosemary Hennessy in "Open Secrets," "instills in peoples a passion for justice and nudges their good sense in new directions. Organizing creates new forms of consciousness that move us beyond our comfort zone to defy our culture's prescribed categories." Creating a feeling for justice, for alternative lives, for sisterhood, was no less important for feminists in the past.

SUFFRAGE PRINT CULTURE

Most women learned about feminism through print sources. Socialist and labour newspapers, as we have seen, were important incubators of debate about the vote. International suffrage magazines from Europe and the United States circulated among Canadian suffragists, creating political linkages, knowledge, and feelings of cross-border solidarity. Print culture was also critical to the cultivation of a distinctly French women's movement in Quebec.

Nineteenth-century writer Joséphine Dandurand contributed to a lively conversation about women's role in French Canadian society through her articles for Quebec newspapers, her short stories and plays, and the magazine she founded, *Le Coin du Feu* (1893–98), the first French Canadian periodical edited by a woman. Dandurand's elite status – she was the daughter of a premier, the wife of a senator – gave her the time and financial resources to write and the necessary social connections to the publishing world. Despite her place in the ruling class, Dandurand's cultural work was viewed warily by religious and conservative elites, who fretted about the negative effects on Quebec society of any hint of women's intellectual independence.

Dandurand did not endorse suffrage, a premature demand in her view, but she nonetheless used *Le Coin du Feu* to spark a conversation that circled *around* feminism. The women's movement, she believed, allowed women to extend their important familial roles to much-needed improvements to Quebec social and cultural life. Women could do philanthropic work, engage with social issues, and develop their own intellects – the latter was crucial for Dandurand, whose chosen charity involved dispensing free books to those who could not afford them. *Le Coin du Feu* printed other writers' views of suffrage and discussions of literature, family relations, and social reform, as well as the more traditional topics of childrearing, fashion, health, and cooking. Dandurand's cultural connections also extended to Europe. Progressive Quebec thinkers were often oriented intellectually toward France, which recognized Dandurand's efforts to develop French Canadian culture by bestowing the title of "officier d'academie" on her in 1898. Later, the Fédération nationale Saint-Jean-Baptiste (FNSJB) paper, *La bonne parole*, nurtured similar international linkages as a means of reaffirming the importance of women's engagement beyond the home. Articles on women's Catholic social activism in France were a subtle means of countering the Quebec church, as some French clergy argued there was no contradiction between Catholicism and women's suffrage, no hostility between Christianity and women's ability to vote.

Only one English-language woman's paper was devoted solely to suffrage: *The Champion*, published by the Victoria Political Equality League (PEL) primarily for the BC women's movement. Despite its short two-year run (1912–14), *The Champion* helped to fashion both a public sphere for feminist debate and a space for internal movement dialogue. As an intellectual forum, an organizing tool, and a manifestation of culture, it provided an important venue for feminist expression of all kinds. Its aim was to promote a fair deal for women in employment, education, and the law by fostering a unified coalition of women rather than an organization representing any "one religious creed, Political party, or Social Class." Although the PEL's aims were laudably inclusive, its day-to-day activities, encompassing afternoon parlour study groups, mirrored its white, middle-class, and professional membership.

Although it focused especially on British Columbia, *The Champion* printed international coverage, designed to make Canadian suffragists feel part of a larger, like-minded, and thoroughly righteous global movement. International news provided proof that the female franchise actually *worked* in practice. It offered hope: the vote had been achieved elsewhere without violence or militancy, and far from destroying the family, it led to progressive reforms to protect it. Reports from New Zealand, where suffrage for white and Indigenous women came in 1893, and Australia, with federal suffrage for white women in 1902, concluded that the "drawbacks were nil, the positive gains unquestionable." The "moral atmosphere had been purified," and countless reforms "dear to women's hearts" had been legislated in Australia, including "Sunday Closing, Age of Consent, Children's Courts, Prevention of Sweating, Suppression of Indecent Advertising, Hours of Labor for Women and Children, Prohibition of the Opium trade, Gambling and Smoking." Another *Champion* column praised California women who used their new voting power to secure a law that punished "lazy fathers" who did not support their dependants: these men were forced to labour on public works and turn their wages over to the family. Suffragists' enthusiasm for this brand of legal regulation reflected their desire to protect vulnerable women and children but also their tendency to blame poverty and destitution on the moral failures of the working class, rather than their meagre economic prospects.

The Champion experimented with various means of communication to get its message across: poems, editorials, provincial organizing reports, letters to the editor, and even a mock men's column. It is not hard to imagine suffragists' immense pleasure in finally having the discursive upper hand after enduring years of public ridicule in the press. Feminists savoured the opportunity to treat their political debates with respectful gravitas but also to lampoon their opponents, satirize mainstream culture, and create their own identity. The "Men's Cosy Corner," for instance, was partly serious, raising questions about men's role in supporting suffrage, but also satirically tongue-in-cheek. Written by Uncle Pry, it offered advice on "all men's little personal affairs" as well as hints for their cocktail attire, recipes, manners, and deportment. In more serious pieces, the *Champion* generated the self-image that suffragists desired: they portrayed themselves as heroic pioneers in the history of the Canadian West, doing equal work with white settler men on the frontier. Together, they could enjoy an auspicious future of building the nation, if that one "stain of inequality," women's lack of the vote, were rectified.

Although *The Champion* was a unique suffrage paper, other social reform magazines, including *Women's Century* (1913–21), endorsed by the National Council of Women of Canada, the FNSJB's *La bonne parole* (1913–58), and the Vancouver-based *Western Woman's Weekly* (1917–24), also touched on suffrage issues. International suffrage papers added another layer to the cultural construction of the Canadian movement. Enthusiasts such as Flora MacDonald Denison, dedicated to the ideal of feminist internationalism, sent intermittent reports on Canada to the International Woman Suffrage Alliance paper, *Jus Suffragii*, but its Canadian coverage was still sparse, usually emanating from a few cities such as Toronto. Canada was not particularly prominent in the international organizations and could not claim to be a global suffrage leader, as Australia and New Zealand were, though Canadian publications always kept their eye on feminist news outside the country.

Sometimes Canada seemed to be the backward colonial cousin. The British Women's Social and Political Union (suffragette) newspaper, *Votes for Women*, viewed the smaller Canadian movement through a rather condescending lens: it was underdeveloped, in need of the enlightened leadership of the mother country. *Winnipeg Free Press* journalist Lillian Beynon Thomas told researcher Catherine Cleverdon that British claims to tactical superiority rankled Canadian suffragists: "We resented very keenly that some English women came out and tried to stampede us into violent methods" for which we were not "ready." *Votes for Women* reported that Canadians were inspired to act after British suffragettes toured their country, and suffragette leader Emmeline Pethick-Lawrence offered extensive opinions in the paper after a short stay in Victoria with her brother and sister-in-law, who was also a Women's Social and Political Union (WSPU) supporter. Canadian feminists, she asserted with authority, had

more allies and did not face the "blind prejudice" of the old country. Thus, "if the women were to bestir themselves now, and if
strong political leadership were to be evolved, I believe they could
get the vote within a year." After their decades of organizing, one
wonders what Canadian feminists thought of this assessment.

Most women, however, did not learn about suffrage from international publications, but from Canadian newspapers, often of
a regional bent. In a geographically diffuse nation in which the
rural population still dominated, newspapers offered a lifeline
to the women's movement. The women's column in the farm
newspaper, the *Grain Growers' Guide* (GGG), was a case in point.
Published in Winnipeg, the GGG promoted economic and social
co-operation among farmers, challenging the power of large
private corporations. From its inception in 1908, the paper endorsed suffrage, not just on the women's page, but on its editorial
page. The first editor, E.A. Partridge, announced that women's
equality was an intrinsic part of the co-operative ideal, and he
scathingly dismissed male opponents of suffrage as narrow-
minded autocrats. If "men wanted freedom of the mind," they had
to give it to women too: most men who objected to the franchise
simply feared the "loss of their own prestige and power to play the
tyrant."

Suffrage talk was also a staple of the GGG women's page.
Under the direction of Francis Marion Beynon, it became a dynamic forum for debate about the vote, legal reforms, farm labour,
women's oppression, and family relations. Beynon provided the
usual advice on managing a home and raising children, but she
also wrote critically about the connection between women's un-
paid farm labour and their second-class status in the family and
society. An open, unmediated stream of letters from readers became the means of facilitating what Tracy Kulba and Victoria
Lamont call the GGG's "radical democracy" in action. Women and
some male correspondents rallied back and forth, debating,

decrying, and explaining women's inequality. For every correspondent who advised women to follow and cherish their husbands, many others criticized women's confining role as economic
slave to her male master in the family. A series of cartoons featuring John Tightwad, a patriarchal tyrant who excluded his wife
from all financial decisions, elicited intense debate among readers, not the least because it struck at the heart of women's complaint that their labour built farms, but provincial dower laws
denied them a stake in them. Female correspondents, however
geographically isolated, could have a conversation in print about
problems that touched their lives, and some used the opportunity
to raise controversial issues, such as male violence against women
and children or birth control.

The medium – debate – was the feminist message: democracy,
not only in letter writing, but in real life, should be the goal of all
co-operative progressives. Yet the GGG echoed some of the same
cultural prejudices of other suffrage organizations. The ideal rural
settler was imagined as British, English speaking, and Protestant.
Southern and eastern European (and Catholic) immigrants were
less preferred interlopers – though they might be *assimilated* to
superior Anglo-Canadian laws, culture, and traditions. As Partridge
once editorialized about the vote, "What an outrage to deny to the
highest minded, most cultured native-born lady what is cheer-
fully granted to the lowest browed, most imbruted foreign hobo
that chooses to visit our shores."

Like Francis Beynon, journalist Flora MacDonald Denison
used her regular newspaper column in the *Toronto World* to stimu-
late a public dialogue about women's social roles, reform, and
suffrage. She injected political commentary into a medium – the
women's page – that was previously devoted to fashion, romance,
personal advice, and recipes. Denison was born in Belleville,
Ontario, to a middle-class family that valued education but
was plagued by money woes, leaving her responsible for her own

Canadian Suffrage Association president from 1911 to 1914, Flora
MacDonald Denison was one of the most internationally oriented
Canadian suffragists. More unconventional and radical than
other feminists, she was one of few Canadians to proudly call
herself a "suffragette" in solidarity with the British WSPU.

upkeep when she left school at fifteen. After working as a teacher
and a seamstress, she set up her own small tailoring business in
Toronto, an experience that gave her a front-row perspective on
the difficulties that working women experienced in surviving on

minimal wages. Inspired by a meeting with Emily Stowe, she became a suffragist and, with Dr. Augusta Stowe-Gullen, revived the flagging Toronto Canadian Suffrage Association (CSA). A working mother with a son to support, Denison was not affluent, but she subsidized and housed the CSA office, and she self-funded her trips to international suffrage meetings in Europe. Had she lived to write an autobiography, her name might be synonymous with the history of suffrage, but she died at a relatively young fifty-four in 1921, leaving us only intriguing fragments of her unconventional ideas.

Denison was inspired by the writing of American poet and democracy advocate Walt Whitman; she was later designated Canada's first eco-feminist, as she ran a wilderness retreat for Walt Whitmanites, spiritualists, and other non-conformists at Bon Echo, now a provincial park. Feminist writer Charlotte Perkins Gilman, who promoted the collectivization of housework to free women from domestic labour, was also her mentor, as was South African Olive Schreiner, whose book *Woman and Labour* became a foundational feminist text validating women's paid work outside the home. Theosophy and spiritualism also claimed Denison's interest. She penned a fictionalized biography of her deceased older sister, *Mary Meville*, a psychic whose gifts she believed were denied by the small-minded strictures of convention and Christianity. British labour leader Kier Hardie was one of her heroes, and like many socialists, she was highly critical of organized religion, including the Christian churches' prohibitions on divorce and family planning – issues that other suffragists shied away from.

Denison's column encouraged women to contemplate these challenging ideas and imagine how they might use their vote to create a different society. She advocated for state-funded mothers' pensions for widows and child care centres (or crèches) for impoverished working mothers. The low wages of women workers earned her rebuke, and she was particularly critical of Canada's hierarchical "caste society," in which the affluent looked down their noses on the honest labour of ordinary men and women. Denison would have fit comfortably within the nineteenth-century Knights of Labor, who similarly valued the dignity of all labour, or today, with activists who are horrified at the indefensible wealth of the 1 percent. "Do I really have a right to two coats when my brother only has one?" she asked. "Have I a right, even as mistress of a Government House to 500 gowns, while my sister has not enough to cover her nakedness, she having done more in her life to produce wealth than I?"

Denison insisted that women *deserved* the vote, as a human right, as a step toward full democracy, and as a fulfillment of personal autonomy. However, maternalist ideas were also intrinsic to her world view. As scholar Janice Fiamengo notes in *The Woman's Page,* Denison's columns spoke to the "practical knowledge and emotional commitment" of women's mother work, pointing to the social problems that deeply touched their families. If women were to address the issues that threatened the home, such as sanitation, pure water, or the "protection for girls from sexual predators," they must secure a political voice. The protection of children, like the safeguarding of humanity, gave women no choice but to speak out. They could do so effectively only with the vote.

Beynon, Denison, and many other female journalists played an important role in constructing a feminist counterculture rooted in reasoned argument and an affective feeling for suffrage. They cultivated social dialogue, a smorgasbord of new ideas for women to contemplate, and a vision for the future while also nurturing a sense of emotional and political urgency as they detailed women's day-to-day experiences of suffering and exploitation. Unconventional ideas, however, also generate backlash. Denison's more radical views and suffragette sympathies would eventually land her in hot water, and not simply from anti-suffrage men. She was reviled by some conservative Toronto suffragists, who by 1912 had formed a new suffrage group, quietly pushing her aside and insinuating that her modest class background was an embarrassment. A nasty private letter to Denison asked why she did not "stick to her own class" and let more reputable women assume the leadership they deserved.

SUFFRAGE CULTURE IN INTERNATIONAL CONTEXT

If Beynon and Denison put suffrage on the women's page, it was still a long way from the front page. The British suffragettes, associated with militancy and civil disobedience, *were* featured on the front page, indirectly giving the Canadian movement more visibility. The term "suffragette" was originally derogatory, referring to British women who disrupted and heckled the political meetings of men. It was then claimed by these same women as a badge of honour, a moniker that distinguished them from the more sedate suffragists, who used legal, non-militant tactics. The notion that only the suffragettes of the WSPU were radical is contradicted by the range of radical ideas and complex alliances within the British feminist movement. However, as British historian June Hannam concludes, the "passion, intensity of feeling and flamboyance" of WSPU property destruction and civil disobedience, along with the state's severely punitive responses (imprisonment and force feeding), elevated the suffragettes to the limelight of the movement, which is still true today.

Flora MacDonald Denison provided a personal link to the British suffragettes. She gave a speech at one of their London rallies after attending an International Suffrage Congress, where she met Emmeline Pankhurst. Denison subsequently organized Pankhurst's first trip to Canada in 1909 and used her *Toronto World* column to provide an alternative view of the WSPU, dispelling the media image of the suffragettes as aggressive, angry, unwomanly, and irrational. Nor was she alone. Winnipeg journalist Lillian Beynon Thomas also refuted the antagonistic, mannish image of the suffragettes, and socialist Mary Cotton Wisdom declared in her *Cotton's Weekly* column that criticizing suffragettes for blowing up a few mailboxes while ignoring the "hourly violence" visited upon them by the British government was pure "bunk."

During Emmeline Pankhurst's Canadian lecture tour, the press focused on the WSPU destruction of property, which is now interpreted by historians as the result of over forty years of organizing disappointment and suffragists' reaction to the male violence that greeted their initially peaceful protests. Reporters constantly asked Canadian feminists whether this culture of violence would cross the Atlantic. Canadian suffragists distanced themselves from WSPU tactics, without actually condemning them. Most stressed the calm, rational, peaceful character of their own movement, though a few, such as a young Toronto poet and university student, Laura McCully, hinted that their patience with petitions was wearing thin. She and a fellow militant, she intimated, were ready to "torment members of parliament, march through the streets, or raid sleepy legislatures." McCully was recruited to the cause as a university student, and her writing points to another cultural outlet for budding suffragists: women's literary societies, clubs, and university journalism. She published her poems in the University of Toronto student newspaper, the *Varsity*, and wrote for local papers about women's rights. "The time is past when women will be satisfied with a 'rattle' or a halo," she warned. "The former is infantile, the latter obsolete. What we want from men is candor, justice, self-control. What we offer is help – a 'help' meet for men."

McCully's attraction to the suffragette style of protest was shared by a small group of WSPU sympathizers in Victoria, the home of many British émigrés. Canadians who wanted to embrace militancy, however, were better off moving to Britain. Gertrude Harding, from a New Brunswick farming family, did just that. When her international travels took her to London, she joined the WSPU, worked as an organizer, participated in its campaigns of public disruption and property destruction, and eventually became part of the elite female bodyguard that protected

Although Canadian suffragists were influenced by diverse political ideas imported from Britain, including labour and socialist writing, most newspapers after 1912 were obsessed with just one group – the militant "suffragettes" associated with the Women's Social and Political Union. Canadian suffragists did not support similar methods of property destruction, but they did condemn the violence directed against suffragettes, including the cruelty of the Cat and Mouse Act. Passed by the British Parliament in 1913, the act allowed for the release of suffragette hunger strikers in prison who resisted forced feeding and were near death. Once their health recovered, they were reincarcerated, and the process began all over again.

Emmeline Pankhurst from re-arrest after the infamous "Cat and Mouse Act" of 1913 allowed the police to release suffragette hunger strikers and then promptly reapprehend them.

Canadian suffragists appeared staid in comparison. Disruptive *tactics*, however, are not necessarily the same as radical *ideas*. To assume that Canadian suffragists were boring and conservative because they employed peaceful strategies ignores the risks that women ran simply by organizing and speaking *in public*, occupying space not usually allowed them.

WIDENING THE COUNTERCULTURE TO POPULAR CULTURE

As forms of comment that convey feeling, make an argument, or elicit laughter, cartoons were an important resource for suffragists. In the absence of photographs, sketches of suffrage leaders were often used as illustrations, humanizing their words and bringing them closer to readers. Satirical or lesson-based cartoons, using recurring symbols and characters, were also common. The broom, often associated with women witches, was reclaimed by feminists as a symbol of women's purifying activism. In a *Grain Growers' Guide* cartoon, a virtuous suffragist named Dame Canada sweeps the corruption of the liquor interests and political patronage into a bonfire, helped by her muscular mate, John Canada. In countless other cartoons, women use domestic utensils – brooms, dusters, mops, and pails – as instruments of decontamination, attacking corruption, special interests, white slavers, corporate monopolies, and bribery. The idealized suffragist was a housewife working hard at nation building or a pioneer farmer settling the land, both the exact opposite of wealthy, leisured women. In one *Montreal Herald* cartoon, a suffragist holding her "Votes for Women" sign is surrounded by children in rags and overworked factory women. They all point an accusing finger at the symbolic anti-suffragist: a complacent, inactive, fashionably dressed upper-class woman, dripping in jewels.

Suffrage cartoons predicted a rosy future once women won the vote, showing numerous blights on society swept away, pushed over cliffs, run out of town. Conversely, those who feared suffrage were portrayed as the greedy and intransigent economic or political interests who benefitted from the misery and exploitation of others. Whereas social reform messages about women's purifying roles were evident, so too were cartoons suggesting that they had a right to democracy, freedom, and equality, thus reflecting the dualistic nature of suffrage arguments. John Bengough, editor and cartoonist for Canada's satirical magazine *Grip,* sketched a victory cartoon when Ohio women secured the vote, showing banners reading "government of all the people by all the people" and "not sex but citizenship." Sympathetic allies such as Bengough and labour journalist Phillips Thompson used *Grip's* penchant for biting satire to support the female franchise. The paper skewered the courts' lax treatment of abusive husbands, ridiculed the law

GRAND TRIUMPH FOR THE WOMAN SUFFRAGISTS.
MR. MOWAT TAKES THEIR PETITION INTO HIS CONSIDERATION!!

In this *Grip* cartoon, which appeared on 24 November 1883,
Ontario premier Oliver Mowat consigns a suffrage petition
to oblivion. Co-edited by Knights of Labor journalist Phillips
Thompson, *Grip* was cynical about Mowat's meeting with
these earnest suffragists.

profession's refusal to allow female lawyers, and lampooned politicians such as Ontario premier Oliver Mowat for hypocritically
claiming sympathy for suffrage but then quietly throwing their
petitions in the garbage.

An emerging group of feminist cartoonists in the United
States used their skills to create alternatives to the anti-feminist
cartoons that were so pervasive in the mainstream press. In their
work, the shrill, crowing hen is supplanted by the suffragist as
statuesque Greek goddess, holding up the torch of Justice and

Humanity. *The Champion*'s cover features such an image, borrowed from a British publication. An enlightened suffragist
stands in the foreground, set against a background of huddled,
poorly clad, oppressed women, presumably the impoverished
people whom the suffragists would uplift and aid. Rather different feminist cartoons graced the pages of labour and socialist papers, which were less likely to show working-class women as
mere background to middle-class women's good works, and more
likely to foreground their exploitation by the forces of capital.
A cartoon in which capitalist employers push a wage-earning
woman off a cliff and into the abyss of the white slave traffic is
one good example.

Suffrage cartoons were not differentiated solely by class: they
also exposed racial and ethnic prejudices. A common middle-class
motif was outrage that the uneducated working-class man, the
Chinese immigrant, and the "Indian" could vote but not the educated, white woman. A *Grain Growers'* cartoon showed a woman at
the back of a queue for a polling booth, with Aboriginals, "coolies,"
and other undeserving men ahead of her. The blatant race and
class prejudices intrinsic to such cartoons also appeared in a poem
published by *The Champion*. "Ma Can't Vote" made it clear that
educated and responsible Ma, who understood the tariff and
world politics, would be a more intelligent voter than her own un-
informed husband, their working-class coachman, and the husband of Ma's downtrodden domestic – the latter oppressed by her
own drunken husband but of course not by her female employer.

Suffragists also sought alternatives to the stock storylines
presented in silent movies, which ridiculed them as authoritarian
wives who dominated and emasculated their husbands or as
villainesses who victimized their families by deserting the home
for politics. As the masses flocked to the new burgeoning entertainment of five-cent movies, the cinema made for powerful
anti-suffrage propaganda. In one of the more vicious examples,
A Busy Day (also called *The Militant Suffragette*), Charlie Chaplin

appears in drag as an aggressive suffragette who fights with the police but is ultimately distracted by her own intense jealousy of a more attractive woman. Pushed into the ocean at the end of the film by her ashamed male companion, she drowns, presumably neither missed nor mourned.

The British suffragette was featured in many movie scripts: she is invariably a scowling, overbearing, demanding woman who strikes fear into the hearts of normal men. She is inevitably a bad mother, leaving ruined families and abandoned children in her wake. In *How They Got the Vote*, a suffragette mother almost destroys her cowering daughter's life by forbidding her romance with a handsome suitor, though he employs both magic and ingenuity to outsmart the heartless mother, winning the day for youthful, heterosexual romance. Films portraying women's misguided attempts to ape men by taking on masculine jobs were one of the most common comedic methods of exposing the sheer *impossibility* of gender equality. Women were prisoners of their passive, frivolous, helpless personalities, and many plots ended with them begging men for help or scurrying back to where they belonged – the home.

American suffragists took the threat of anti-feminist cinema seriously, countering with semi-documentaries and dramatic movies that they encouraged or co-produced, such as *Votes for Women* (1912) and *Your Girl and Mine* (1914). Both were screened in Canada. *Votes for Women* combined appearances of real-life American suffragists Jane Addams and Anna Howard Shaw with a fictional story about a corrupt senator whose suffragist fiancée converts him to the cause. Melodrama, romance, and the resolution of a happy marriage were still standard fare in suffrage movie plots, probably to assuage fears that feminism bred familial disorder and marriage breakups. Suffrage movies also became educational opportunities. At each Montreal showing of *Your Girl and Mine*, writes historian Laura Carlson, the Montreal Suffrage Association ensured that a member was on hand to speak about the film's theme, the "unjust laws affecting women and children at home and in industry." Although these films probably had a countervailing educational impact, they could not overcome the immense power of the Hollywood machine, churning out endless anti-feminist fare.

Movies were forms of entertainment, ideology, and consumption. The North American suffrage movement emerged along with consumer capitalism, so material goods, advertising, and spectacle were all part of its culture. North American suffragists adopted nascent advertising techniques, including billboards, walking sandwich boards, and window displays, as well as marketing countless suffrage souvenirs through mail-order catalogues. Such paraphernalia included the standard political buttons and banners, and almost everything else imaginable: dolls, pins, hats, valentines, playing cards, dishes, fans, salt shakers, clothing – and more. Campaigners also used celebrity endorsements (as today, actresses were good advertisements: Canadian Mary Pickford was one), scripted public events, and dramatic spectacles. Suffrage pageants, created through silent tableaus or pantomimes, told a story through elaborate costumes and dramatic symbolism. When Canadian suffragists attended a giant suffrage march in Washington in March 1913, a pageant was enacted on the steps of the Treasury Building: a woman dressed as the Spirit of Woman appealed to characters named Truth, Knowledge, and Equality. She finally knelt at the Altar of Freedom, as Hope shows her a vision of Liberty.

Canadians were less ostentatious, but they too understood the necessity of reaching out to the populace while also creating a feeling of comradeship and collective purpose among themselves. People who campaign against stubborn prejudice and the status quo need to feel part of an oppositional community that shares a set of principles and the hope they are on the right side of history. From small meetings set up by BC organizer Dorothy Davis in the hinterland town of Chilliwack to large assemblies in

Toronto's Massey Hall arranged by Flora MacDonald Denison, public events were used to build an exhilarating sense of purpose and strength. In 1911, when Emmeline Pankhurst visited Toronto, two thousand people turned out to hear her speak; her address was followed by an elaborate banquet celebration and speeches praising the work of local suffragists. Likewise, Victoria suffragists marked the end of a tour by their provincial organizer with a banquet at the Ritz Hotel, speeches, and awards. But banquets, like afternoon teas, reflected the exclusive nature of the middle-class movement, one reason that socialist and labour feminists organized separately.

Suffragists also followed the tried-and-true path of holding bazaars and other fundraising events to create a sense of community and finance the cause. A surviving suffrage quilt, created in Senelac, Saskatchewan, suggests that some items were handmade to mark victories or perhaps to be auctioned off for money. Fundraisers were also types of performance. In Victoria, the Suffrage Bazaar, reported in *The Champion,* involved a rummage sale in the form of an "original burlesque" (one assumes without the scanty costumes), in which a Mrs. Grundy and the Mad Hatter auctioned off "a choice lot of prejudices, superstitions, fallen idols, curios, second hand costumes and antiquated notions." Touring photographs of suffrage events, satirical skits, countless musical performances, singalongs of suffrage songs, and poetry readings were all enjoyed by suffragists across Canada. Although often presented as a humourless lot, they also liked to poke fun, including at themselves. *The Champion* reported on a Halloween party attended by costumed suffragists and their supporters at which a wizard (anti) and a witch (pro) engaged in a staged debate. The witch won.

PUBLIC PRESENTATIONS

Middle-class suffragists were cautious about their public self-presentation. Events were carefully planned and the appearance

Canadian women probably bought suffrage memorabilia from US catalogues. This homemade quilt from Senelac, Saskatchewan, with the names of the suffragists in the Women Grain Growers, suggests they also created their own.

and actions of the participants contemplated for their symbolic impact. Balancing feminine respectability with the assumed audacity of a public, political presence was often a concern. In Victoria, the Political Equality League (PEL) entered a float in the annual city parade, with the intent of delivering a visual message that was awe-inspiring yet also decorous. The float was preceded by three heralds mounted on black horses, wearing suffrage colours and using trumpets to proclaim the justice of the cause. Then came suffrage standard-bearers on horseback. Then the float, decorated with wisteria vines and featuring standing women draped in white, who represented the six countries and eleven American states in which women could vote. Another woman, Liberty, stood on a pedestal, with British Columbia at her feet, praying for freedom. "Citizens are we" proclaimed a banner held by the voting women. "Why not B.C.?" rhymed a second banner that represented the PEL. After such intense planning, winning fourth prize for the float must have been a disappointment.

Claiming the public space of the streets on women's *own* terms, however, was a more risky and daunting act. Montreal suffragists staged a Suffrage Exhibition in a downtown storefront to display their ideas, while some suffragists used local fairs to set up booths, distribute newspapers, and accost the public with political pamphlets, though they usually did so with trepidation. Women who organized a Victoria tag day (where women collected donations on the streets) admitted afterward in *The Champion* that many volunteers did not show up, probably fearing verbal harassment from the public. The brave ones who did participate were relieved when the most hostile response was a jibe from a man who assumed that all feminists were in search of husbands: "Sorry women, I'm already married." Suffragists might occasionally disrupt an anti event – they interrupted one such meeting in Toronto, demanding to be heard – but middle-class Canadian suffragists constructed a cultural image *of themselves* as reasonable, dignified, calm, and that supposed Canadian trait, polite.

Even American suffragists were initially worried that they might be seen as unfeminine or undignified if they marched in demonstrations (or "parades"). Aleta Dey, the heroine in Francis Marion Beynon's Canadian suffrage novel of the same name, struggles with her own shameful terror about an upcoming parade. She dreads making a "distasteful" public exhibition of herself, with spectators staring at her disapprovingly from the sidelines. A conservative male friend unkindly confirms her fears by telling her she will degrade herself, as the parade is "disgustingly unwomanly."

This may explain why eighteen Toronto suffragists joined the massive Washington parade in March 1913, timed to coincide with President Woodrow Wilson's inauguration: there was reassurance to be had in numbers. Canadian participation was an act of solidarity and an emotional investment in international sisterhood that helped to sustain the spirits of suffragists. Flora MacDonald Denison organized the Canadian contingent of rival Toronto suffrage groups, who put aside their differences and travelled together by train. Three male supporters, including Denison's ardently pro-suffrage son, Merrill, still in high school, were also part of the delegation. The Canadian marchers met for a public send-off with well-wishers at Toronto's Union Station. The *Toronto Globe* reporter who covered the event was rather surprised that the "quiet" members of this "handsome" group were actually suffragists. Unlike the stereotypical unattractive and fearsome suffragists, they seemed so very normal.

Canadian newspapers portrayed the marchers as something of an oddity but commented positively on their nationalist garb, which included caps decorated with red maple leafs and the word "Canada." Denison's fourteen-year-old American niece, who walked with them, was wrapped in the Union Jack. The marchers claimed that some approving onlookers shouted "way to go Canada" as they passed, though they also encountered dismissive jeers, including "it was too cold to vote up at the North Pole." Indeed, the procession was plagued by the problems that Aleta Dey dreaded: men threw things, shouted obscenities, and jostled and manhandled some of the marchers. Why the police failed to protect them from violence later became the subject of scandal. No one, however, questioned the American suffragists' racist decision to segregate the parade, with white women leading the march and African Americans at the back.

Canadians were becoming less timid about public display by the outbreak of the First World War. A self-named "leader of the

Most Canadian suffragists favoured Mock Parliaments
and meetings over large demonstrations, but these Toronto
suffragists joined the massive 1913 Washington parade that
demanded votes for women. Denison saved her program as
a keepsake: its cover shows suffragists' self-portrayal as
gallant knights for justice and their use of performance
and spectacle to promote their politics.

Finnish labour and socialist suffragists in the Fort William
summer festival parade, advocating for both workplace and
political rights, 1911 or 1912.

militant section" of the CSA, Miss Browne, boasted to the Toronto
media that she would "welcome a term in jail," though the CSA
leadership denied that it had adopted militant tactics. In the
summer of 1914, Laura McCully and her firebrand comrade at the
university, Helen Cunningham, "President of the Women's Political Club, Militant Section," organized twelve new suffrage locals, accepting everyone from "college grads to socialists." Helen
and Laura's repertoire included open-air meetings and speeches
in towns outside Toronto, the first of their kind, they claimed.
Socialist suffragists also joined labour movement, ethnic, and
socialist parades. In Fort William, Ontario, Finnish socialist suffragists marched under banners demanding both the vote and an

eight-hour day, and in 1913 Toronto suffragists finally joined the annual Labour Day parade, a first they made much of.

Most Canadian suffragists, however, opted for the respectable spaces of theatres, halls, and churches rather than street corners or open-air meetings. Mock Parliaments, with their carefully crafted display of irony, satire, and humour, fit these preferences well. Kym Bird's reconstruction of the few remaining Mock Parliament scripts, in "Performing Politics," suggests that women's public performances incorporated both "safe, moderate reverence" for the parliamentary system and more courageous critiques of the gendered division of labour and the reigning ideology of femininity. The first Mock Parliament, held in Winnipeg in 1893 and organized by Dr. Amelia Yeomans and the WCTU, was timed as "pre-performance publicity" for a suffrage petition that was presented to the legislature. Although it adhered closely to a simple debate format, subsequent Mock Parliaments incorporated more elaborate satirical renditions of male legislatures. These were fairly safe, genteel forms of protest, but they undoubtedly empowered women, some of whom were apprehensive about speaking out or performing in public.

News of the popularity of the Mock Parliament spread quickly across feminist networks. While visiting Vancouver in 1913, Lillian Beynon Thomas attended a parliament presented by the University Women's Club, and on her return to Winnipeg, she urged the PEL to follow suit. The group researched its performance by attending a suffrage debate at the Manitoba legislature, during which Premier Rodmond Roblin waxed eloquent about his love for his mother and his reverence for all women, whom he urged to remain "queen of the home." The pompous and irrational arguments of anti-suffrage legislators were mimicked the very next night in a debate titled "Should men have the vote?" staged in Winnipeg's impressive Walker Theater and later memorialized in McClung's novel *Purple Springs*. After male supplicants presented their arguments for suffrage, the female legislators complimented them on their "manly" attractiveness but rejected their petition – for their own good. Imitating Roblin's gestures and speech, McClung declared that man was "made for something higher and better than voting ... Politics unsettle men and unsettled men means unsettled bills, broken furniture, broken vows, and divorce. Men's place is on the farm." Her clever parody of Roblin brought the house down.

THE NEW WOMAN

If women were to envisage an egalitarian future, imagination and creativity were required. Novels, verse, and short stories infused with a feminist consciousness also contributed to an emerging oppositional movement culture. Reading feminist fiction was a symbolic act that connected individual women to a larger community, allowing them to question what was unacceptable in the present and to imagine something different in the future. American and British novels about suffrage circulated in Canada, though most Canadian authors wrote *around* but not directly *about* the suffrage movement. They were not particularly interested in the modern realist novel that was emerging in Britain, still partial to the nineteenth-century melodrama with its romance, convenient plot surprises, emotion, and pathos. But realist conventions were gaining ground, offering socially conscious authors a means of raising feminist issues.

Nellie McClung did embrace suffrage as a theme in her novels. Her fiction has been characterized as didactic and entertaining melodrama with a social reform slant, though some contemporary literary critics typify her writing as moralistic "Sunday school lessons." Her trilogy featuring irrepressible Irish immigrant Pearl Watson, starting with *Sowing Seeds in Danny*, raised a long list of feminist issues: temperance, domestic violence, women's nurturing qualities, an idealized family, the environmental causes of social ills, a discriminatory legal system, political corruption, and the shame of affluent idle women who were unconcerned with women's oppression. In the final book, Pearl represents Canada as a "land of the second chance" for poor but ambitious immigrants: she has progressed from domestic servant to schoolteacher and is married to a doctor. More importantly, she is also a feminist, suffragist, and temperance advocate. Through Pearl's story, McClung idealized her own principles and made suffrage seem the logical and heroic culmination of the campaign for purity, social responsibility, and human compassion – all of which are Pearl's qualities.

Whereas many authors remained wedded to romantic, moralistic, and melodramatic formats, some women were grappling with a changing social environment in which feminism loomed large. What did modernity and equality mean for women? Could they embrace work, independence, even politics, without jettisoning motherhood? How did they experience and interpret their changing social, educational, and work roles? Short stories featuring the New Woman provide a fairly diverse sample of Canadian fiction that dealt with these questions. The short story was an especially popular medium for female authors: it could be written in snatches around other duties, and there were many possible venues for publication in magazines and newspapers. In the first two decades of the twentieth century, the *Canadian* magazine alone published over three hundred stories by women.

From our perspective, the gender messages in New Woman short stories seem rather unadventurous: few digressed from an ending with happy heterosexual pairing. But in the process, women tackled questions of independence, freedom, work, and matrimony. Jean Blewett's story "The Experiences of a Woman Bachelor" depicts the close friendship between a homemaker and an independent, educated woman who lives away from her family and searches for intellectual relationships with men. It raises questions about women's choice to marry or not. The "not" option is portrayed quite positively. "Leave all this foolishness [marriage] to us," writes the homemaker to her friend, we "who know nothing of the delights of brand new womanhood, who can't write books, speak on platforms, box, fence, run, row or analyze our emotions, [while we] hang on to our embroidery frames ... and hug our chains." Blewett's heroine, the independent woman, crossed over into her non-fiction advocacy writing. In a *Collier's Weekly* magazine article titled "The Canadian Woman and Her Work," she called for both women's suffrage and a more enlightened male and female citizenship; it was reprinted by the Canadian Suffrage Association as a pamphlet.

Authors also wrote about the appalling costs of patriarchy when husbands exercised dictatorial power over their wives, misleading them, denigrating them, battering them. Mazo de la Roche touches on the theme of violence in an ironic, tragic manner, suggesting at the end of her story "Canadian Ida and English Nell" that marriage for the heroine was an illusory trap more than a happy ending. Sometimes women fought patriarchal oppression in small ways, as does the farmer's wife in a story by Adeline Teskey, "A Common Man and His Wife: The Ram Lamb." The farm wife's small rebellion, saving a ram lamb from slaughter, sets her on a larger path toward dignity and self-sufficiency, despite her husband's tyrannical control of the household – exactly the issue raised in Francis Beynon's GGG columns. The undervaluing of women's farm labour is also raised in "Carried Forward," an unusually pessimistic story by McClung. A farmer is annoyingly self-pitying at his wife's funeral, but his complaints have more to do with his loss of a valuable "chattel" than with grief: "It would have been easier to lose every horse in the barn," he tells the other mourners.

Short stories written by non-Anglo immigrant and working-class women, or poems in the labour press, often looked at the world differently, stressing women's struggle with material want and social exclusion. Late-nineteenth-century labour poet Marie Joussaye, for example, did not advocate for the vote as much as for better conditions for female workers. Her famous poem "Only a

Working Girl" pleaded for more dignity and respect for working women, too often looked down on by bourgeois men and women alike. Icelandic Canadian feminist Margret Benedictsson's fictional writing criticized male domination but also expressed a decidedly working-class immigrant understanding of multiple inequalities. In a short story titled "The Widow," Benedictsson explores the agonizing choices faced by an impoverished mother who is unable to feed her children after the death of her husband. When she tries to give away his political book on human rights, hoping for some compassion at the very least, she encounters the mean-spirited hypocrisy of the affluent and respectable, including the local Christian minister. Icelandic Canadian author Laura Salverson also incorporated themes of poverty, marginalization, and oppressive working conditions into her fiction set in a turn-of-the-century immigrant community. In "Hidden Fire," she describes a young farm wife who is literally worked to death. On her deathbed, aware that her husband will probably soon remarry to replace her indispensable work on the farm, she wishes only that her daughter may escape her fate and be allowed to "play" rather than be "a'slavin for another woman."

Women writers of mixed-race parentage addressed the double discrimination of gender and race in their short stories. "A Red Girl's Reasoning," by Mohawk English performer and writer Pauline Johnson, featured an independent, spirited Metis daughter of a fur trade marriage, who, on her own marriage to a white man, discovers that racial prejudice lies just beneath the surface of his devotion to her. Her unwavering claim that her mother's Indigenous culture is equal to white culture, her direct confrontation of her husband's racism, and her courageous decision to leave him are a very different kind of New Woman statement. Johnson's work usually prioritized racist oppression above that of patriarchy, but her literary double vision did encompass a sense of her dual identity as both "Redskin and woman." Her commitment to gender equality was influenced by Western feminist ideas but was also firmly grounded in Aboriginal traditions that valued women's power and influence as community leaders.

Sui Sin Far (Edith Eaton), a Chinese English immigrant to Montreal, also wrote about the difficult in-between existence of bi-racial women in the racist culture of North America and the intersecting oppressions of patriarchy (both white and Chinese) and racism. Her complex "Story of One White Woman Who Married a Chinese" features a white working-class woman named Minnie, her dictatorial white husband, his middle-class, white "suffragette" friend, and Minnie's second husband, a Chinese man who comes to her aid after her first husband abandons her. Told from Minnie's view, the story explains why a woman might choose a Chinese husband's respectful, quiet manliness over a white man's domineering control – despite his claim to support women's rights. The piece is also about far more: Sui Sin Far probes the tense interactions between a middle-class suffragette and a working-class woman, between the aggressive version of white manhood and more gentle Chinese manhood, and between Minnie and her progressive husband, all of which make for a complex work. Critics have rightly pointed out that both the suffragette and the Chinese man display stereotyped gender and racial characteristics, but the story nonetheless complicates our understandings of feminist writing in the early twentieth century. The tragic ending to the sequel story, with the Chinese husband killed by racists, suggests a more pessimistic view of social equality and tolerance than that of white, middle-class feminists such as McClung.

Some white women writers also tried to explore the intersection of gender, race, and class relations. In "The Assimilation of Christina," Jean McIlwraith tackles both class and race prejudice. The story describes an unfolding romance between a working-class Scottish domestic and an Ojibway man, both denigrated by the dominant social order: she because of class, he because of race. No doubt, he is something of a romanticized noble Indian, but he is still more honourable than Christina's snobby, stuffy (and useless) white, upper-class employers, something that she comes to understand only by confronting her own racial prejudices. Flora MacDonald Denison's short, unpublished story about cross-racial romance ("Pateeka: A Romance of the Northlands") echoes this idealization of the noble Native but nonetheless ends with the validation of interracial marriage. Grace, a young and wealthy American, is taken to the Canadian North for a rest cure by her widower father, and a young Iroquois man, Pateeka, guides them on a canoe trip that restores her to health. When romance blossoms between Grace and Pateeka, the father is unnerved but moved to acceptance by Grace's declaration: "I love this man. He is not a graduate of Yale or Oxford, but he is a graduate of the great university of Nature, and belongs to the old aristocracy of this continent."

Both Francis Marion Beynon and Nellie McClung wrote short stories involving Aboriginal women in the Prairie West. Though shaped by ethnocentric assumptions about Aboriginal life, Beynon's story "Noonie" also subtly undermines white settlers' fearful stereotypes of their now dispossessed, poor Aboriginal neighbours. McClung wrote only two stories involving Indigenous characters, but critics have endlessly dissected them, while drawing different conclusions. In "Red and White," a "half-breed" woman named Minnie Hardcastle and a "full-blooded Cree" man, Johnny Starblanket, face many barriers to their romance, from white racism to his mother's suspicion of Minnie's mixed parentage. The epitome of degeneracy in the narrative is a white member of Parliament, presented as lascivious, corrupting, and dishonest. Johnny and Minnie are more noble, forthright, and courageous, though they still exhibit "innate" racial tendencies, whether these are a weakness for drink, a feeling for the land, or easily aroused anger – even after their superior "mission" education.

Johnny and Minnie abandon the corrupt, white south for a brighter future in the purer Aboriginal North, a choice interpreted by critics of McClung as a sign of her segregationist, racist tendencies but by sympathetic academics as her support for the protection of Indigenous culture. Whichever interpretation you accept, the story does reflect most suffragists' views that Indigenous people were culturally disconnected from white society, needing protection and education but not inclusion in debates about women's rights. The despicable white MP complains about Minnie's pride and unbecoming assertiveness, claiming that "half breed girls take on airs" after their time in industrial schools. "I'll bet that black-eyed jade wants to vote," he remarks with emphatic disdain. McClung disparaged such racism, even though her view of Aboriginal women remained clouded in paternalism.

CREATING A FEELING FOR SUFFRAGE

A few paragraphs can't do justice to the breadth of New Woman short stories, let alone other feminist newspapers, novels, poetry, and visual display, but they indicate the vibrant, broad landscape of debate regarding women's changing social roles. Discussion about votes for women was nurtured by an emerging movement culture and oppositional feminist community that both reflected and fostered the more specific political struggle for the franchise.

When a woman threw in her lot with the suffragists, she was taking a social leap beyond her prescribed gender role, placing herself in the unwelcome limelight of scrutiny as a "disgustingly unwomanly" woman. Future generations of feminists, also subject to belittling denigration for their "outlandish" ideas, became all too familiar with this experience. The emotional bonds created through co-operative work, attachment to others of like mind, investment in a vital project, and enjoyment of a common culture all countered feminists' isolation and sustained the suffrage project.

Moreover, other forms of feminist cultural expression exist in languages other than English and French: they are waiting to be discovered. Rather than talking about *a* suffrage culture, we could speak of multiple countercultures, as white, middle-class women created images and performances about their struggle that clearly differed from the expressions of immigrant, racialized, and working-class women. It is critical to reinsert Pauline Johnson's and Sui Far's writing on women, colonialism, and the oppressions of racialized women back into suffrage history. Doing so expands and complicates our understanding of feminist debates before the First World War. When that global conflict broke out, the suffrage movement encountered its most difficult, and ultimately insurmountable, divisions to date.

I feel I am in no way justified in using my own and other women's energies on behalf of the Suffrage cause when the war ... needs us so urgently. Though political freedom is near to my heart, yet at present there is a far greater issue at stake – the freedom of the whole Empire.

CONSTANCE BOULTON, *WOMEN'S CENTURY*, AUGUST 1915

The women of England have no quarrel with the women of Germany. Both were standing together like sisters, asking, pleading and petitioning that International Arbitration keep peace between nations and that women be given the power of the ballot to assist in protecting their homes and make their laws ... Their voices were not yet strong enough to make a dent in the murderous power of militarism.

FLORA MACDONALD DENISON, *WAR AND WOMEN*, 1914

SEVEN

DEBATING
WAR AND PEACE

This cartoon, which appeared in the *Brantford Expositor* on
8 December 1917, shows pro-war women as aggressive and loyal
defenders of the nation. It advises those women enfranchised by
the Wartime Elections Act to use the vote as a weapon in the
election, returning a pro-conscription government to power.

DURING THE FIRST World War, media stories and pictures of women working in munitions factories often celebrated their patriotic contribution to the war effort and focused on their non-traditional labour in difficult industrial jobs that were normally reserved for men. Yet a fictional story about a female munitions worker by J.G. Sime may have hit the mark more accurately. In "Munitions," the heroine, Bertha, has laboured unhappily for years in the stifling confinement of domestic service. During the war, she escapes her servant status by securing a factory job making armaments and discovers an exhilarating "freedom," not from hard work and exploitation, but rather in living outside her workplace, socializing with other workers, sharing ribald stories, and living for herself. War work represents neither patriotism nor liberation, but rather a pragmatic search for less oppressive paid labour that is necessary for daily survival.

"Munitions" and other stories in Sime's collection *Sister Woman,* published at the end of the war, offer a startlingly realistic view of the social conditions of industrialization, poverty, and urbanization that so worried social reformers. Sime's writing, however, avoids their sermonizing, fears of working-class promiscuity, and intent to improve the moral character of working women. Her unconventional heroines are working women, prostitutes, unwed mothers, mistresses, charwomen, and immigrants, all portrayed with compassion and understanding as they struggle with restrictive social norms, love and loss, dependence and autonomy, maternity and economic troubles.

Sime's radical challenge to outmoded sexual mores suggests that the First World War (1914–18) was transformative, altering both women's morals and their work roles. Yet we should be careful about jumping to conclusions: after all, the book sold a mere 250 copies and was not well received. The question of whether the war shook up gender relations is closely connected to the suffrage story. Many popular histories insist that the vote was won because women's labour and loyalty proved their mettle during the war, despite scholarly evidence questioning this singular explanation and despite the fact that some women did not attain the vote until much later. Myths tied to patriotic versions of history, however, are difficult to disrupt. Although the war hastened the achievement of suffrage in some provinces, it was never the sole cause of these successes, and the federal franchise had a more tortuous history that was bound up with the controversy over conscription – the compulsory enlistment of men in the armed forces. The war also divided women as never before. Class, language, ethnicity, ideology, and region shaped their experiences of this conflict, differentiated their politics, and sundered any semblance of feminist unity, exposing for us the illusion of gender as the only point of division in women's history.

PATRIOTISM AND HISTORY

Just before the war broke out in August 1914, suffragists of all stripes felt that victory was in sight. Confidence and resolve were evident: "The women of today," declared the Canadian Suffrage Association pamphlet *Canadian Woman and Her Work,* are "in line" for the vote and will not back down: already sharing social "power and responsibility ... we are marching towards the highest kind of citizenship." The newly formed socialist Social Democratic Party placed suffrage prominently in its platform, trade union federations had finally endorsed the female franchise, some municipalities allowed women to vote for school boards, and suffrage bills were being contemplated in provincial legislatures across the country. Suffrage picnics, meetings, teas, petitions, and Mock Parliaments were reported from cities, villages, and rural areas throughout Canada: from Roaring River in northern Manitoba, to North Bay in Ontario, to Fernie in British Columbia. Suffrage could no longer be misconstrued as a political cause supported by a small group of privileged urban women. In some provinces, multiple suffrage organizations thrived, though this also reflected divisions within the movement.

Two years before the war, the Canadian Suffrage Association was granted a private audience with Prime Minister Robert Borden, another indication that suffragists thought politicians were listening. Flora MacDonald Denison opened the meeting, telling Borden that he would be remembered in history as a visionary statesman if he provided decisive leadership on the suffrage issue. She reminded him that his Conservative predecessor, Sir John A. Macdonald, initially included women in the 1885 franchise bill, that widows and spinsters voted municipally, and that even Republican Teddy Roosevelt was now a convert. Situating Canadian intransigence in an international context was key to her pitch: Canada was being humiliated for lagging behind its fellow dominions, Australia and New Zealand, and Ottawa should reward its peaceable suffragists before things digressed to the "terrible state of affairs" in Britain, where government "obstinacy" had produced suffragette militancy. She closed with the observation that even the National Council of Women, a conservative organization that never endorsed anything controversial, now supported suffrage.

Augusta Stowe-Gullen then asked a practical follow-up question about the relationship between federal and provincial voting lists, which provided Borden with a convenient escape hatch. Since the provinces controlled who voted, he directed suffragist lobbying to the provincial premiers – and indeed, the former Liberal prime minister, Sir Wilfrid Laurier, had similarly fallen back on this excuse. Borden must have heaved a sigh of relief after this very polite encounter. In Britain earlier that year, he met with a far more demanding Women's Social and Political Union suffragette delegation, which claimed it had "branches" in Canada (something of an exaggeration; there seems to have been just one). Reported word-by-word in *The Champion,* this encounter put Borden in the hot seat. The delegation insisted that Canadian laws discriminated against women and that female British emigrants would soon be avoiding such a backward country, heading instead to Australia or New Zealand, where they were truly "valued." British militancy, they warned, might soon migrate to Canada if stubborn governments (like his) refused to listen. Borden was a little piqued at such "threats," assuring the women that no Canadian laws were "unjust to women."

When war was declared, the female franchise was probably the last thing on Borden's mind. Precipitated by empires struggling for power and control over territories, markets, and colonies, the conflict was global in scope, drawing in reluctant and aggressive participants, colonies and colonizers, civilians and soldiers, men and women. Massive battlefield losses in the most atrocious conditions, new armaments and chemical warfare, and unprecedented civilian mobilization made this a war like no other. Interpreting suffrage history in the context of total war is complicated: first, there were many interconnected issues at stake, including women's wage labour, moral regulation, and ethnic discrimination, all concerns taken up by suffragists. Second, this unprecedented war spawned unprecedented mythologizing. In subsequent years, experience, fact, justification, rationalization, and myth were hopelessly entangled, as historians, artists, and political writers tried to make sense of the tragic and pointless slaughter, in the process creating founding folklore about the Canadian nation. Feminists produced their own myths, insisting that the war should be etched in historical memory as a watershed for women, transforming gender roles. Even recently, after scholarly writing has criticized the watershed theory, popular writing and film-making persists in claiming that the war had liberating effects for women, suffrage among them. Why did women cling to the view that war work proved their worth, leading to the vote?

For one thing, women said so. Middle-class, professional, and politically astute women hoped that their pro-war contributions *would* alter their second-class political status. The ranks of organizations such as the NCWC, the Red Cross, and the IODE swelled, and women used their wartime roles as volunteers, fundraisers, recruiters, and allies of the Borden government to stake out a claim for enhanced respect. At the Women's War Conference, called in 1918 by the federal government, they asserted their historical significance by representing themselves as the Mothers of Consolidation, walking in the footsteps of the Fathers of Confederation. Even French Canadian female reformers, adamantly opposed to the government's conscription policies only the year before, claimed in *La bonne parole* that the conference marked the first time in Canadian history that "les femmes ont été officielle-ment consultées par le gouvernement et priées de donner leur avis dan les questions nationals."

Similarly, *Women's Century* endlessly alleged that war work proved women's worth as full citizens: Canadian women were creating a new "soul" of the nation, contributing to a "nobler conception of the state." Women became virtual engines of their own self-promotion. Even labour newspapers, more skeptical about political change, claimed that the war would endow women with a new status and greater opportunities, so that the country could never revert to the old gender order. Nor did such claims evaporate after the war. In the 1924 BC election, Mrs. J.Z. Hall, a candidate for the Provincial Party (a conservative party), campaigned for office by promoting herself in the *Western Woman's Weekly* as "Vancouver's best known woman war worker." She was not referring to her wage labour in munitions, but rather to her genius in organizing auxiliaries and raising funds from the locus of her "Killarney estate."

Second, politicians said so. As women won the vote in provincial legislatures in 1916, 1917, and 1918, anti-suffrage politicians invoked the war as the rationale for their about-face. As they introduced suffrage bills, they puffed themselves up as patriots rewarding patriots, citing women's loyal war work as a cause for their change of heart. To be sure, many suffragists proclaimed their pro-British, imperialist sympathies from the very start of the war, offering to help in any way possible, from raising funds, to knitting socks, to pinning white feathers (symbols of cowardice) on men who would not enlist. Some suffragists, such as Prairie journalist Cora Hind, denounced all anti-war women and men as traitors, while others established suffrage war auxiliaries to channel their efforts into volunteer work supporting the troops. How could this patriotic point of view not become part of the public message of suffrage victory?

VICTORIES

There were other factors that contributed to suffrage triumphs. In Manitoba, the unpopular and corrupt Conservative government of Sir Rodmond Roblin was swept out of office in 1915 by an electorate tired of pork-barrel politics. Suffragists had cleverly hitched their wagon to the incoming Liberal Party under T.C. Norris, and their support for the Liberals was rewarded with a suffrage bill. But even these allies had to be watched for backsliding. The night before the suffrage bill was presented to the legislature, newspaperwoman Lillian Beynon Thomas discovered that it did not allow women to run for office. She leaked the disturbing news to her sister Francis Marion Beynon, who was attending a Grain Growers' convention. Between Beynon's threat to introduce a resolution there and Lillian's suffragist networks in Winnipeg, they mobilized enough support to nip the discrimination in the bud. The next day, animosities melted away in an atmosphere of mutual congratulation, as suffragists were welcomed into the galleries of the legislature to witness this historic moment. In return, they applauded the legislators with a rousing rendition of "For He's a Jolly Good Fellow." Nonetheless, Francis Marion Beynon reminded her *Grain Growers' Guide* readers that this was no effortless victory but rather the outcome of years of political "drudgery" by tireless workers who slowly but surely shifted public opinion in favour of suffrage.

Saskatchewan and Alberta passed their own suffrage bills in 1917. In all three Prairie provinces, the link between temperance and suffrage, always seen as sister causes, was important. The emotionally charged atmosphere of war provided temperance advocates with the rhetorical ammunition to win prohibition plebiscites in 1915 and 1916. Nationalist, imperialist, alarmist rhetoric was used to persuade the public that ending the production and sale of alcohol would protect soldiers' health and conserve agricultural resources for the war effort. Prohibition was equated with the battle against Germany and made into a patriotic loyalty test; European immigrants who were previously unsympathetic to prohibition felt pressured to support it or be assailed as enemy traitors. The pro-war propaganda that inundated Canadians through daily newspaper articles, posters, recruiting, and public events was also critical to suffragists' victory. The never-ending claims that the war was being fought for liberty and democracy created an embarrassing conundrum for anti politicians. Surely it was hypocritical to trumpet one's fight for democracy in Europe but deny it to pro-war Canadians – even if they were women?

In Saskatchewan, the recently unified rural and urban suffrage groups had an influential ally in the pro-suffrage, male-dominated Grain Growers' Association. The expansion of women's volunteer organizations, from Homemakers Clubs before the war to Red Cross groups during the war, also mobilized more and more women, who worked alongside suffragists ready to convert the politically hesitant. Moreover, a 1912 Saskatchewan suffrage bill had not elicited fierce opposition: MLAs from all parties had declared their sympathy in principle. The premier's rather insincere refusal to act on suffrage was whittled away over the next few years as petitions proliferated, and he could no longer claim that women were "disinterested" in the vote. But most important, says historian Elizabeth Ann Kalmakoff, was the ruling government's careful measure of its "short term political self interest," since further delay would cost it future votes. In the moment of victory for white women, suffragists made no mention of the bill's disenfranchisement of Chinese and First Nations voters.

Despite a 1914 suffrage petition with twelve thousand signatures, Alberta premier Arthur Sifton said he was unconvinced that the issue had rural backing, so suffrage organizations roused support from their powerful allies in the United Farmers of Alberta, which had officially endorsed suffrage three years before. By 1916, continuing pressure from rural and suffrage associations, along with the Manitoba precedent, sympathy for temperance, as well as the war, clinched Sifton's reluctant agreement to grant the vote. But unleashing unfettered democracy, unchecked by any class or ethnic qualifications, clearly worried many bourgeois politicians. When Edmonton City Council passed a radical bill giving *all* residents a vote, it was vetoed by the provincial legislature, not because it added women, but because there was no property qualification. Sir John A. Macdonald's "stable property holders with a stake in society" were still imagined as the ideal electorate.

In other provinces, suffrage accompanied a change in the ruling party, or it was an about-face expedient decision of a governing party that wished to stay in power. Many middle-class members of the suffrage lobby in British Columbia abandoned their campaign for war work in 1914 but returned to it in 1916, now sensing that a potential alliance with the Opposition Liberals would guarantee them success. The resignation of resolutely anti (or "antedeluvian") Conservative Richard McBride changed the political landscape, though the new premier, Billy Bowser, announced that "women would not get the franchise in his lifetime, if he could help it." He couldn't. When the government introduced a provincial referendum on women's suffrage in 1917 – which ironically did not allow them to vote – suffragists were divided on whether to campaign for it or denounce it. The referendum passed, but labour suffragist Helena Gutteridge was disenchanted with both the Liberals and the Conservatives: in her view, they were equally hostile to working women and the labour movement.

By 1917–18, the writing was on the wall for provincial politicians joining the queue of converts. Long-time anti, Ontario's Conservative premier William Hearst, who also qualified as antediluvian, switched sides suddenly in 1917. Perhaps he wanted to leave a progressive legacy, but his decision was more probably aimed at garnering women's votes in the next election for *his* party. His turnaround also resulted from behind-the-scenes pressure exerted by federal Conservatives. Seeing conscription as a future issue, they wanted to court as many pro-war, Conservative voters as possible, and imperialist Ontario was perceived to be full of them – women included.

Similar shifts within the ruling elite occurred in Nova Scotia, the last province to enfranchise women during the war years. By 1918, Nova Scotia suffragists had new allies: a prominent local judge, the Social Service Council of Canada (an influential religious reform group), and a Halifax newspaper. A 1917 suffrage bill, put forward by Opposition members of the legislature, passed two readings and seemed destined to succeed, only to be unexpectedly scuttled by the Liberal premier. This disingenuous action united women's groups in righteous anger: a newly organized Nova Scotia Equal Franchise League, led by Eliza Ritchie, mobilized popular pressure from below, and a bill succeeded in 1918.

Leading Halifax feminists such as Ritchie, writes Maritime historian Ernest Forbes, represented "an elite of talent and education," but this does not necessarily mean that they were sedate and acquiescent. One of the most influential, Edith Archibald, the socialite wife of the president of the Bank of Nova Scotia, had the confidence of her social status to *be* outspoken, whether about the vote or her highly intolerant views on the superiority of Protestant Christianity. Archibald came from the very highest echelons of society and did not support social causes that challenged the economic status quo, but she did advocate very strongly for suffrage.

Historians initially suggested that there had never been a protracted struggle for the vote in the Maritimes, though it was suffragists who initially implied this to historian Catherine Cleverdon. Eliza Ritchie claimed that a "weight of indifference" hung over their cause for years, and Halifax journalist Ella Murray similarly reported that the movement was "spasmodic," never penetrated the entire province, and was fractured by internal leadership contests. Perhaps significantly, the province lacked a strong contingent of labour and socialist suffragists, who mobilized in cities such as Vancouver and Winnipeg. Nova Scotia suffragists did put aside their campaign for many years, not convinced that the time was ripe, but the vote was always perceived as just one of multiple strategies to further women's equality, along with educational, temperance, and other reforms. Suffragists increasingly appealed to the public using maternal feminist arguments, and during the war, they diverted their attention to patriotic work – and after the Halifax explosion to disaster relief. However, by the end of the war, suffrage was imminent in Britain, and the 1917 precedent of some women voting federally under the Wartime Elections Act would have alerted astute politicians that the battle to keep women out of the polling booth was over. With a shift in the political climate at the top, and women's organizing from below, a suffrage victory was ensured.

Each provincial case was unique, but words such as expediency, political advantage, and pragmatism are used repeatedly to explain the cascading successes of provincial suffrage. Perhaps these triumphs did not represent the noble change of mind that suffragists had hoped for, but this was not to discount their years of organizing, laying the groundwork for success. In subsequent decades, new explanations for wartime victories complemented the popular refrain that women were rewarded for their war work. Former Prairie suffragists who wrote to Catherine Cleverdon in the 1940s alleged that their "pioneering" spirit and highly valued farm labour resulted in Prairie women winning the vote first (by a year, mind you). Over time, their claim that the "pioneering cooperation and partnership" of white men and women settlers led to political egalitarianism aroused some skepticism. Were farm women really valued more because they were scarce labour? Did the patriarchal characteristics of Ontario farm families somehow evaporate when people moved west across provincial borders? What about the underlying ethnocentrism of the progressive groups on the Prairies? Although the Prairie co-operative movement undoubtedly aided suffrage, there was also persisting opposition to other rights – such as dower laws and equal pay – which suggests that there was no ideal region where women were valued equally with men.

WAR AS A WOMEN'S ISSUE

All suffragists agreed that war was a women's issue. But they disagreed on why and on what roles feminists should play in the conflict. The war reaffirmed the importance of international organizations and transnational ideals for Canadian suffragists, even if pro- and anti-war feminists adopted divergent positions in this global struggle. Before the First World War, many feminists in Canadian and international organizations staked out optimistic claims of women's ability to steer nations toward disarmament, negotiation, and peace. Using maternalist arguments, suffragists maintained that, had women been enfranchised, war might have been avoided. As life-givers, they could have prevented the tragic loss of lives on the battlefield; their reform proclivities would also manoeuvre humanity away from aggressive masculinity and territoriality in favour of governing for human welfare. Ironically, some of these suffragists were proud defenders of the British Empire, itself constructed on the basis of armies, aggression, territoriality, and the subordination of Indigenous populations.

At the beginning of the war, this assumed connection between women and peace was earnestly reiterated by Flora MacDonald Denison in her 1914 pamphlet *War and Women*. She warned of the impending tragedy of the current "deadly" conflict but claimed that war might eventually be "evolved out of" human existence. Men, she believed, had been socialized to support "combat and dominance through force," whereas women were more "constructive" in their thought. But these roles were not biologically predestined: men had the intellectual and moral capacity to live in peaceful co-existence, even if women had to lead the way. The idea that men were hardwired to "promote" war was repeated by Nellie McClung in her popular 1915 book, *In Times Like These*. The human cost of war – the loss of one's child – was felt "most deeply by mothers." Men, in contrast, had created war as "romance, legend and tradition, surrounding it with a false glory." Even so, as a pragmatist, a Liberal, and an empire enthusiast, not to mention a mother with a son at the front, McClung supported the war. She claimed that Germany's 1915 sinking of the *Lusitania* ocean liner had opened her eyes to the violent "evil" of German autocracy. Denison's assessment was more radical: "No one nation is to blame; if we cultivate race hatred and militarism, we will get war."

The majority of middle-class and liberal suffragists were war supporters, lending their hand to military recruiting campaigns, volunteer work, fundraising, and perhaps most important, legitimization of the government's war aims. A few super-enthusiasts (including Toronto poet Laura McCully) tried to create Home Guards of uniformed women, marching, drilling, ready to defend the home front. Suffragists' quick change of heart from avowals of maternal pacifism to bellicose pro-war rhetoric appears rather hypocritical, but their support for the war was shaped by more than ideas about women's innate maternalism. The cross-class ethnic and racial loyalty to Britain and the empire, especially by recent British immigrants, was critical. So too was the close association of the more affluent suffrage leaders with leaders of the wartime state. The government's unprecedented propaganda campaign – posters, newspapers, and public events – informing Canadians about Germany's brutal atrocities against women and children also had a formidable effect. Germany became the socially constructed "axis of evil" of that time. Nor should we discount the emotional impact of women's personal grief for soldiers who lost their lives, remembered every day in newspaper casualty lists and memorialized on women's own bodies with black armbands and mourning dress.

Many suffragists put aside political organizing and reform work, save for temperance. Despite evidence that soldiers at the front preferred to make their own choices about alcohol (though they were often not consulted), the Woman's Christian Temperance Union and its suffragist allies argued for sober soldiers, dry canteens in military camps, and an end to a rum ration in the trenches. Suffragists also aided the federal government's registration of available manpower and pushed for the substitution of women for male workers in munitions work, as well as the provision of female welfare supervisors to provide "moral aid" to these factory women. Moral aid, however, was also a new form of surveillance of working-class women's sexuality, and calls for women to take up munitions work showed the distance between working-class and middle-class women. Writers in the middle-class reform magazine *Women's Century* were eager to substitute women for men in munitions work, but this was not *their* work. The majority of the munitions girls, as Sime's story indicates, were working-class individuals who were willing to put up with difficult conditions in their search for better wages. Handling dangerous substances for ten or twelve hours a day was not patriotism, except for those who did not have to do it to earn a living.

Not all suffrage agitation ceased. Following some provincial victories, a National Equal Franchise Union was cobbled together after a WCTU conference in 1916, and it petitioned for the federal vote for women. The Canadian Suffrage Association, including long-time stalwarts Dr. Margaret Gordon and Flora MacDonald Denison, continued to advocate for suffrage and also called for the international arbitration of disputes between nations to prevent wars. This stance was anathema to more assertively imperialist and pro-war women who criticized the CSA's misplaced priorities, if not downright disloyalty. How can we possibly persist in doing suffrage work, asked well-to-do conservative suffragist Constance Boulton, a member of the National Equal Franchise Union, when "the freedom of the whole Empire is at stake?" Boulton and like-minded allies had a role model in British WSPU leader Emmeline Pankhurst, who toured Canada in 1916, promoting her view that women must put aside their suffrage work in order to defend the Empire. Feminists who dared to differ, including her daughter Sylvia, were dismissed as foolish and wrong-headed. Boulton was in agreement: she saw no distinction between even a whiff of pacifism and "ignorance, cowardice and treason." They were all the same to her.

ANTI-WAR SUFFRAGISTS

A minority of suffragists were critical of the war, though some remained involved in volunteer, Red Cross, and refugee aid. Flora MacDonald Denison was deeply conflicted. She publicly endorsed the conflict as a fight against "autocracy" and for democracy, but she also argued in her pamphlet *War and Women* that its immense "horror" could be justified only by a completely reconstructed post-war society, in which "sex autocracy," the slum, caste differences, and all "parasitic idleness" were abolished. The "shame of the millionaire and the pauper" in Canadian society, she averred, must become a thing of the past. But during the war, she quietly slipped away from the nastiness of patriotic Toronto, working in Napanee to put her son through school, retreating to her wilderness resort at Bon Echo, and moving to New York State to aid the 1917 suffrage campaign there. Denison's secondment by the American movement was unusual for a Canadian. Praising her "experience, prestige and gift for stirring a large number of people organizationally," New York suffragists hired her to travel the state, giving lectures and setting up new suffrage groups.

A few Canadian anti-war suffragists were more forthrightly pacifist: they organized meetings, circulated anti-war material, and wrote for newspapers – though only socialist papers were sympathetic. Anti-war suffragists were enmeshed in international anti-war networks, communicating through personal correspondence, print culture, and very occasional meetings, but censorship and the difficulties of travel made these transnational lifelines challenging to sustain. Like their British and American counterparts, Canadian feminist pacifists often came from or moved toward alliances with the labour movement or the left, for three reasons. First, labour was supportive of the war effort but also critical: unions called for the conscription of wealth, arguing that working-class men were doing their share as army recruits, while profit was being made hand-over-fist by a wealthy few, often with strong connections to the government in power. Second, socialists already had a critique of imperialism and its natural extension into global wars, just like the one currently being fought. Third, the costs of war were particularly high for many working-class and farm women: slowly introduced soldiers' stipends barely supported their families, and wartime inflation ate away at household budgets. Labour and socialist women initiated their own Next of Kin organizations, not to knit for socks for soldiers, but to advocate for adequate financial aid to working-class families hard hit by the war.

It is no surprise that the daughter of suffragists James and Adeline Hughes, Laura Hughes, rebelled against the wartime status quo. Her eighteenth birthday present from her father was a lifetime suffrage membership, and she had grown up in the midst of social reform circles and political debate, though also from the right-wing side of her family, as her uncle, Sir Sam Hughes, was the Conservative minister of munitions. Perhaps losing her brother, Chester, in battle in 1915 sharpened her anti-war beliefs. Hughes was part of a small group of Toronto suffragists who were critical of the war, including Denison, Dr. Margaret Gordon, social gospeller Alice Chown, and socialist Harriet Prenter, but she was initially inspired by international anti-war organizing. In 1915, she attended the International Women's Peace Conference in Europe, led by American pacifist Jane Addams, where another lesser-known Canadian was also influential behind the scenes. The group presented European leaders with a proposal for peace, which was written by Julia Grace Wales, a Canadian who taught English literature at the University of Wisconsin (opportunities for such women being nil in Canada). Her social gospel and reform leanings, and her own transnational education, had encouraged her interest in international affairs. Her pamphlet *Continuous Mediation without Armistice,* written for the Wisconsin Peace Society, became the proposal that influential US and international peace advocates promoted across North America and Europe.

Laura Hughes returned to Canada passionately committed to building a new pacifist venture, Our Women's Peace Party, in what can only be called a very hostile environment. Hughes was such an embarrassment to her Tory uncle that he offered to buy her a plot of land on the Prairies if she would just disappear into rural ignominy. Hughes's anti-war views propelled her into the labour movement; she went to work undercover in a factory that produced soldiers' clothing and then exposed its substandard working conditions in a local labour newspaper. Some trade unionists saw her investigative mission as that of a middle-class do-gooder, but it represented a key part of her anti-war philosophy. In her view, war was created not only by masculine aggressiveness, but also by economic greed; it was sustained by a ruling elite who profited economically and socially from the control of working people and the suppression of opposition politics. In the parlance of the 1960s, war was the product of the "military-industrial complex," propped up by a sympathetic state. Her experience of constant social denunciation explains her move to Chicago, where she married a conscientious objector and remained connected to the women's international peace movement. She did not return to Canada.

It is easier to envisage Laura Hughes seeking out kindred pacifist spirits in Toronto than it is to imagine organizing against the war from northern, rural Manitoba. Yet one of the most effective suffragist pacifists, Gertrude Richardson, created a network of anti-war women from the kitchen table of her farmhouse in the tiny outpost of Roaring River. A British working-class immigrant, Richardson married a local farmer who shared her interest in the co-operative movement and the social gospel, but she also arrived in Canada with a developed critique of imperialism. In Britain, her Christian socialist family actively opposed the Boer War; her father had died a few days after a severe beating by a pro-war vigilante at a pacifist meeting. Transplanted to Manitoba, Richardson founded the Roaring River suffrage society, proselytized in nearby towns, and became vice-president of the Manitoba Political Equality League. She corresponded with countless feminist and social gospel reformers across the West, and wrote prodigiously about women's equality for newspapers in Britain and Canada. Representing the respectable, devout, Christian impulse of the suffrage movement, she was also a reminder to Manitoba politicians that it had strong rural support far beyond the confines of Winnipeg.

At the beginning of the war, Richardson devoted her time to humanitarian war relief and exposés of the physical and mental

mistreatment of conscientious objectors (COs) by army personnel in Canada and Britain (where her brother was incarcerated as
a CO). Over time, her anti-war writing became more focused, impassioned, and socialist. In 1917, her regular column in *Women's
Century* disappeared, either because the paper censored her writing or due to her own disgust with its unabashed militarism. As
its editors bragged, all pacifist literature they received went
straight into the waste basket. Richardson wrote instead for the
Canadian Forward, published by the socialist Social Democratic
Party, and she coordinated an international clearing house of peace
activism, sharing news emanating from Germany, Australia, the
United States, Britain, and Canada.

Richardson transposed her suffrage maternalism into her
anti-war work. She believed that women's "mother hearts" shaped
their pacifism, though this was not simply about biology: motherhood is "more than physical," she wrote, "it is a deep spiritual
possession, a love for humanity, a longing to protect, conserve,
guard and save" – and thus to put an end to the "horror" of war.
Socialist feminist ideas also shaped her critique of war: militarism was the outgrowth of capitalism and its close ally imperialism, which conquered and enslaved subject populations. The
unchecked search for profits and imperialist power struggles
led to the current contest between empires, made all the more
acute by male aggressiveness. The enemy, she said in words that
horrified pro-war suffragists, "is neither Germany nor Austria,"
but the "spirit of cruelty and conquest in the conditions of
war and militarism, the oppression of the other and all of the
weak, and the institutions of slavery in every form." Although
Richardson had not previously criticized Canada's treatment of
Indigenous peoples, she now began to question the internal consequences of "our own Empire."

She suggested political tactics that embodied pacifism rather
than militancy: signing anti-war pledges, boycotting jingoistic

newspapers, walking out of religious services that promoted the war. Women should go to prison in lieu of CO men, she suggested near the end of the conflict, and she herself would undoubtedly have done so. Despite her fervent column and letter writing and her belief in internationalism, Richardson felt intensely isolated, geographically and socially. The cessation of hostilities also brought tragedy. Severe health problems combined with anguish over the war led to nervous breakdown and institutionalization for mental illness.

Whereas Richardson's pen was her primary weapon, urban-based labour suffragists used mass meetings, alliances with socialist and labour activists, and political writing to get their pacifist message across. Helena Gutteridge remained active in the coalition of BC suffrage groups, but she did not share their enthusiasm for the war, which she characterized in the *B.C. Federationist* as a product of hypermasculinity and capitalist monopoly. If the war represented the best that "male statecraft" could achieve, she wrote sarcastically, it was time for women to become involved in the "councils of the nations." Their experience as mothers might act as an "antidote to the false conception of man that places property and possessions at a higher value than human welfare." For Gutteridge, war abroad and the "starvation" of working-class families at home were twin products of a system geared toward profit, not people.

Concerned with the war's deleterious economic effects on working women, especially during the recession of 1914, Gutteridge collaborated with Laura Jamieson and others to create an employment bureau to help women locate jobs, though it too incorporated inequality, accepting white-only hiring policies in some occupations. Gutteridge always faced difficult political choices; the war merely made them more acute. The middle-class allies with whom she worked for suffrage were uncomfortable with her anti-war politics, but now she encountered suspicion among her labour allies too. The *B.C. Federationist* shifted from supporting suffrage to criticizing it, as labour activists suspected that it would produce a legacy of conservative female voters. They also feared that the wartime practice of hiring women to do men's jobs would lower wages and permanently take away men's work.

Winnipeg suffragist and pacifist Helen Armstrong encountered more unqualified support from fellow labour and socialist anti-war allies. She too organized against the economic privations accentuated by the war. She established the Women's Labor League, which organized low-paid female retail clerks into a union; lobbied for better support for war widows through a Next of Kin association; and protested the treatment of imprisoned immigrants from enemy nations and the neglect of their impoverished families. Like other pacifist socialist women, Armstrong believed that the war machine was stoked by capitalism and imperialism, and given the pervasiveness of government censorship, anti-war activity had to be incessantly public. She participated in anti-conscription rallies, which often prompted violent attacks by militarist vigilantes. Her daughter recalls in the film *The Notorious Mrs. Armstrong* that her mother had once stood between the vigilantes and male pacifists and came home "covered in bruises from head to toe." As she discovered two years later when she was arrested during the Winnipeg General Strike, the chivalry so often promised to women by anti-suffrage men quickly evaporated when it came to the state's treatment of working-class troublemakers such as herself.

CONSCRIPTION AND THE WARTIME ELECTIONS ACT

It seemed that war had replaced the female franchise as the most contested terrain, and suffragists were deeply divided on the subject. Political differences became yawning chasms in May 1917, when the federal Conservative government announced its intention of introducing conscription: its Military Service Act was duly passed in August. In September, Prime Minister Robert Borden followed up with the Wartime Elections Act (WEA). He subsequently convinced some pro-conscription Liberals to join his coalition Union government and then announced that the next federal election would be held in December 1917.

Conscription was divisive for suffragists, in ways both predictable and more complex. Even though the Quebec Fédération nationale Saint-Jean-Baptiste (FNSJB) supported volunteer work for the war, it opposed conscription as a coercive measure "qui menace nos fils et nos libertés." Insisting on its patriotism in a protest letter to Borden, the FNSJB denounced conscription as an affront to the very liberties for which the country was supposedly fighting. Rural women's organizations, especially in the West, were not enthusiastic, as they believed that family farms were differentially hurt by the forced enlistment of young men. Labour and socialist suffragists were more likely to be critical, though British-identified workers were always more supportive of war. Even the middle-of-the-road National Council of Women of Canada was divided. With eight local councils in favour and seven against conscription, the national organization quietly avoided taking a stand, though *Women's Century* insisted that all *good* women supported conscription and would "willingly give their sons so that Liberty and Justice may prevail on this earth." Ideological battle lines had become hardened by hyperbole.

The Wartime Elections Act was designed to ensure that Borden's pro-conscription government won the upcoming election. True, the prime minister had a problem on the horizon: with some women enfranchised provincially, others not, how would Ottawa manage the question of female suffrage, given that federal voters' lists were based on provincial ones? His bigger problem, however, was finding men who were willing to enlist in a war that seemed an endless list of casualties. To create an electorate that would be sympathetic to his pro-conscription agenda, the WEA gave the vote to women who had close relatives – sons, brothers, fathers – serving overseas in the British or Canadian forces, as well as to widows of soldiers. At the same time, it *dis*enfranchised

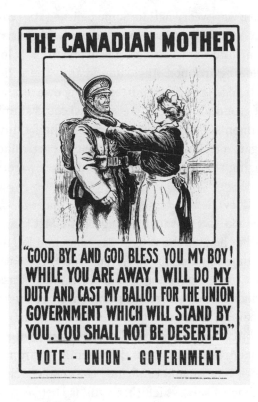

Pro-war posters drew on maternalist images just
as suffragists did. This government campaign poster
for the December 1917 federal election, in which
conscription figured prominently, linked women's
activism to their patriotic defence of the nation.

conscientious objectors and anyone who was designated an
enemy alien. The latter category applied to immigrants who were
born in an enemy nation (which included sprawling European
empires) and had become naturalized Canadian citizens after
1902, unless they had a son, grandson, or brother serving in the
military. To remove someone's citizenship rights based on place
of origin was unprecedented, yet the government found much

approval in a war-weary nation. Some believed that conscription was required to end hostilities more quickly, but restrictions on the "foreign" vote were also welcome expressions of long-standing prejudices against non-Anglo immigrants. The Military Voters Act also extended the vote to nurses serving overseas, a small but significant group, since they (like soldiers) could simply vote for the government or the Opposition, and if their riding was not named, organizers could assign the vote to a particular constituency, swinging the vote in uncertain ridings toward the Union government.

Borden knew he had some suffragist support for the WEA in English Canada. In a private meeting, Nellie McClung suggested to Borden that he give the vote to Canadian and English but not "foreign" women as a temporary expedient. Faced with howls of protest, McClung later recanted, but the damage was done. The Wartime Elections Act tore suffragist and women's reform organizations apart: it made the divisions between pacifist and war supporter more acute; confirmed the gulf between English and French women; separated equal rights feminists from those who sought social reform; and confirmed the suspicions of socialist feminists, who had always felt that a gulf lay between themselves and liberal and conservative feminists.

Some suffragists opposed the WEA due to its denial of democracy. Local Councils of Women in Regina and Victoria refused to endorse it, as did the Manitoba Political Equality League (contra McClung). *Grain Growers' Guide* women's columnist Francis Marion Beynon publicly chastised McClung for her failure to defend democracy, an exchange captured dramatically in Wendy Lill's 1985 play, *The Fighting Days.* Toronto suffragist Harriet Prenter, who had marched side-by-side with conservative Constance Hamilton in the 1913 Washington suffrage parade, now lambasted Hamilton and her allies for their support of the WEA, a piece of "vicious class legislation" that was "a far greater menace to us than many legions of foreigners." These upper-class women, Prenter charged, were "patriotic pagans," interested in military training for boys in public, not private schools. Working-class sons, she feared, were to be nothing more than "cannon fodder in war."

In Quebec, where the war had never been popular, French Canadian feminists expressed their anguish over the WEA. Marie Gérin-Lajoie could not accept votes for women if they were to be based solely on the military service of male family members: the FNSJB decried the injustice "faite à tant de femmes en ce pays par la loi électorate en temps de guerre." But differences over the WEA also blew up in the anglophone Quebec women's movement, culminating in an impeachment trial of the president of the Montreal Local Council of Women, Dr. Grace Ritchie-England, a suffragist who supported the war but not conscription or the WEA. Ritchie-England's crime was offering her own opinion publicly, without council endorsement. The WEA was a cynical "piece of unsurpassed effrontery," she thundered, which defied "every fundamental principle of British justice." Her views were shaped by her loyalty to anti-conscriptionist Liberal Wilfrid Laurier and to French Canadian women reformer friends (unlike many Anglos, she was bilingual), but it was also a product of her equal rights feminism. Protests also came from feminists in the West. Violet McNaughton privately told pacifist Gertrude Richardson that she sensed increasing "revulsion" with the unending "senseless slaughter" of Canadian soldiers and publicly voiced her opposition to the WEA disenfranchisement of the "foreign born" in her *Western Producer* columns.

Suffragists who approved of the WEA believed that women whose relatives were in the forces had a more deserving stake in such political decisions. Justifying the WEA in the pro-war *Women's Century,* Constance Boulton argued that it rewarded women who had made the ultimate sacrifice of their sons, in contrast to the "slackers" who remained behind. The *Western Woman's Weekly* agreed that rejecting this achievement would dishonour, "desert and shame" husbands, fathers, and brothers serving overseas, and would set women's suffrage "back a black half century." Arguments also circled back to racist and ethnocentric characterizations of the foreign and Quebec vote as disloyal and unpatriotic. "Once a German, always a German," *Women's Century* intoned about "alien" immigrants. Other scare tactics emerged. *Women's Century* repeated unsubstantiated anecdotes that Canadian soldiers had encountered Canadian Germans who were fighting for the other side, evidence that these "foreign" immigrants could not be trusted. The WEA's "selective draft" of female voters, wrote another supporter, was bestowed on the "trusted true patriots." If a few "noble and unselfish" war supporters whose relatives were not serving overseas were disenfranchised, that was too bad, but they should understand the "higher" good involved.

Pro-conscription suffragists drew heavily on international connections and solidarities to substantiate their cause; they reported positively on almost every aspect of the British war effort and cultivated imperialist loyalties, situating Canadian women in a warm circle of loyal allies defending democracy. Although usually considered inconsequential to the American movement, Canadians could now brag about their limited federal enfranchisement. Toronto pro-war suffragist Constance Hamilton testified before a US Congressional Committee in 1918 as a support to American suffragists. She reassured legislators that the Canadian experience proved that granting suffrage did not weaken the nation in war, but rather strengthened it.

English Canadian suffragists who opposed the WEA were feminists inclined toward equal rights arguments for the vote, advocates of unequivocal democracy, and labour and socialist women. Francis Marion Beynon, removed from her job with the *Grain Growers' Guide* due to her anti-war views, commented on the WEA from her self-imposed exile in the United States. The December 1917 election, a resounding triumph for Robert Borden, was a "threefold betrayal": first, of the democratic right to vote in a contest that was free from manipulation; second, of the immigrants who were "lured to Canada to build the country" and then denied their rights; and finally, of the soldiers who thought they were fighting for "a free and honourable Canada" rather than for the politicians and financiers who had made it into a "little Germany." Prophetically, Beynon called the WEA a "monstrous act of injustice that has already roused bitter race hatreds that will endure for generations."

THE TRAGEDY OF ALETA DEY: FRANCIS MARION BEYNON'S EXILE

"Almost without exception," Francis Beynon wrote in June 1917, "one will find in the ranks of the most fervent patriots those who are getting rich out of sweated labour and profiteering." Two weeks later, her regular column in the *Grain Growers' Guide* (GGG) was a "Good-bye" message; she had already left for that mecca of writers, New York City, to join her sister and brother-in-law, also journalist exiles from Canada's wartime intolerance. Beynon had become too fiercely anti-government; the press censor's surveillance of her writing may have been a factor in her dismissal. Her pre-war distrust of militarism sharpened into full-blown opposition to war and a deeply felt despair that liberty and democracy had been sacrificed to racial hatred, militarism, and unchecked capitalist profit making. In New York, Beynon penned a thinly disguised semi-autobiographical piece of fiction, *Aleta Dey*. Published in 1919, this novel shows the suffrage movement at its most divided.

Francis Beynon's feminist and anti-war views were years in the making. Before the war, her GGG women's page concentrated on other issues, from better management of the home to dower rights, and her early wartime columns were not resolutely pacifist. Although she referred to the conflict as an "international calamity" and "a hot-bed of racial hatred," she conceded that Canada's participation was a "necessity." Like many temperance advocates, she used the emergency to argue for prohibition. But by

Francis Marion Beynon's courageous novel, *Aleta Dey,*
immortalizes the anti-war suffragist as a noble martyr to the
preservation of democracy. After moving to New York City in 1917,
Beynon published some short stories and edited *The Lookout,* the
paper for the Seamen's Church Institute. She only returned to
Canada shortly before her death in 1951.

1915, she expressed doubt about Nellie McClung's characterization
of women in her book *In Times Like These* as more peace loving, and
she praised international socialists who had the courage to oppose
the war. Two years later, her anti-war views were unequivocal.

Descriptions of Aleta Dey's childhood in the novel offer insight into Beynon's growing radicalism. Aleta is reared in a strict,
repressive Methodist family, in which discipline, strapping, and
absolute obedience to the church ("Churchianity" being distinct

from Christianity) were valued more than natural curiosity. Escaping to the city to work as a journalist, Aleta finds intellectual freedom and a cause: suffrage. Her relationships with two men are used as the plot device to explore various contradictions of feminist and pacifist politics, though the novel also has its share of romanticism and melodramatic twists. Aleta is inexplicably, guiltily attracted to McNair, a conservative, anti-suffragist, and a drinker, though his intemperance most disturbs her. In Aleta's world, men who drink are ineligible: marrying them is a surefire recipe for heartache and poverty. Her childhood friend Ned, a secular anti-war socialist, is McNair's foil and clearly the man Aleta *should* be in love with.

Aleta's interactions with other suffragists also reveal the fissures and hypocrisies exposed by the war. A prominent suffragist belligerently confronts her at a meeting and denounces a US congresswoman who voted against the war. Aleta notes that freedom of expression was the *point* of suffrage: every person is allowed to voice his or her views, and she reminds the pro-war suffragist that "you urged women be given the vote because they would be opposed to war." The woman is outraged, responding, "I meant they would be opposed to wars that are past, like the Crimean War or the Boer War, not wars in our time." In her close Winnipeg milieu, Beynon had witnessed an increasingly intolerant, conformist, repressive state and civil society. Her brother-in-law was fired by the *Winnipeg Free Press* for merely shaking hands publicly with Labour MLA Fred Dixon after an anti-war speech, and Dixon, also Beynon's friend, was badly beaten by pro-war vigilantes.

Aleta's conversations with her two suitors and her fellow suffragists expose the contradictions of politics and personal life, a topic that few other Canadian suffragists explored in fiction or non-fiction. How do we reconcile our romantic attraction to people who don't share our politics? she asks of her relationship with McNair. How do we work with suffragists who share that one goal but have other disagreeable ideas? Aleta's childhood friend

Pauline, also a suffragist, is preoccupied with her own selfish version of individual rights, not with transforming an unequal society. Pauline denounces socialists, supports the moral surveillance of working-class women, and heartlessly dismisses the poor as "lazy beggars" who want to grab what others have. How do we conquer our own feminine fears of speaking out publicly about unpopular causes? Beynon also asks. Aleta admits that she often "drags her shirking spirit" into any public debate. Even though she does not respect her opponents' ideas, she dreads the public derision of hers.

When McNair enlists, Aleta cannot shake off her "sick at heart" worries about him, yet she cannot be a cheerleader for a war that is grounded in economic inequality and irrational hatred. The suffragists in the novel are no more virtuous than others in this regard. A woman whom Aleta previously saw as politically reasonable now offers bloodthirsty directives to her fellow Red Cross volunteers: "Those German swine will all have to be killed off." Female war supporters insist that Germans all tell lies but refuse to confront Canada's own autocratic tendencies in suppressing news stories and stifling dissent. A society woman corners Aleta at an event and challenges her pacifism: "She levelled her lorgnette at me fearsomely. 'But the atrocities my dear, the atrocities. Surely people who do things like that ought to be exterminated.'" Aleta reminds the woman of the atrocities against African Americans in the United States, resulting in torture and death, and of imperialist atrocities in Africa against the peoples of the Belgian Congo. "As I remember it those were only coloured people," responds her adversary. "There is a vast difference between crucifying a white man and hanging a coloured one." Yes, Aleta retorts sarcastically, "I have no doubt their naked bodies have quite a different effect against the sky."

When Aleta participates in an anti-conscription rally, she is badly beaten by soldiers. She dies, a martyr to the cause of liberty but also to a feminism that has not compromised its soul. At the end of the novel, she is critical of Ned's socialism, fearing that it too will bring single-minded solutions. She rejects revolution in favour of social democratic reform and insists, in the vein of the social gospel, that the redistribution of wealth will not be enough. Humanity needs a spiritual regeneration, a return to the principles of love, liberty, democracy, and absolute freedom of speech. The novel is a uniquely intimate, painful glimpse into feminist politics, as we share Aleta's trajectory from dedication to disillusion with the suffrage movement. A raw, introspective reflection on her inner political turmoil, it is a poignant rendition of the divisions sundering Canada's wartime feminism.

WAR'S END

The war years were marked by both advancement and setback for suffrage. At their conclusion, having awarded some women the federal franchise in 1917, the Borden government then extended it to white women on the same terms as men. In 1918, Parliament passed the Act to confer the Electoral Franchise upon Women, and women were given the right to run for federal office in 1919. Electoral reform in 1920 abolished property qualifications for voters, moving Canada closer to universal suffrage for its white citizens. Yet, during the war years, the fragile unity and feeling for suffrage that had been crafted over the past forty years was sorely tested and found wanting. Nor was it salvaged during the peace that followed.

From time to time, men as well as women break into print to claim equal suffrage has been a failure? Is this true? ... Those who sought the suffrage had not in mind a glorified seat in parliament – the last thought was self aggrandizement. Rather, they carried the vision of a deserted wife or a widowed mother with a flock of needy little ones. Immediately following suffrage, three far-reaching acts were placed on the statute books, all aiding women: equal guardianship, equal pay and widows pensions.

SUSIE LANE CLARK, "SUFFRAGE HAS BROUGHT
INCALCULABLE BENEFITS TO WOMEN, SAY PROPONENTS,"
23 OCTOBER 1937

EIGHT

OLD AND NEW
AGENDAS IN PEACETIME

Quebec feminist Idola Saint-Jean created the
pro-suffrage paper *La Sphère féminine* and supported the struggles
of working and professional women for legal rights.

WHEN IDOLA SAINT-JEAN, leader of the Alliance Canadienne pour le vote des femmes du Québec, took a delegation to the Legislative Assembly of Quebec in the 1920s to argue for women's provincial suffrage, she encountered mocking comments about her femininity and sexuality. One member of the assembly, vying for cheap laughs from his fellow legislators, asked if she would like to "wear his trousers." Undaunted, Saint-Jean ran for a federal seat in 1930, using her platform as an Independent candidate to advocate for women's suffrage. Political opponents publicly derided her as an "old maid." Other anti-suffragist detractors in Quebec asserted that feminists should return to their maternal duties in the home, but Saint-Jean did not fit the domestic mould. She was something of a radical, a literati and single working woman, though she had adopted an African Canadian girl who lost her parents in the Spanish influenza epidemic of 1918. Her adopted daughter did not survive the 1920s.

Saint-Jean's upbringing was initially quite traditional. Educated in a Catholic convent, she then became deeply involved in Montreal literary and theatre circles as a poet and actress. Her passion for theatre and the arts led her to Paris, where she studied acting and took courses at the Sorbonne. Saint-Jean's unusually venturesome intellectual exploration and exposure to European political debate undoubtedly shaped her later perspectives and her courage to stand outside the mainstream. On her return to Montreal, she secured a position as a French language teacher at McGill and taught diction at the Monument-National cultural centre and the working-class Mechanics Institute. As a member of the Fédération nationale Saint-Jean-Baptiste (FNSJB), she was introduced to suffrage and became one of the two key leaders of the Quebec struggle by the 1920s.

She founded a new feminist magazine, *La Sphère féminine,* and used her first editorials to address the woman question rather bluntly: "For centuries, one half of humanity has dictated to the other half its will and way of thinking in religious, political, and judicial spheres." Saint-Jean's vision of "redistributive justice" was also attuned to the class dimensions of female oppression. Some "gentlemen" were "crying" that women's labour would result in a "deserted home," she wrote sardonically. They took note only when women demanded entrance to "intellectual" and professional jobs but didn't care when they did "inferior manual work, washing the floors of offices."

Idola Saint-Jean's tenacious promotion of women's rights in Quebec throughout the 1920s and 1930s is a reminder that the suffrage struggle did not end in 1918. Nor did all feminist agitation. Post-mortems on what women would do with the newly acquired federal vote began immediately after 1918. By the end of the 1920s, the mainstream media often claimed that women had retreated to the domestic sphere and failed to make their mark on politics, invariably citing one factor: few women were elected to office. Conservative senator Grattan O'Leary, writing in *Chatelaine* magazine in 1930, offered condescending confirmation of their irrelevance: little more than political "window dressing," they did not vote in a female block, and contrary to feminist predictions, their votes had not dispelled all "evil things" from society. Vancouver suffragist and judge Helen Gregory MacGill disagreed. In the same magazine, she pointed to men's assumed superiority and women's internalized inferiority and reminded *Chatelaine* readers that suffrage had always been "a means and not an end." Women's "special knowledge" was needed more than ever if Canada were to solve the urgent issues of the day. Analyzing their defeat in the 1930 federal election in the *Chatelaine* article "Why I Failed to Be

Elected," a group of female candidates all lamented the common Achilles heel of women who ran for office: negative news coverage, lack of party support, and meagre campaign funds. Co-operative Commonwealth Federation (CCF) candidate Beatrice Brigden added that nine out of ten defeated women in 1930 had run for alternative farm, labour, or socialist parties. They faced double prejudice, as women and as radical critics of society – not a surefire way into Parliament.

Grattan O'Leary's notion that the interwar years became a trough of feminist inactivity has been remarkably resilient in historical writing. "After gaining the vote in the period from 1916–1920, the women's movement simply sputtered," claim two legal historians in a recent treatment of the Persons Case. The periodization of feminism into waves – first (suffrage), second (1960s), and third (1990s) – perpetuates this unfortunate distortion. Yet the wave and trough image is contradicted by the themes of this chapter. Some women and men continued to agitate for the provincial vote until 1940, and suffragists, along with a new cohort of feminists, threw themselves into many old and new reform causes, though not necessarily electoral politics. The fleeting unity of the suffrage battle fragmented into multiple feminist ideals, organizations, and novel visions of emancipation.

THE STRUGGLE CONTINUES: THE MARITIMES
In the Maritimes, New Brunswick, Prince Edward Island, and the Dominion of Newfoundland did not enfranchise white women until 1919, 1923, and 1925, respectively. Some historians initially described their delay as a sign that the suffrage movement had absorbed the region's sedate conservatism. Even feminists who recounted the struggle for the vote gave this impression: "No lobbying was necessary" by 1919, reminisced Mrs. Lawlor of New Brunswick for historian Catherine Cleverdon, "so the women stayed home, had afternoon tea and shook hands all around." Yet

the legislation had been delayed by the same forces of opposition, especially the discourse of separate spheres, that women met in the rest of English Canada. Years of slow and steady lobbying, including efforts to draw in more rural support and collaboration with the Woman's Christian Temperance Union (WCTU), laid the groundwork for post-war success.

New Brunswick suffragists were sharply divided over the Wartime Elections Act, but once peace was declared and Conservatives and Liberals commenced their partisan jockeying, it was only a matter of time until one party or the other would – for reasons of political expediency – bring in a measure long avoided. Provincial legislators who had been fierce opponents could now announce their conversion by wrapping themselves in the flag and declaring they were rewarding women's patriotic war work. Yet New Brunswick women had to wait another fifteen years for the right to run for the legislature; by 1934, this democratic deficit was too embarrassing to sustain and was rectified.

In Prince Edward Island, suffrage petitions initiated by temperance supporters were presented to the legislature in the 1890s, but a movement dedicated singularly to suffrage did not materialize. Women's interest in the vote was perhaps muted by other debates about democracy, notably getting rid of a provincial, appointed upper house (or senate). The issues that often galvanized suffragists in other provinces were also solved incrementally by PEI legislators: a prohibition bill, single women's municipal voting rights in Charlottetown and Summerside, married women's property legislation, and women's right to run for school trustee. A 1918 suffrage resolution in the legislature went down to defeat, but a change of governing party again precipitated a turnaround by politicians. The newly elected Liberals (1919) received suffrage petitions from constituents, including the rural Women's Institutes, and were also lobbied internally by their women's Liberal organization. Success came in 1923. One point of debate was whether (and how much) property holding was required for voters, a vestige of nineteenth-century class elitism that had not yet disappeared from thinking about the franchise.

In Newfoundland, the Conservatives replaced a discredited, corrupt Liberal government in 1925, and a commitment to women's suffrage accompanied the change in the ruling party. Newfoundland suffragists had redirected all their energies to volunteer labour for the Women's Patriotic Association (WPA) during the First World War, but in 1920 they established the Women's Franchise League to petition and plead with elected officials anew. Travelling across the island, suffragists used the WPA network to build new support; by 1925, they had amassed twenty thousand signatures on a petition. Newfoundland suffragists had for many years looked outside of Canada for intellectual inspiration and organizational models, linking up with the British Dominion Woman Suffrage Union (BDWSU), the Europe-based International Woman Suffrage Alliance and, later, the American women's movement. Through the alliance newspaper, *Jus Suffragii*, they appealed for international speakers – someone "eloquent and attractive" – who might "tour the Island," especially when one of their most active leaders, Armine Gosling, was wintering in Bermuda.

The members of the Newfoundland group, notes Margo Duley in *Where Once Our Mothers Stood*, were popularly portrayed as "grand dames out of touch with the true feelings of homespun Newfoundland women," yet, like many Canadian suffragists, they promoted social reforms intended to alleviate the burdens of poor and working women. Newfoundland suffragists, it is true, faced considerable derision for decades. As suffragist Agnes Ayre recalled, when they lobbied for the vote, "it was not surprising to find some otherwise delightful people fly into terrific rages and order us out of their offices."

Though certainly mocked, the core of the Newfoundland group were affluent, well-educated, and well-established members of St. John's society. The *St. John's Evening Telegram* supported their cause in 1925, argues historian Sean Cadigan, not as an equal rights issue, but because it thought that enabling the wives and daughters of the business and professional elites to add their say to political life would be beneficial and would perhaps help clean up rampant political corruption.

Newfoundland politicians justified their change of heart in 1925 by claiming they were simply moving with the changing times. Women of the Victorian age supposedly never wanted the vote, as it did not impinge on their pure and secluded lives, but now women's responsibilities could no longer be limited to the home circle. For their part, suffragists reminded legislators that their public roles primarily involved social reform, not a desire to appropriate men's roles. Women's ardent wartime WPA work, justified in familial and patriotic language, was further reassurance of their safe incorporation into existing class and gender structures. Still, the House of Assembly could not resist one last vestige of paternalism. The suffrage bill allowed men to vote at the age of twenty-one, women not until twenty-five, a restriction that imitated the 1918 British Representation of the People Act, which allowed only women over thirty, with property qualifications, to vote (the ages were equalized in 1928). Somehow, women were *not quite* adults on the same level as men.

QUEBEC'S DISTINCT SUFFRAGE BATTLE

A different struggle unfolded in Quebec, reflecting the province's distinct religious, cultural, and political history. Anti-feminist arguments that suffrage was un-Christian and would destroy the family were heard across English and French Canada, but Quebec women fought a more difficult battle. Their experience was perhaps more in tune with that of French and Italian women, who also received the vote only in the 1940s. Quebec's Liberal premier (1920–36) and ardent anti-suffragist, Louis-Alexandre Taschereau, boasted proudly about this connection, maintaining that the majority French population in Quebec was "imbued with the [European] Latin spirit," which in his mind meant that women should remain in the home on their pedestals of purity and domesticity. Anglophone suffragists such as Isabella Scott had no patience with Taschereau's tributes to Quebec's Latin mentality, which she relayed, laced with incredulous sarcasm, in her reports to the international suffrage paper, *Jus Suffragii*. French-English tensions, both long-standing and accentuated during the war, inevitably seeped into the Quebec movement, which nonetheless tried valiantly to find avenues of bi-cultural accommodation.

With the advent of peace, both English and French Canadian Quebec suffragists shared a moment of hope that national and international suffrage advances might inspire Quebec to accept the vote for women. French Canadian feminists pointed optimistically to international precedents showing that the female franchise did not contradict the tenets of Catholic femininity. In England, noted the FNSJB paper, *La bonne parole*, Catholic Women's Leagues were educating women in their new civic role as voters, and women's votes in New Zealand had reduced electoral corruption and did not cause "le dissension dans les familles." Pro-suffrage writing from the other motherland – France – was always strategically used in the paper to suggest the compatibility of suffrage with French culture (contra Taschereau). Women were awarded the vote in other lands, argued dedicated suffragist Marie Gérin-Lajoie, because people rightly believed in the "justice of their judgment, the effectiveness of their work, their special domestic knowledge."

Officially, *La bonne parole* was a vehicle for social reform and was neutral on the issue of votes for women. No editorial criticized the Quebec MPs who all voted against the federal 1918 suffrage bill, but once it passed, the paper urged women to exercise their civic duty and vote federally, especially in a time of post-war loss and national rebuilding. Any hope that the federal franchise would be imitated in Quebec was soon dissipated, and anticipating a long struggle, the suffrage movement regrouped. Given the reality that a predominantly francophone province would never be won over by an anglophone group, the Montreal Suffrage Association disbanded in 1919. Anglophone suffragists reconvened around the nondescriptly named Montreal Women's Club, which just happened to have a franchise subcommittee. As the Newfoundland women did, this group, including Isabella Scott, looked across the Atlantic to the International Woman Suffrage Alliance (IWSA) and the BDWSU for inspiration, in part because other Canadian suffrage organizations had folded. In 1925, *Jus Suffragii* reported that the Canadian Suffrage Association was no longer affiliated with the international group due to lack of interest in English Canada.

Isabella Scott wrote for the alliance newspaper *Jus Suffragii* and travelled to London to attend BDWSU meetings. Later renamed the British Dominion Women's Citizen Union (BDWCU), this Commonwealth group routinely passed resolutions urging the Quebec government to join the rest of "civilized" North America, to stop "disadvantaging" Quebec women in comparison to *all* other provinces and countries by enacting women's suffrage. English Canadian Quebec suffragists clearly felt marginalized and frustrated. Scott wrote repeatedly to international groups about Quebec's "unjust, humiliating and degrading" laws, under which women were virtually "slaves" in the family hierarchy, and she once claimed that the French element was "holding back" the struggle. Quebec prided itself on being different, she lamented, as it embraced the "medieval," the "antique," role. Pragmatically though, Scott conceded that resolutions attempting to shame the Quebec government, if passed at a *British* conference, might actually make English-speaking suffragists even more "unpopular" in the province.

Scott knew that an English-French partnership in Quebec was also essential to success, and she threw her support behind a new bi-cultural organization formed in 1921. At the urging of Idola Saint-Jean, the FNSJB initiated the Comité provincial pour le suffrage féminin, with both English and French co-chairs. Emboldened by the (apparently false) rumour that Premier Taschereau might be sympathetic to a private member's suffrage bill, two hundred women headed to Quebec City the next year to present their case, only to be told by Taschereau that his government would never accept their request for the vote. His obdurate refusal was in contrast to the placatory pleas of suffragists such as Gérin-Lajoie who reassured politicians that they had no intention of "destroying" the home or abandoning motherhood, indeed quite the contrary. Year after year, a pilgrimage of suffragists trudged to Quebec City to make their case through petitions, meetings, private members' bills, and special pleadings. A predictable drama unfolded with each attempt: the women had a sympathetic politician present a bill; the government used party discipline to vote it down; the women announced in defeat that they would continue their fight.

In 1927, the Quebec suffrage movement split, though not on language lines. Idola Saint-Jean founded a new group, the Alliance Canadienne pour le vote des femmes du Québec, and the Comité provincial pour le suffrage féminin became the Ligue des droits de la femme under leader Thérèse Casgrain. Both groups were bi-cultural, and both studied, publicized, and lobbied the government concerning women's legal and social disadvantages. The Alliance Canadienne kept its links to the IWSA but focused its efforts on more grassroots local mobilizations, trying to reach working-class women whom Saint-Jean believed had been ignored by middle-class suffragists. Though there were tensions between the two groups, they co-operated on the yearly pilgrimages, and their respective leaders, Saint-Jean and Casgrain, became known as the two "lionesses" of the Quebec movement.

Thérèse Casgrain represented affluence and political connections. She came from a wealthy Quebec family, her husband was a Liberal member of Parliament and Speaker of the House of

Commons, and she was socially well connected, exemplified by her presence at Prime Minister Mackenzie King's dinner parties (where, as her autobiography tactfully relates, the entertainment was the very eccentric Mackenzie King playing the piano while his dog sat beside him and sang along). A clever public advocate, private lobbyist, and person of immense persistence, she was a liberal reformer who followed the rules of the game but played them so well that she was helpful to the cause. "I am not a suffragette," she wrote in *La bonne parole,* fearful of the image of the man-hating feminist. We must exercise "de modération, de mesure et de sérénité," she insisted, stressing women's "inherent maternal qualities" as the rationale for the vote. Still, her political choices later in life, such as running for the CCF in Quebec, took courage, swimming against, not with, the tide.

Idola Saint-Jean would not have graced the prime minister's dinner parties. She was more outspoken than Casgrain (who labelled her brand of feminism as rather "bitter"), and the issues of work, welfare, and economic independence – from enforcement of the minimum wage to women's right to their own bank accounts — were high on her list of causes. She bravely supported a major strike of garment workers in Montreal in 1937 led by a left-wing union, and when a Quebec member of Parliament suggested in 1935 that unemployment could be solved by the dismissal of married female workers, she countered with resolutely feminist rhetoric in *La Sphère féminine:* "Prétend-on refuser aux femmes le droit de vivre et de jouir de la dignité et de l'indépendance que le travail confère à tout être?" Rather than drawing solely on the discourse of maternalism, Saint-Jean emphasized natural rights, democracy, egalitarianism, and republicanism. Women should not receive the vote as a "favour," she argued, but because they were an integral part of society, intelligent and free, as were men. Her blunt support for equal rights and her methods of direct grassroots engagement contrasted with

Casgrain's "seduction" of the ruling elites, argues historian Diane Lamoureux, and this may be why Saint-Jean was singled out for lewd, sexist, and demeaning comments by male opponents.

No matter how inspired the leadership of these two women, Quebec suffragists faced intractable obstacles, particularly the Catholic Church. Throughout the 1920s and 1930s, it remained opposed to suffrage. In our more secular age, imagining the pervasive influence of the church may be difficult, but it was deeply implicated in Quebec history, cultural practices, family lives, and sense of "la survivance": it had provided education, social welfare, advice, and solace for generations. Gabrielle Roy's moving and insightful novel *The Tin Flute*, about a working-class family as it struggled to survive in Depression Montreal, offers a feeling for the church's immense authority over daily life. The family matriarch, Rosanna, would never think of disobeying the church, no matter how much her own life of sorrow and toil directly contradicted its teachings.

Moreover, the real issue was the *Quebec* Catholic Church. In some European countries where women had the franchise, the church was pragmatically attempting a rapprochement with female suffrage in hopes of mobilizing women voters against its most hated enemy, communism, and in support of its many moralizing projects. When Marie Gérin-Lajoie travelled to Rome for a conference of Catholic women in 1922, she was elated to see that the church was about to accept a resolution allowing women to vote but furious when a last-minute clause was added, clarifying that they must still obey the wishes of their *local* clergy. In other words, Quebec women must follow the dictates of their bishops. Henri Bourassa, still fiercely anti-suffrage, and with more influence than Gérin-Lajoie, had lobbied the Vatican for this clause.

Pressured by the church, Gérin-Lajoie withdrew from suffrage work, though she turned her formidable efforts to other feminist causes. Her comprehensive knowledge of the Quebec civil code informed her advocacy for legal reforms that would aid women's economic autonomy, such as married women's right to their own wages. But when it came to the vote, Quebec feminists evaded direct confrontation with the Catholic hierarchy. In a 1938 CBC Radio interview, for example, Casgrain avoided any negative mention of the church, almost blaming Quebec women for being "slower" to obtain the vote, as they were not generally "club women." Her 1972 autobiography, written after Quebec's Quiet Revolution, more forthrightly acknowledged the church's purposeful, effective antagonism to suffrage.

Suffrage also had more support in urban areas, particularly Montreal, but not in rural areas. Farm women, coping with large families and unending labour, did not necessarily feel that electoral politics spoke to their needs. In 1915, the provincial government launched Les Cercles de Fermières du Québec, an organization for farm women that consciously reinforced this position, cultivating the message that French Catholic women should devote their primary efforts to the family, not to involvement in politics. The cercles did validate women's farm labour and promote some social reforms, but their magazine was a venue for anti-suffrage articles and petitions, including church-sponsored ones. Rejection of suffrage by an influential group such as the cercles hurt the cause, providing politicians with visible proof that ordinary women did not want the vote. Other church-sponsored organizations were also created as antidotes to feminism, including auxiliaries for Catholic boarding school graduates and the Catholic Women's League. The league became the womanly voice of the church on moral issues, warning about the perils of dancing, immodest clothing (sleeveless dresses), "garçonism" in fashion (the boyish flapper style), and of course, sex outside of marriage. Even the progressive FNSJB bowed to these pressures, setting up its own "indecent clothing sub-committee."

Like other Canadian suffragists, francophone women met with ingrained patriarchal ideas about gender and the family, but in Quebec, these were closely interwoven with discourses about nationalism, Catholicism, rural preservation, and the survival of French Canada. Well into the 1930s, Fadette, the anti-suffragist columnist in *Le Devoir,* warned young Quebecers against imitating English Protestant values: to do so would threaten not just the family, but cultural, national, and linguistic survival as well. In nationalist discourses, as historian Andrée Lévesque notes in *Making and Breaking the Rules,* rural depopulation and French emigration out of the province were seen as harbingers of the decline of French Quebec. Women's reproductive, maternal role – the "revenge of the cradle" – was still seen as a solution. Concerns about protecting Quebec's version of French Catholicism infiltrated the suffrage debate, and since the FNSJB had always stressed the primacy of women's familial role, it had trouble convincing Quebecers that maternal concerns should extend beyond the home to the legislature.

Also, what about women who had no children or whose experience of marriage and motherhood entailed poverty, violence, and disappointment? Middle-class maternal discourses did not necessarily provide solutions for them, a problem that Idola Saint-Jean recognized well. Those who stood outside the idealized gender order were open to marginalization and ridicule. Even Casgrain recalled the shocking wake-up call for suffragist lobbyists as they were greeted with male laughter, ridicule, and humiliation on their Quebec City pilgrimages. Male supporters were suspect too. When one member of the Quebec legislative assembly presented a women's suffrage bill, his chair was pulled out from under him as he sat down, leaving him seriously injured. Such schoolboy tactics were routine, and Casgrain remembered countless small instances of humiliation. One suffrage delegation spent twelve hours outside a committee room, waiting for its scheduled appointment, only to be sent away. Deliberate snubbing sent a clear message: this space belongs to men.

Given these formidable barriers, perhaps we should ask why suffragists finally succeeded in 1940. The contradiction (and reassurance) that Quebec women already voted federally was probably one reason. As labour journalist Éva Circé-Côté wrote in the trade union paper *Le Monde ouvrier,* the sitting female member of Parliament, Agnes Macphail, was "la preuve vivante" that women were the equal of men. Quebec suffragists were also able to cash in on advertising practices that earlier campaigners had barely touched. They used donations from American suffragist Carrie Chapman Catt to hire women as sandwich-board walkers in Montreal, distributed leaflets at the Montreal market, and teased sympathetic articles out of various newspapers. They also used a new strategy: radio. Communicating through the air waves broke down the urban-rural barriers and spoke to women directly in their homes. Broadcasting in English and French, Idola Saint-Jean explained the basic arguments for women's equal rights and cleverly cast the struggle in nationalist terms, portraying modern suffragists as part of the long lineage of Quebec heroines. She reminded her listeners that Patriot Louis-Joseph Papineau's mother once voted, and she celebrated the contributions of white female settlers to early Quebec as they established manufacturing, hospitals, and agriculture, and protected the colony against "Iroquois attacks." Casgrain also innovated with the air waves as political communication. Her weekly CBC program, *Fémina,* offered women-centred news, shrewdly presented with a pro-suffrage slant.

As in other provinces, both suffrage organizations sought out allies. When the Trades and Labour Congress held its annual meeting in Quebec in 1927, the Alliance Canadienne persuaded it to pass a supportive resolution and include suffragists in its lobbying delegation to Premier Taschereau. Three women, representing Catholics, anglophones, and francophones, were carefully selected to join the delegation to emphasize the linguistic and religious collaboration at the heart of the suffrage struggle. Strategic alliances with both elite and grassroots groups were forged. Casgrain lobbied high-ranking federal Liberals to pressure their recalcitrant provincial Liberal counterparts who opposed suffrage, whereas Saint-Jean focused on mobilizing urban working women for the cause.

A small and embattled organized left, along with the trade union movement, also added its voice to equality for women. Writing under a male pseudonym in *Le Monde ouvrier*, Éva Circé-Côté not only defended the dignity and rights of working women, "ostracisées" by the "dames de la société," but also made the case for suffrage, even though she had previously opposed it. Now, she asked drolly, why were the Quebec bishops even "more Catholic" than the pope himself in opposing women's right to vote? Pro-suffrage labour and socialist feminist voices, however, were still rather marginal in Quebec. In France, historians argue, the decline of a previously vibrant socialist feminist suffrage lobby in the 1920s and 1930s was one factor delaying suffrage – perhaps a political consideration in Quebec as well.

To make the case for political rights, suffragists focused public attention on the gender discrimination that pervaded family law, property ownership, and the economy in Quebec. The Ligue des droits de la femme persuaded the provincial government to set up a commission of inquiry (the Dorion Commission) to determine whether family law in Quebec's civil code needed modernizing. The four appointed commissioners were more interested in protecting the traditional Catholic family than in substantial reform, but the commission hearings provided feminists with a golden opportunity to publicly air countless examples of legal discrimination. Married women, for instance, were still unable to claim their own wages. Suffragists were also adept at showcasing the more egregious examples of an outdated sexual double standard, citing Quebec marriage laws in which a husband was allowed to separate from his wife if she were "adulterous," whereas the wife could do so only if her husband were adulterous *and* had his "concubine" (mistress) living in their home. The public hearings for a federal Royal Commission on Provincial Federal Relations (the 1931 Rowell-Sirois Commission) also provided suffragists with a

REALLY, THIS IS SO SUDDEN

This English Canadian interpretation of suffrage in Quebec,
which appeared in the *Toronto Daily Star* on 22 February 1940,
portrays French women being seductively wooed by men who
"gave" them the vote, an image that obscures their long legal
struggles in that province.

chance to expose gender discrimination. The Ligue des droits
de la femme's legal counsel, Elizabeth Monk (who was not allowed to practise law in Quebec), made a compelling case in
her public presentation that Quebec's many forms of legal discrimination led directly to poverty for women and the children
they supported.

Allies, publicity, lobbying, and political connections: in a sense, the vote was achieved in Quebec in a manner not unlike that of other provinces. In Quebec too, a political party that was on the outs accepted suffrage for the kudos and womanpower it offered, and when a regime change occurred, the party paid its due with a suffrage bill. After the Union Nationale, a nationalist right-wing party, took power in 1936, the ousted Liberals for the first time allowed women to attend their convention, expecting they would present a resolution supporting suffrage. They did, and it passed. When a Liberal government under Premier Joseph-Adélard Godbout was re-elected in 1939, there was one last hurdle to overcome: church opposition. Rather than contradict the anti-suffrage bishops, Godbout offered to resign as premier, but he astutely warned the church in private that the man who replaced him would be an anti-clerical Liberal. Perceiving suffrage as the lesser of two evils, the Catholic hierarchy put its anti-feminism on hold, though not with much grace.

SUFFRAGISTS' AGENDA AFTER THE VOTE

Women did run for office after 1918, though with varying polit-ical agendas. In Montreal alone, Grace Ritchie-England, who had vehemently opposed the Wartime Elections Act, ran for Parliament in 1921 as a Liberal, though later in the decade she became so annoyed with the Quebec Liberal Party that she urged women to refuse all Liberal election work until it gave them the vote. When Idola Saint-Jean ran as an Independent, she secured an impressive three thousand votes, and Rose Henderson, a prom-inent suffragist and commentator in *Women's Century,* took a turn to the left after the war and ran as a Labour candidate.

Most women, however, did behind-the-scenes party work rather than risk public scrutiny on election platforms. Many suf-fragists also claimed that they were more interested in actual reform than in careers as politicians. When asked to reflect in 1937 on the legacy of the vote, Vancouver suffragist, municipal activist, and CCFer Susie Lane Clark argued that women were less interested in "glorified seats in parliament" than in legislation to aid disadvantaged women, and on this count, suffrage had brought "incalculable benefits."

Many suffrage groups across the country did not disband after the First World War. They reformulated their goals, merging suffragist views of women's collective, maternal political power with a new commitment to act as "women-mother citizens." Women spoke with confident conviction of their new divine opportunity to purify politics and reconstruct society. Practically, they created venues and organizations to educate women about their new public roles. Speakers, meetings, and women's papers explained the parliamentary system and citizen responsibilities to women, who were often imagined as political neophytes. In Vancouver, a Voters Educational League temporarily attempted a non-partisan model of individual political education, but a rival organization, the New Era League (the name capturing suffragists' immense optimism), founded by Susie Lane Clark, had more longevity and some success mobilizing women in support of mothers' allowances and many civic reform issues. Newfoundland suffragists transitioned into a new League of Women Voters, designed to agitate about legislation relating to women and children, whereas Saskatchewan's Political Equality League developed a post-suffrage "Plan of Work," audacious in its optimism, calling for the nationalization of public utilities, international arbitration to end war, changes to the Criminal Code, education reform, and equal pay.

Suffragists' long-cherished social and moral reforms were now their legislative priorities: property rights for wives, a minimum wage for women, pensions for widows, aid to deserted wives, anti-VD regulation, and a maternity allowance for expecting mothers. In British Columbia, suffragist Mary Ellen Smith, the first woman member of the provincial legislature, placed many of these reforms at the heart of her platform. A British immigrant,

Artist Emily Carr created this cartoon for *Western Woman's Weekly*.
It appeared on 7 February 1918 and expressed the suffragists'
optimism about their post-suffrage agenda of mothers' pensions,
equal pay, and a host of other reforms.

Smith forged a political partnership with her husband, Ralph
Smith, a miner, preacher, suffragist, and Liberal-Labour member
of the BC legislature. When he died, she ran successfully for his
seat in 1918 as an Independent Liberal. She built an electoral
base not only out of "loyalty to his memory," but also by drawing
on her volunteer work in the women's reform community, in

causes ranging from the IODE to separate courts for juvenile offenders.

Under the banner "women and children first," Smith helped to realize suffragists' maternal feminist agenda, creating a coalition that championed an Equal Guardianship Act that allowed women equal custody of their children, mothers' pension legislation, financial aid to impoverished single mothers with children, and a female minimum wage. She was less successful with other demands, such as women's right to sit on juries, and she persisted with suffragist prejudices, speaking out against Asian immigration and in favour of eugenic sterilization legislation. Often, it was not one woman, but collaborative efforts that translated maternal feminism into public policy. In Ontario, trade unionists and women reformers successfully collaborated to persuade the new Farmer-Labour government to introduce a female minimum wage law, intended to protect the most vulnerable workers from super-exploitation.

If there was one reform that had defined English Canadian suffragists, it was temperance. Prohibition legislation was achieved alongside the vote in some provinces, and even the federal government briefly experimented with prohibition. For women who became suffragists to combat the liquor interests, the vote appeared a resounding success. That this became one of their greatest disappointments was apparent only later in the decade, when many provincial governments abandoned prohibition for state-regulated sales of liquor – a great moneymaker and a concession to new social norms about drinking. The WCTU now seemed old-fashioned to younger women keen to experiment with the new forms of fun portrayed in the movies, such as drinking, smoking, and dancing. To temperance suffragists, the freedom to imbibe appeared a rather slim cultural victory and highly indulged personal pastime, especially in the face of remaining injustices against women. Other suffrage achievements, such as eugenics legislation in Alberta, look less to us like victories and far more like mistaken pathways, but they were reflections of one group of suffragists, who stressed moral regulation and restraint more than equality and emancipation.

The exaggerated claims of suffragists about transforming society had always been overly optimistic, and even suffragist legislative victories in the 1920s and 1930s were often circumscribed in their final incarnation. For instance, in many provinces mothers' allowances (or pensions) were intentionally kept meagre to encourage working-class women to re-enter the labour force, and recipients were heavily scrutinized for their moral rectitude. In British Columbia, racist policies denied Asian Canadian women access to mothers' pensions altogether. Provincial minimum wage laws, though well intentioned, often became a maximum wage ceiling for women, keeping their scanty earnings far lower than men's. This is not to denigrate suffragist *hopes* that such reforms would help, and some did make life a little more bearable for working-class women. Arguably, they show suffragists as successful mothers of the welfare state. We also need to measure these political outcomes against the goals of suffragists. Many were small-l liberals at heart: they had always endorsed pragmatic, gradual, parliamentary reform, and as the war showed, feminists could be drawn into the ruling class in limited, but to them, satisfying ways.

After the war, these same feminists claimed victories of political inclusion, as select women were appointed to movie censor boards, consumer organizations, and mothers' allowance boards, appointments that shrewdly incorporated professional, educated, middle-class women into bureaucratic circles of expertise. A smaller group of suffragists, never interested in radical change, ran for election on conservative platforms that promoted patriotic values, economic protectionism, and anti-immigration policies. Conservative Canadian feminists were never quite as powerful as the more ferocious female contingent of the American radical right. These women embraced the state-orchestrated, repressive red scare of the 1920s as a means to destroy "Miss Bolsheviki" in the United States, which in their mind included moderate as well as left-wing feminist reformers. Animated by their hatred of socialism, pacifism, and the Bolshevik Revolution in Russia, American conservative women had some success in blocking suffragists' maternalist reforms, even those of a modest liberal nature.

Canadian suffragists, like those in the United States, were never a politically homogeneous group. Class and ethnic tensions over who would be included on the voters' list surfaced as soon as suffrage was achieved. Some Ontario suffragists argued for the installation of literacy qualifications to keep the riff-raff from voting, especially the "hordes of aliens" and dangerous communist Bolsheviks (one and the same in some minds). Emmeline Pankhurst, who became a Canadian citizen during the 1920s and used Victoria and Toronto as her base for North American speaking tours, exemplified the hardening of political lines. Although she had once been friendly to labour, she was now an ardent imperialist, Conservative, anti-socialist, and anti-communist. Her new cause was the anti-VD movement (or social hygiene), which called for a single standard of sexual purity for men and women. In her mind, social hygiene was connected to combating Bolshevism, as sexual promiscuity and communism were both insidious and infectious mental diseases. Hundreds of women continued to pack Canadian auditoriums to hear her lectures, but one wonders what her former admirer, Flora MacDonald Denison, who spoke on behalf of the Independent Labour Party after the war, thought about Pankhurst's turn to the right.

Rifts in the fragile edifice of suffragist coalition were dramatically displayed when class conflict swept the country immediately after the First World War. In Vancouver, the anti-labour, anti-strike Citizens Committee recruited its supporters *through* the conservatively inclined *Western Woman's Weekly,* and the 1919 General Strike in Winnipeg separated suffragists into irreconcilably

Suffragists disagreed about one of the most explosive class confrontations in Canadian history: the 1919 Winnipeg General Strike. The confrontation was fuelled by postwar inflation, stagnating wages, and unemployment; working-class demands for the right to unionize in the face of employer opposition; and the international inspiration of the Russian Revolution. What began as a strike over union recognition in one industry turned into a general strike of all Winnipeg workers, followed by sympathy strikes across Canada. More liberal, middle-class, and affluent suffragists saw merit in the government's use of legal devices and police measures to defeat the strike. Socialist, labour, and working-class suffragists situated their political loyalties with striking workers.

opposite camps. Opposing the strike, Nellie McClung stated she was appalled at the "arrogance" of labour's tactics. On the other side of the conflict, Women's Labour League organizer Helen Armstrong ended up in prison for her role in aiding the strike.

During the next two decades, rifts sometimes widened into gulfs. In Vancouver, local lawmakers tried to prohibit white women from working as waitresses in Chinese restaurants, using the racist rationale that they needed protection from the corrupting influence of Asian men. The waitresses mobilized and repeatedly marched to city hall to protest the law and the loss of their jobs, arguing that their employers treated them well. As Lilynn Wan shows in "Out of Many Kindreds and Tongues," the left-wing Women's Labour League and Mothers Council supported the waitresses, but other white female reformers stood solidly behind

This cartoon, which appeared in the *Vancouver Strike Bulletin*
on 20 June 1919, captures the class divisions that the Winnipeg
General Strike exposed and the resentment of labour and socialist
women toward middle- and upper-class strike breakers.

the anti-Chinese legislation. They earned the intense ire of the
waitresses, who denounced them as a "bunch of fussy old bridge-
playing gossips who are self-appointed directors of morals for the
girls of Chinatown."

Debates about party allegiance, legislative agendas, and even voting rights were sometimes just as contentious after the war as they had been during it. Differing views were aired on whether women should move into existing parties, set up new ones, or try independent non-partisan activism. After decades of frustration with Liberals and Conservatives who had blocked suffrage, there was understandably a desire for new approaches to politics. In both Vancouver and Toronto, the idea of a Woman's Party was floated as a means of maximizing women's electoral impact. Using unfortunately coy language, the Vancouver group argued that the party would be "like a girl with two beaux, we could keep both political parties guessing." The Toronto Woman's Party, modelled on a similar, if short-lived effort in Britain, found itself under fire from other feminists, even after it hastened to clarify that it was a lobby group, not a party running for office. It was treated with derision by Western Prairie suffragists and dismissed by labour movement women as a mere front for Tory politics, which in a sense it was, promoting empire, patriotism, and the existing social order.

Yet abandoning the "old line" parties was also appealing to Prairie suffragists. In Saskatchewan, Violet McNaughton and Zoe Haight urged women to support whatever policy and candidate was superior. Surely this would keep politicians honest and democratically responsive. Haight took her convictions to heart and ran as a Non-Partisan League candidate in the Saskatchewan election. Although Haight was unsuccessful, Albertan Louise McKinney became the first woman elected to the Alberta legislature in 1917 on the Non-Partisan ticket. Nellie McClung liked the idea of non-partisanship but succumbed to Liberal overtures and ran successfully for the party in Alberta. But it was not always an either/or choice. McClung and United Farmer MLA Irene Parlby represented opposing parties in the legislature but collaborated on feminist reforms such as dower rights.

Female candidates fared better in local electoral contests, where they could run for office outside of established party politics and also more easily combine political work with care of their families. Arguably, their new influence was felt most strongly at the local level – school boards, city councils, community organizations – a theme explored more fully in upcoming volumes in this suffrage series. In Calgary, a middle-class English immigrant, Annie Gale, backed by a non-partisan Women's Ratepayers Association, was elected to city council after the war, promoting a platform reminiscent of maternal feminism: protection of child labour, control of food prices, milk purification, and better health care. Vancouver labour suffragist Helena Gutteridge was also elected as an alderman during the 1930s. Her social justice agenda included subsidized low-rental housing and public ownership of utilities. She also vigorously opposed efforts to fire married women as a solution to Depression unemployment. Suffrage was an ongoing battle for Gutteridge. The city's restrictive, property-based municipal voting laws excluded many renters, women without a legal share in their family home, and Indigenous and Asian residents. Gutteridge proposed universal suffrage for all Vancouver residents, to the adamant opposition of her fellow councilmen.

A few suffragists not only ran for but also aspired to office. Emily Murphy's campaign to have women appointed senators morphed into what is now called the Persons court case. It later became a symbol of women's political equality, but the case centred primarily on Murphy's quest for a Senate seat. The offspring of an affluent, influential Toronto Conservative family, Murphy enjoyed many of the benefits that social status could offer, but a Senate seat proved elusive. After moving west with her husband, she made her name as a social reformer, suffragist, and popular writer under the nom de plume of Janey Canuck. Appointed as a police magistrate in Edmonton in 1916, she was something of a

This photo appeared under the headline "Baby Carriages Head Mother's Day Parade" in the *Vancouver Sun* on 13 May 1935. Like Gutteridge, Vancouver labour and socialist women embraced new working-class causes in the interwar years, including demands for adequate welfare for the unemployed and their families and abolition of military-like relief camps for unemployed men.

Judge Judy of the time, eschewing formalized court procedures for blunt commentary and her own recommendations for the prisoner's rehabilitation. But her methods included harsh lectures and strict sentences, especially for moral crimes involving promiscuity, prostitution, or child neglect. Her ire was not directed solely at women. The lawyers who represented prostitutes, she claimed, were little better than pimps, and she held Chinese men responsible for the drug trade – and thus white women's downfall.

The Persons case took off when Murphy and four other prominent suffragists (now known as the Famous Five) sent a petition to Ottawa, asking for a legal decision on whether women were "persons" under the Constitution (then called the British North America, or BNA, Act) and thus eligible for the Senate. The Department of Justice said no. The government of Prime Minister

Mackenzie King tossed this hot potato to the Supreme Court of Canada, which also said no, based on a very narrow reading of the BNA Act. In its view, the Fathers of Confederation did not *intend* women to be office holders. A final appeal to the British Judicial Committee of the Privy Council (still possible in the 1920s) reversed the Supreme Court judgment. In a progressive decision, Lord Chancellor John Sankey described laws against women holding public office as a relic of the "barbarous" past. The Persons case did not result in substantial political or legal advances, only in female senators, but it became a symbol of equality, and as such, it has overshadowed women's other political organizing (wrongly, some believe). Ironically, Sankey's progressive view of the Constitution as a "living tree" that evolved with the times re-emerged much later with the Charter of Rights and Freedoms, 1982, and subsequent Supreme Court decisions that *did* advance women's equality.

PEACE AND IMPERIALISM

The Persons case exemplified the varying paths that women took after suffrage. Those in the communist Women's Labour Leagues ridiculed the Liberals and Conservatives who aided Murphy's campaign. Why, they asked, would we want women appointed to an undemocratic, corrupt, elite Senate? In the 1920s, suffrage coalitions fragmented into diverse priorities. Class, culture, region, language, and ideology shaped women's politics, though a few campaigns could always unify unlikely allies. Suffragists also turned their broad political vision into single-issue campaigns, such as rural improvement for farm wives, access to professional occupations, educational reform, labour rights, and international peace. If we trace just three of these – peace, education, and labour – we can dispel the idea of a post-suffrage trough of inactivity.

In the aftermath of a devastating world war, former suffragists and newly politicized women contributed to mixed-gender organizations that were dedicated to diplomacy and world peace, such as the liberally inclined League of Nations. They also built distinctly feminist peace groups, most notably the Women's International League for Peace and Freedom (WILPF, or WIL). Feminists Violet McNaughton, Rose Henderson, Alice Chown, and Laura Jamieson transferred their suffrage idealism to the WIL, which argued that wars could never be eradicated until economic and social inequality – including gender and racial oppression – was vanquished and colonialism challenged. WILers were motivated by various ideals, including humanist tolerance, social co-operation, maternalism, and anti-capitalism, but they were in agreement that wars were precipitated by territorial ambitions, greed, prejudice, and the propensity to use violence in settling disputes. Vancouver suffragist Laura Jamieson provided indispensable organizational leadership to the WIL, and by the 1930s, small chapters had been founded across the country, attracting author Laura Salverson, Agnes Macphail, the first woman MP, and Lucy Woodsworth, wife of CCF leader J.S. Woodsworth. WILers organized visiting international speakers, including women from formerly enemy nations (not always welcomed in the 1920s), interacted with their international body, and wrote, pamphleted, petitioned, and lobbied the public and politicians.

Rose Henderson's personal pathway from reforming suffragist to outspoken pacifist is instructive. She was radicalized by the First World War and the labour revolt of 1919. A well-educated, middle-class reformer, she was dismissed from her job as a probation officer with the Montreal Juvenile Court in 1919; her new passion for socialist politics had become a problem. When Henderson testified before a 1919 federal Mathers commission investigating labour unrest in Canada, she called for radical, transformative social change: "remove the profiteers ... abolish child labour ... nationalize [medicine]." "The real revolutionist," she told the commission men, perhaps thinking of her own metamorphosis, "is the woman."

After 1919, Henderson redirected her life toward labour, socialist, feminist, and pacifist causes. Her pamphlet *Woman and War* portrayed war as an extension of ruling-class and capitalist avarice: tragically, working-class men became cannon fodder, their blood "coined into profits on the battle fields." During the world war, women had been used as substitutes in male jobs and to promote recruitment, but now they should become the vanguard against all wars, a force of maternal leadership and redemption for society. Though presented in maternalist rhetoric, Henderson's analysis reflected the WIL's firm belief that wars were triggered by territorial ambitions and social inequalities. Henderson was developing what feminists today often term an intersectional analysis: as her biographer, Peter Campbell, notes, she "did not focus on any one of the major hierarchies of power in capitalist society, but rather on them all."

Although Henderson and other WIL women were highly attuned to imperialism abroad, they did not generally detect it at home. Feminists seldom discussed Canada's internal colonialism and the dispossession of Indigenous peoples, though some wrote to the international *Jus Suffragii* concerning injustices against Six Nations women. *Jus Suffragii* reminded its readers of the historic traditions of woman-centred Indigenous self-governance, as exercised by the Six Nations: "These people have long had the referendum and woman suffrage and other sage laws." The discussion, however, was not sustained. One might expect that feminist pacifists who were suspicious of European imperial conquests could see parallels in Canada. In the 1920s, most did not. Irene Parlby promoted educational efforts to foster ethnic and religious "tolerance," but she was silent on the status of Indigenous and Metis Albertans. Prairie feminist Violet McNaughton admired Gandhi's efforts to secure Indian independence from Britain, yet in the 1920s she imbibed the dominant version of white settler progress in Canada. Aboriginal peoples, she thought, were unaccustomed to farming and had thus been inevitably displaced by white settlers, who were better able to develop the land. Her views, however, would later change.

Canadian feminists' relative silence on Aboriginal issues, save for those who were interested in the preservation of Aboriginal arts, contrasted to the stance of a small cadre of Australian feminists who protested state Aboriginal policy, including forced child removal and violence against women. They used organizations such as the BDWSU to urge the protection of Indigenous women globally and to pressure their own government through international embarrassment. Though couched in the language of concern for the less advanced races, their organizing did initiate a discussion about Australian state policies of child removal, long taken for granted. The few Canadians involved in the BDWSU were often Quebecers, who used it for different ends: to pass resolutions shaming the Quebec government for its failure to join the "civilized world" by enacting women's suffrage. For both Australian and Canadian feminists, internationalism operated as an inspiring ideal of collective solidarity but also as a pragmatic strategy to sway opinion on their home turf about their chosen issues.

Transnational discourses of British imperialism and white superiority remained strong during the interwar period, though by the 1930s, some pacifist feminists were beginning to think about the intersection of gender and race oppression, as new ideas about the brotherhood of man, human rights, and racial equality were advanced by racialized groups and their few white allies. WILers Violet McNaughton and Laura Jamieson gave speeches in this vein at the Pan-Pacific Women's Association international conference (drawing together women in the Pacific Rim nations), held in Vancouver in 1937. Jamieson voiced her hope that the presence of Chinese and Japanese delegates would encourage more "tolerance towards Canada's own Asian population," which still lacked any voting rights in British Columbia.

EDUCATIONAL POSSIBILITIES

The Canadian Pan-Pacific Women's Association delegation was led by Mary Bollert, dean of women at the University of British Columbia, an educational reformer and founder of the Parent-Teacher Association in British Columbia. Bollert and other inter-war liberal feminists believed that women's opportunity, economic progress, and civic enlightenment depended on their access to higher education and the professions, some of which were still out of reach. When anglophone Quebec feminists were not lobbying their recalcitrant provincial government for the vote, they too focused on education, lobbying the intractable powers-that-be at McGill University to open up all programs – such as architecture – to female applicants. After their written pleas achieved nothing, they met with the university principal, Sir Arthur Currie, in 1929. By his own proud admission (and to their disgust), they reported to *Jus Suffragii* that he was "a very decided anti-feminist from whom we received no encouragement." Opposition to equality in Quebec was rooted not only in the Catholic Church, but also in elite English institutions that were impervious to change.

Feminist educational reform had multiple goals, ranging from the transformation of the public school curriculum to equal access to university programs. The WIL's peace advocacy overlapped with educational campaigns that were critical of a war-oriented curriculum. Schools promoted militarism, the WIL stated, by encouraging male cadet training and teaching the glories of war but remaining silent about peace. The WILers backed up their arguments with studies of the "biased, propagandistic" history texts used in the schools. Feisty CCF MP and WILer Agnes Macphail, never one to sugarcoat her views, publicly criticized cadet training, asking why "we take our boys, dress them in uniforms and teach them to strut along to martial strains with their foolish little guns and swords." She was soundly condemned for her unpatriotic disloyalty.

In the 1930s, pacifist feminists Rose Henderson and Ida Siegel ran successfully for the Toronto School Board, where they tried to put their feminist anti-militarism into action. Not surprisingly, in British-proud, imperialist Ontario, they encountered stiff opposition from other board members, who saw no problem with existing texts or cadet training. However, after Siegel unearthed the unsavoury, corrupt practice of rewarding Toronto teachers financially for every cadet they recruited, the program was temporarily halted. The WIL campaign against the veneration of war led to conflicts with conservative women's organizations across the country. In Vancouver, Laura Jamieson ran afoul of the IODE when she protested the "war pictures" it had donated to the Vancouver School Board. For Jamieson, such displays glorified war; to the IODE, they commemorated Canada's glorious contribution to the recent war.

Because some women had secured the right to vote and run for local boards of education by the late nineteenth century, educational reform was a well-trodden path of feminist activity. Nineteenth-century suffragists often rationalized their involvement in maternalist terms, as education was closely connected to the needs of children and families. As soon as women were eligible to stand for the Victoria Board of Education in 1889, WCTUer and suffragist Maria Gordon Grant successfully ran for office. For temperance advocates such as Grant, schools also were logical venues for anti-alcohol education. Still, not all women justified their educational activism in maternalist terms. After being elected to the Toronto School Board in 1892, suffragist Augusta Stowe-Gullen used her position to argue for equal pay and women's right to be school principals, based on their merit, skills, and talent. She had to endure mocking jibes from male board members when she defended the right of female teachers to dress as they pleased, even in bloomers, which the men claimed were a shocking abandonment of decorum.

By the interwar period, feminists used school board elections, as Stowe-Gullen had, to address the needs of one of the largest groups of female workers: teachers. Clustered in the lower grades, denied administrative positions, and paid much less than men, they were often far from happy with their second-class status. In Calgary, a group of Labour Party women made school board issues their cause célèbre, addressing intersecting gender and class inequalities. They supported teachers' collective bargaining rights, equal pay for women, limited class size, and free school clinics that offered medical and dental care to children. The Labour Party's Amelia Turner, a socialist and suffragist since her teens, was first elected to the Calgary School Board in 1926 on a platform of free school books for all students. This was a pressing class issue at the time: paying for school texts was a financial barrier for poor and working-class children, contributing to their low numbers in high school.

LABOUR, ETHNICITY, AND THE LEFT

Many women in the labour movement also seized the opportunity to enlarge their political sphere after the vote was won. Women's and men's different occupational roles were left largely unquestioned, but labour feminists had other equality issues on their to do list. Working through trade unions, labour parties, and union auxiliaries, they called for equal pay, the unionization of underpaid women, and social security provisions for working-class families. Since labour women's organizations were often local, sometimes fleeting, we know relatively little of this political work, but many took a two-pronged approach, focusing on improving the conditions of women's wage labour and alleviating the burden of homemakers' domestic work. The United Women's Educational Federation of Ontario (UWEFO), founded in 1920, defined its role in class and feminist terms; according to historian James Naylor, it positioned itself as the working-class version of the National Council of Women. Following up on the efforts of earlier labour and socialist feminists, it self-identified as the "champions of womanhood, children, and the home" for working people. At its most radical, the UWEFO hoped that "capitalism would pass peacefully into oblivion," and at its most pragmatic, it lobbied for free health care, school meals for children of the unemployed, and healthy, public leisure for working-class children.

Although the UWEFO later lost its radical edge, other women's labour organizations, dotted across the Canadian map, picked up the slack. In Manitoba, social gospeller Beatrice Brigden followed Rose Henderson's move to the left after the war. Her change of heart was precipitated by the labour revolt of 1919 and the Methodist Church's marginalization of its radical ministers who supported the Winnipeg General Strike. Brigden resigned from her position of teaching sex education for the Methodist Church and became a self-described "pioneer for the labour movement." She organized the annual Western Women's Labor Conference, a non-partisan women's group dedicated to working-class political activism across the Prairies. Embracing the socialist motto "Production for use, not for profit," the conference discussed strategies for opposing war, protecting workers with unemployment insurance, and improving women's working conditions. When it ceased meeting in the 1930s, Brigden sought a new political home that might welcome her commitment to the "dignity and equality" of all women and men. Her feminist, egalitarian views led her to the CCF, the new social democratic party, which called for the eradication of capitalism and equal pay for women in its founding Regina Manifesto of 1933.

Labour party, pacifist, and socialist feminists often found their way into the CCF. But this social democratic option did not appeal to left-wing activists whose political goals were shaped by very different class and ethnic experiences. Finnish socialist organizer Sanna Kannasto, for instance, criss-crossed the country before and after the First World War, travelling in the most impoverished circumstances, often on foot, to spread the word about women's and workers' equality. Her feminism, radical in its critique of religion and marriage, was also firmly rooted in a perception of capitalism as *the* major impediment to women's emancipation.

By the 1920s, Kannasto had become a household name in the Canadian Finnish community. She turned her attention to building up the membership of the communist Women's Labor Leagues, which attempted to unionize female workers, including domestic servants; promote birth control clinics; and advocate for ample social provisions for working families, including free state medical care. Influenced by European socialists such as Clara Zetkin, the leagues' understanding of gender equality drew inspiration from the radical gender reforms of post-revolutionary Russia. Kannasto's fiery speeches attracted the attention of the RCMP, with its mandate to nip radical agitation in the bud. Imprisoned and interrogated during a speaking tour in Alberta, Kannasto pleaded that she could not speak English but managed to "charm" the prison warden into lending her his typewriter. She wrote to friends from her cell, boasting that, despite their "cruel cross examinations," the police "have not succeeded in making me angry or nervous, and thereby cry and confess. I am as if made of iron. God help the people when I can again be in the middle of a crowd."

Whereas the Finnish Women's Labor Leagues connected female equality to communism, other women mobilized primarily around the bonds of ethnicity or race, creating solidarities that reflected their mothering work, desire for community, and concerns about racist discrimination. In Windsor, Ontario, African Canadian women's participation in church activities and motherhood clubs during the 1930s evolved into Hour-a-Day Study Clubs, affiliated with the local chapter of the National Council of Women of Canada. The Hour-a-Day women were committed to maternal self-education and charitable and social service work for their own community, including raising scholarship funds for African Canadian students. They also pursued issues of political concern, asking how they might preserve their own community's history and identity, create links with other women's groups, and open up occupational doors for their children, who were excluded from education and jobs due to racism. At the time, young African Canadian women were barred from attending Ontario nursing schools; the study clubs took up this cause, pressing both the University of Toronto and the Ontario government to end such racist discrimination. Women in the study clubs might not have publicly labelled themselves feminist, but they were equality-seekers, in the tradition of the suffrage struggle and beyond.

A GLASS HALF FULL

If we scan the landscape of women's politics during the interwar period, we find many examples of equality-seeking women, stretching from the dominant stream of pragmatic liberal feminism to the more marginal idealism of communist women. The interwar period was not simply about disappointment and retreat: a trough this was not. On the one hand, some women had to continue their battle for the vote. Others with the vote in hand directed their energies into political parties, but far more devoted themselves to new causes and organizations, in which they could express the unfulfilled idealism of the global suffrage movement: the desire for a world without war, exploitation, or male domination.

Perhaps these divergent streams of feminism make it hard for us to measure the outcome of suffrage. Canada was not unique in this regard. In Britain too, says Maria DiCenzo in "Our Freedom and Its Results," a proliferation of feminist causes created a mistaken view of post-suffrage "defeat," when in fact many women were voicing new "resilience and determination" to confront inequality. Some pragmatic British suffragists concluded that the glass was half full: reforms were effected in small, incremental ways. Alberta politician Irene Parlby was of a like mind. Interviewed on CBC Radio in 1938, she lauded the "quiet steady work" of women after suffrage and pointed with pride to incremental gains, such as the creation of child welfare clinics. Susie Lane Clark, who had observed that suffragists never sought "glorified seats in parliament," agreed. She made her case by citing a key feminist victory, women's equal custody of their children, a legal advance so taken-for-granted today that we might forget the anger and pain of women who were denied this basic right in the past.

Other women saw the suffrage glass as half empty. Socialist feminists especially had always assumed that gender equality was only half the battle; true emancipation would entail freedom from exploitation, unemployment, and economic want. Dissatisfied with small concessions and cognizant of resilient structures of class and gender inequality, they also feared the emergence of more devastatingly cruel forms of oppression, as the Depression unfolded and fascism spread over Europe. They were not wrong.

If we are to save future generations from making the mistakes of today ... women must know and understand the problems that exist within and without our homes ... We must take an intelligent stand, without emotionalism, in accepting people of varied races as equals ... To be a great nation, Canada must destroy the virus of rot that affects our national life, and among other vices, race prejudice ranks high.

MURIEL KITAGAWA, "I STAND HERE TONIGHT,"
1945–46, AND "THE PROBLEM OF THE JAPANESE
IN CANADA," 1948

Under the present Indian Act the "enfranchising sections" are merely masks to a series of ways and means whereby the Indian can be parted from his beloved homelands.

BIG WHITE OWL, "THE VOTE IS A POWERFUL TOMAHAWK,"
NATIVE VOICE, APRIL 1960

NINE

VOTES FOR
ALL WOMEN

Japanese Canadian delegates on the House
of Commons steps, Ottawa, 1936. The parliamentary
committee rejected their pleas for the vote. *Left to right:* Samuel
I. Hayakawa, Minoru Kobayashi, Hideko Hyodo
(Shimizu), and Edward Banno.

IN 1936, HIDEKO HYODO posed for a picture on the steps of the House of Commons in Ottawa, after delivering a brief to a parliamentary committee on elections and franchise acts. A Vancouver teacher and community leader, she faced the camera squarely, impeccably attired in hat and suit. Her male companions had also addressed the committee. All four were asking for the vote. All were Japanese Canadians. The rationale for denying Hyodo this basic democratic right was her assumed racial identity and place of origin, though she was born and educated in Canada. Her exclusion was part of a long history of racism against Asian Canadians, implemented by the state, enshrined in law, and popularly supported by many Canadians.

Hyodo is never mentioned as a suffragist heroine, yet her 1936 address to the parliamentary committee on behalf of the Japanese Canadian Citizens League was an important part of the struggle for human rights in Canada. For the parliamentarians who heard her speak, she should have been a reassuring symbol of Canadian patriotism. She was committed to the Christian education of young people through United Church Sunday Schools, and she argued that Japanese Canadians could create a rich hybrid Canadian identity that combined their "commitment to Canadian goals" with the "idealism, loyalty and filial piety inherent in Japanese culture." Her eloquent appeal fell on unreceptive ears. If she had been offering a hybrid Scottish Canadian culture, her listeners might have been impressed, but other than expressing surprise at her excellent English, this Liberal-dominated committee was unmoved: it rejected voting rights for Japanese Canadians.

Unfortunately, most women's organizations of the time were not concerned with the unfinished business of suffrage: exclusion from the franchise based on race and Indigenous status. Chinese and South Asian Canadians could not vote in British Columbia until 1947, and Japanese Canadians and "Indians" had to wait until 1949. All Indigenous people could not vote in federal elections until 1960. Voter exclusion based on race and colonialism was long-standing in franchise history but was increasingly contested after the Second World War, as racialized groups, supported by white allies, campaigned for their rights and as Canadian political life absorbed new international discourses on human rights. Canadians faced a gaping contradiction between their country's wartime rhetoric about fighting against Hitler for humanity and democracy and the reality that the nation had been built on racial intolerance.

The history of Japanese and Indigenous voting rights reveals some of the contradictory ideas about race held by suffragists as well as racialized groups' varying positions on the vote. By 1936, Japanese Canadians had requested the franchise for decades and with good reason perceived their exclusion as a painful racist reminder of their second-class citizenship. Indigenous Canadians, whose exclusion was tied up with colonialism, were more ambivalent. Some Indigenous nations did not embrace the franchise – again with good reason. Whereas feminists had long associated it with equality, progress, and fairness, Aboriginal women saw it differently: as a question, if not a problem, since enfranchisement entailed the *loss* of their Indigenous rights.

RACE AND SUFFRAGIST THINKING

Even after the Second World War, "race" remained a nebulous term, linked variously with skin colour, ethnicity, and culture. French Canadians were sometimes referred to as a race, as were Jews, South Asians (with Sikhs sometimes equated with all South

Asians), Chinese, Japanese, and Indigenous peoples (then called Indians and Eskimos). Racialization, the idea that either biology or culture (or both) created essential inherited differences between humans, was a pervasive, recurring theme throughout the history of suffrage. However, the exact definition of race and justifications for the imagined hierarchy of races – or racism – changed over the course of a century. The racism that Mary Ann Shadd Cary challenged in the 1850s was not justified in the same manner as the racism that Japanese Canadians encountered during the 1940s or that First Nations experienced in the 1960s.

Racialized thinking was embedded in arguments about voter rights, though this was manifested not only through exclusions, but also through people's proximity to the privilege of whiteness. The Conservative Party's rationale for *adding* some Aboriginal people to voters' lists in 1885 was that the better-educated and acculturated ones who owned property had progressed up the ladder toward the higher echelons of white civilization. Drawing on transnational imperialist discourses of white superiority, some suffragist social reformers at the turn of the century believed that the vote could act as a positive measure to Canadianize working-class immigrants from inferior European cultures, described in highly racialized rhetoric.

The idea that there were inherent differences between racialized groups was quite pervasive until the Second World War, but not all women in the suffrage movement were similarly racist. Even though belief in the superiority of white "civilization" was quite pervasive in the white women's movement, to claim it was absolute and unchanging in feminist circles oversimplifies. Feminists had differing, incongruous, and changing views of race. They wrestled with racism in their minds and their midst, sometimes challenging it but also reinforcing its premises. Their ideas about colonialism were also contradictory. As mentioned above, some feminists of the late nineteenth and early twentieth centuries were critical of colonialism abroad, but, like their male counterparts, seldom recognized it on their own doorstep. Sara Jeannette Duncan, an accomplished, internationally known Canadian writer with individualist, elitist feminist views, wrote novels that explored the violent undertones of the British occupation in India, but she believed that British imperialism was Canada's treasured birthright. In *The Imperialist,* a 1904 novel set in Ontario, some of her Aboriginal characters are ignorant voters who are easily bribed with liquor, unable to grasp the importance of the franchise and self-government. To Duncan, the superiority of British civilization in Canada meant the inevitable disappearance of less advanced Aboriginal peoples.

Other pro-British feminists, however, gradually expressed some second thoughts about the Anglo-Saxon, Christian superiority and intolerance that underpinned Canadian nationhood. Nellie McClung was particularly contradictory, grappling with issues of race over her lifetime, first affirming the superiority of British Christian ways but later criticizing racial prejudice. In her autobiography, she claimed early empathy with the Metis uprising of 1885, but like most white settlers, she never defended their right to land, and she saw the Christianization of Indigenous women as highly desirable. She defended non-Anglo "foreign" women against ethnocentric attacks at the beginning of the First World War but turned against them in 1917, when she endorsed their exclusion from voting under the Wartime Elections Act. During the 1930s and 1940s, her views shifted, as she responded with alarm to the rise of Nazism and anti-Semitism. She urged Canada to take in Jewish refugees fleeing Europe before the Second World War and lamented Canadians' failure to welcome these "strangers at our gates." She also earned the ire of her own Liberal Party in British Columbia, when she supported the enfranchisement of "Oriental" Canadians in 1936.

Prairie feminist Violet McNaughton underwent an even clearer metamorphosis. In the aftermath of the First World War, she was silent about the appropriation of Indigenous land for veterans,

seeing Indigenous people as inadequate farmers who would be replaced by more energetic, productive white settlers. Yet, as historian Georgina Taylor documents, her views on Aboriginal peoples
changed over the next three decades. On a personal level, she saw
the poverty and marginalization of Aboriginal life through the
eyes of her adopted daughter, who married a Metis man, but her
exposure to political thinking and events also mattered. Her interwar affiliation to the Women's International League for Peace and
Freedom (WIL) probably helped modify her views. Believing that
racial inequality created social disorder and international conflict,
the WIL publicly exposed colonial atrocities, and the neighbour-
ing American WIL also grappled with racism in its own country.
By the 1940s, an emerging Native rights movement also contributed to McNaughton's rethinking of Indigenous rights. Her *Western Producer* columns now called for "fair play for Indians ... our
first Canadians," and the Aboriginal newspaper the *Native Voice* reprinted her writing to emphasize the importance of such white
allies. "How many of us," McNaughton asked, "are ready to go hand
in hand to meet our native Canadians halfway to promote better
understanding between the white and red races?" Whereas she
had praised Gandhi in the 1920s and ignored Canadian colonialism, she now reversed her approach, asking her readers how Canadians could criticize Holland's colonial role in Indonesia without
attending to "our own native problems."

This is not to claim a rosy picture of feminism always improving, always more inclusive. Women's equality-seeking organizations wrestled with racism and colonialism in partial, inadequate,
incongruous ways. Even those women who challenged racist ideas
often promoted an idealized liberal tolerance of the culturally
separate "other" group: they did not comprehend the deep, systemic structures that perpetuated racism. Moreover, the wider
women's movement – though not feminist – remained imbued
with ideas about British imperial and racial superiority. And it
was not without power. The influential Imperial Order Daughters

of the Empire (IODE) advertised its post–Second World War work as philanthropy, education, and the nationalist celebration of Canada, yet it was saturated with ethnocentrism. The IODE favoured immigrants of British stock, though once Continental Europeans were admitted, it created programs to Canadianize them, assimilating these newcomers to the benefits of British democracy and civilization.

Nor was the IODE the only women's organization intent on incorporating non-white, or non-Anglo women into its charitable orbit by providing them with education, aid, and guidance. The rural Women's Institutes (WI) attempted to extend their reach into the Far North after the Second World War, setting up chapters for white and Indigenous homemakers, claiming that their common maternal and domestic roles mattered more than the colour of their skin. But the colour of one's skin mattered a great deal in the North, as elsewhere. At best, the WI naively denied racism and Aboriginal marginalization, but at worst, as Linda Ambrose shows in "Our Last Frontier," the WI project was yet another attempt at "cultural imperialism" shaped by ideas of Aboriginal inferiority and white women's superiority.

COLONIALISM AND THE VOTE

If such racialized thinking persisted, why did ideas about political equality shift after the 1940s? Why were previously excluded groups now granted the franchise? Three forces were at work: the excluded groups demanded their rights; Canadian political life was influenced by international events and discussions about human rights; and some white allies became more assertive advocates of inclusive voting.

Even after the Second World War, not all Aboriginal Canadians were convinced that acquiring the franchise was worth the risk to their treaty rights. Since the Liberal government's 1898 decentralization of voting lists to the provinces, many Aboriginal Canadians could not vote, though they might become eligible if they "enfranchised," a term that hearkened back, long before Confederation, to the Province of Canada's 1857 Gradual Civilization Act. The thinking behind the act was this: as long as Aboriginal people remained uncivilized, they should have special protection and treaties, but once they were civilized and assimilated through education and property ownership, they could be enfranchised and enjoy the full benefits of citizenship. Integrated into the 1869 Indian Act, the concept of enfranchisement continued to entail the exchange of Indian status, a share in communal lands, and treaty payments for full citizenship rights. Enfranchisement thus translated to a fundamental loss of Indigenous rights, and it was even more restrictive for Aboriginal women, who were automatically enfranchised if they married a white man. They lost their rights forever, as did their children. The Indian Act also allowed Indian agents to enfranchise people and bands without their consent, a means of dispossession that was odious to Aboriginal people.

No wonder enfranchisement was a heavily loaded, negative term for Indigenous people. Those who chose enfranchisement through the Indian Act often did so for very practical reasons relating to increased economic options and independence. During the Depression, for instance, some Ontario Aboriginal women applied for enfranchisement to secure a small payout of band funds and find better-paid work away from their reserve homes. Indigenous applicants had to prove their sincerity and "worth" to Canada, so female applicants had to show they were self-supporting, lived off-reserve, and were "morally upright." Yet very few people applied for enfranchisement. After 1920, only 1,600 people enfranchised over the next two decades, and by the 1950s, a study of BC Indigenous people concluded that enfranchisement had been a complete failure. Aboriginal people, to the chagrin of those who thought that enfranchisement spelled assimilation and thus progress, did not want the vote at the expense of their treaties, culture, and identity.

Forgotten Man

This cartoon, which appeared in the *Native Voice* in February 1947, echoes Constance Jane Cook's view that automatically giving the vote to new immigrants of all "races" while denying it to the First Peoples was insulting. Designating the reservation a concentration camp would have had powerful meaning in the immediate post-Second World War years.

The very word "enfranchise" was defined differently by white and Aboriginal women: for the former, it was synonymous with the vote, but for the latter this coupling was problematic. Interviewed in 1947 for the *Native Voice,* newspaper of the Native Brotherhood of British Columbia, Jane Constance Cook (Ga'axsta'las) asked "why should an Indian have to become enfranchised at all to vote?" In her view, it was an insult that "any British subject" who came to Canada could automatically vote, whereas subjects who were defined as "foreign to British soil" must first become enfranchised. Indians were put in this "foreign" category. Although Cook supported the extension of the vote, Aboriginal people across the country did not speak in unison.

From 1946 to 1948, a Senate–House of Commons Joint Committee on Indian Affairs explored the "Indian problem," including their "eligibility to vote in federal elections." The *Native Voice* endorsed the extension of the franchise, thinking it would increase the visibility of Aboriginal issues, but warned that it must not endanger "title to land and aboriginal rights." Some bands rejected the vote outright, as rather meaningless in the light of pressing economic and social problems and the mobility of Aboriginal people in bush production: "we can hardly say anything definite," replied an Alberta chief to the joint committee, as "most of us are away on our trap-lines or hunting ... Still less are we acquainted with politics." Others were blunter: "What [is] the use of giving us the right of vote if we starve to death or if we do not know what it is all about. First, give us the means of learning how to make a living and what the vote is about." Aboriginal respondents knew their history well, urging that enfranchisement must never be "compulsory," which the Indian Act permitted, a practice described by the Reverend Peter Kelly, an Aboriginal activist, as nothing more than a means to bully and "threaten" Indigenous people into acquiescence.

Almost no Indigenous women spoke or wrote to the joint committee, which is hardly surprising since their governance role was restricted by the state: the Indian Act did not allow them to run for band councils. Peter Kelly did discuss their political rights, recommending that those who married white men be allowed to rejoin their band if they were widowed or deserted – a suggestion that would garner no state interest. This is not to say that Indigenous women were passive, uninvolved, or disinterested. The Indian Homemakers Clubs, established in 1937 and expanding rapidly after the Second World War, provided one outlet for their activism. Although the state established the clubs as charitable and educational methods of integration/assimilation and citizenship training, women used them to define their own community needs, fund chosen causes, raise awareness of Aboriginal social problems, and organize around reform issues. Not unlike earlier maternal suffragists, the clubs used women's domestic skills, concern for the family, and investment in future generations as a mobilizing strategy for social engagement and change.

Although the joint committee recommended granting the franchise to all Aboriginal peoples, Parliament did not concur. In a comedy of Liberal errors, two Liberal MPs tabled a motion in the House of Commons in 1948 to extend the vote to status Indians and then voted against it themselves. Some MPs used the debate to put forward egalitarian and human rights arguments, decrying a history of white paternalism that had kept Indigenous people "dependent and inferior." Liberal MP David Croll added it was time that Canadians stopped treating Indigenous people as if they were backward and realized that they themselves were the backward ones. Others, however, believed that the vote might play a positive role in the "integration" and "gradual assimilation" of the First Nations. The old gradual civilization choice re-emerged: surely, Indigenous people could not hold on to taxation, treaty, and other rights and also join the Canadian polity, some suggested. Paternalism was sometimes inflected with sexism. Would "very old" uneducated Indian women on the Pacific Coast who spoke Chinook rather than English or French even know the difference between a member of the Co-operative Commonwealth Federation (CCF), a Communist, an Independent, or other candidate? asked one MP. With treaty and procedural issues complicating the debate, the motion was withdrawn, with a promise to revisit it the next year.

The next year came twelve years later. By this time, 1950 and 1951 revisions to the Indian Act and the Canada Elections Act had given Aboriginal veterans and their wives the vote, as well as "Indians normally resident off reserves," although they were required to sign a waiver giving up their taxation exemption. In the 1940s, many provinces (Ontario, Manitoba, Nova Scotia, Newfoundland, and British Columbia) enfranchised Aboriginal people and incorporated them into social policy programs, a trend that also occurred in Australia. Aboriginal leaders supported these inclusions as a means of improving desperate health and welfare conditions in their communities, an issue of immediate concern for Aboriginal women. BC Indigenous leader Andrew Paull's plea for Aboriginal women's right to provincial social services was also a critique of colonialism: "[Aboriginal] mothers and deserted wives and widows must be included in all benefits enjoyed by their white sisters ... because in many cases the white people are responsible for these conditions."

The 1960 parliamentary debate about Aboriginal suffrage focused primarily on federal voting rights for Indians (meaning status Indians at the time) who lived on reserves. The vote had been extended to the Inuit in 1950 and to all Northwest Territories residents in 1951; previously, the Northwest Territories was governed by an appointed commissioner and a six-person council. Official inclusion did not necessarily mean practical voting rights. Just as nineteenth-century polls were inaccessible to many rural voters, so too were Arctic polling stations geographically off limits to many Inuit, whom the government did not even try to enumerate. Not until 1962 were ballot boxes finally placed across the Inuit eastern Arctic.

Leading up to the 1960 debate, a 1959 joint committee of the Senate and House of Commons again solicited Aboriginal views on the vote. Whereas the Six Nations expressed ambivalence, in light of their own history and traditional governance practices, the Native Brotherhood of British Columbia was positive, claiming their exercise of the provincial vote since 1949 had given First Nations a "greater sense of pride and responsibility" in their citizenship. Although the *Native Voice* referred optimistically to the extension of the federal vote as "the Indian Magna Carta," there were divergent views, even within British Columbia. The paper printed a dissident editorial by its eastern editor, Big White Owl, who asked how Indigenous people could possibly trust that their treaty rights would be respected after years of being "cheated, robbed, fleeced, despised and trampled on." "We would all feel better," the editors admitted, if "unequivocal [written] guarantees" to treaty rights were given by the government.

That would not happen. The ruling Conservative government made verbal promises of protection, but when a Liberal MP attempted to integrate a statement protecting treaty rights into the legislation on voting, he was ruled out of order. In contrast to the 1948 debate, and certainly that of 1885, there was unanimity over the principle of full voting rights for Aboriginal people. All parties were eager to establish their credentials as advocates of equality and as friends of the Indian. Speeches about the unfortunate failure of Canada's Indian policy were common, and parliamentary debaters emphasized that the vote must be a choice, not a compulsion. Softer language of "integration" rather than "assimilation" was used, though some people saw integration as assimilation masquerading under another name. Old forms of blatant racism were tolerated less. One MP who claimed that Indians in his constituency had been bribed with liquor in the last election was taken to task by other MPs, who demanded proof for this nasty slur. This is not to say that press discussions of the Aboriginal voting issue in the post-war period were not tinged with racism: some were. And some MPs could not escape paternalism even while denouncing it. Indians, they said, would now take "a more direct interest in their affairs"; the vote would have "educational value" for them – as if Indigenous people knew nothing of self-governance!

A few MPs did refer to Canada's history of dispossession. One Toronto MP noted that though Canadians denounce Hitler and Stalin for annexing land not theirs, "we never think of our own share in the tragedy of the Indian who dwelt for centuries in the land we now call our own." Women were rarely mentioned, but in contrast to the 1885 debate in which the "squaw" was feared as a potential ignorant voter, MPs now equated Aboriginal women

Hiawatha Council Hall, Rice Lake, Ontario, during a federal by-election in 1960. The first ballots cast after the extension of the franchise to all status Indians were those of the Rice Lake Band near Peterborough, Ontario. *Left to right:* Lawrence Salleby; Chief Ralph Loucks, deputy returning officer; Lucy Muskrat, poll clerk; and Eldon Muskrat, poll constable.

with forces of progress. One MP lauded an exceptional female chief from Parry Island for "giving leadership to her tribe." Despite their efforts to appear more enlightened, MPs did not discuss another historic wrong: Aboriginal women's loss of their rights when they married a white man. Only nine years later, Indigenous women would initiate human rights court cases and organize specifically around "Indian Rights for Indian Women," demanding redress of this long-standing injustice. However, that is another story entirely.

JAPANESE CANADIANS AND THE VOTE
In the 1948 House of Commons debate, MPs deliberated at some length over the vote for Aboriginal men and women, but they

expeditiously granted the federal franchise to all Japanese Canadians, including those in British Columbia. The ease with which this amendment passed was a remarkable contrast to the reception to Hideko Hyodo's 1936 presentation and earlier parliamentary debates in which Japanese Canadians, both those born in Canada and those who had become citizens, were reviled in racist language as unwelcome interlopers. Japanese exclusion was part of a long history of intense hostility to Asian and South Asian immigrants in British Columbia, though anti-Asian discrimination was also expressed in other provincial and federal jurisdictions. Some provinces, for instance, prohibited white women from working for Chinese employers, and the federal Dominion Elections Act (1920) legally enshrined the provinces' right to exclude voters based on racial origin. In British Columbia, racism was historically constructed through interconnected economic and ideological forces: white fears of economic competition and wage suppression, notions that Asians were so culturally alien that they were unassimilable, beliefs regarding racial hierarchy, and the class opportunism of politicians who manipulated racist fears.

In 1874, the BC government disenfranchised both the Chinese and Aboriginal people, and it specifically excluded the Japanese and Hindus in 1895 and 1907. Since provincial voters' lists were the basis of federal voting, exclusion carried over into that realm as well. Occupations that required one to be a registered voter were also closed to Asian Canadians: this applied to pharmacists, chartered accountants, lawyers, and public servants. In 1904, Tomekichi Homma's court challenge to British Columbia's exclusion of Japanese voters reached as high as the British Judicial Committee of the Privy Council, but it was not successful, unlike the Persons case, which involved discrimination against women. Thus, the province's right to create its own racially defined laws was upheld, justified in the highest court of appeal.

The cultural construction of Asian groups did differ, with Chinese immigrants portrayed as cheap labour, criminal drug pushers, and pimps, the Japanese as untrustworthy and secretive. Japanese immigrants were supposedly unfairly competitive owners of small businesses and industrious small fishers who were bent on controlling the BC economy. There was a common complaint that all Asians clustered in dangerous ethnic enclaves, even though, ironically, racist law and practice limited their educational advancement and economic integration. Anti-Asian rhetoric was also gendered. Suffragists such as Emily Murphy joined the chorus of racists equating Chinese men with white slavers who flouted superior Anglo-Saxon gender norms and felt no compunction in inducing white women into prostitution, corruption, and addiction. Racist fear-mongering found popular outlet in conservative articles in women's newspapers. During and after the First World War, the *Western Woman's Weekly* called for boycotts of foreign-owned businesses and the segregation of "Oriental" children in schools. One reprinted article warned, in words presaging Nazism, that the wartime "slaughter of the white races" left an alarming racial imbalance in the world.

The denial of political and social rights for Asian Canadians was often coupled with demands that Ottawa end their future immigration. Exclusionary immigration laws had historically targeted male and female migrants differently. Asian women were especially unwelcome because they were potential bearers of children, thus enlarging non-white communities in Canada. According to some historians, the federal state's virtual closing of the borders to Asian migration during the interwar period resulted in a short détente of cultural tolerance because whites felt that the Asian population was at least now contained. However, racist discourses did not completely disappear. Anti-Asian rhetoric was endorsed by mainstream organizations such as the nationalist Native Sons and Daughters of British Columbia – in which "Native" meant white settler. State efforts to curtail the economic livelihood of Japanese Canadians continued to go unchallenged, and political rights remained elusive.

Younger, second-generation "Nisei" Japanese Canadians became more outspoken about their lack of voting rights by the 1930s, though the first-generation Issei feared that their protests would arouse another racist backlash against the entire community. Nisei students at the University of British Columbia (UBC) wrote critically in the student newspaper about instances of racist discrimination they experienced on a daily basis. Japanese Canadians, they pointed out, were expected to be accountable as citizens, even though they lacked any voice in their own government. Using the same arguments as earlier women suffragists, they called for "no taxation without representation," reminding white readers that Japanese Canadians had the responsibilities of citizenship but not its attendant rights.

When First World War Japanese Canadian veterans were given the BC provincial vote in 1931, hopes were raised, but prematurely so. No further concessions followed. Nonetheless, white allies, including the United Church, outspoken UBC politics professor Henry Angus, and the left-leaning Canadian Youth Congress, were becoming more numerous and more vocal. New international discourses of humanism and interracial co-operation, combined with the law-abiding success of Asian immigrants, convinced some whites that voting rights should have no colour bar. Some feminists argued that Asians were model citizens who produced stable families and communities through their own self-policing. Former suffragist and Juvenile Court judge Helen Gregory MacGill claimed that the delinquency rate of white British Columbians was fifteen times that of the province's Chinese and Japanese youth, who were governed by a strong system of family authority and respect for their elders. In other words, even white allies who supported Japanese voting rights employed arguments that were designed to assuage racist fears. Some allies claimed that they did not support any *more* Asian immigration, or, like the United Church, they warned that political exclusion would prevent cultural integration and reduce the prospect of Christianization of Asians.

The CCF was the only mainstream political party to endorse the enfranchisement of all "Orientals" (meaning all South Asian and Asian people), but the party sometimes vacillated, intimidated by Liberals and Conservatives who routinely bombarded voters with racist myths about an uncontrollably high Asian birth rate, Japanese dominance of fishing and the grocery trade, and wage suppression by Asian workers. Hoary gender stereotypes were resurrected to incite fears of Asian men exerting corrupting power over white women. "Men of the yellow race will further undermine the white Anglo-Saxons of the province," warned the Native Sons of British Columbia. "How would you like your daughter to apply to a Japanese for a job in the civil service?" "Orientals once our servants," it warned, "are now our competitors" and would soon "become our masters" if they received full citizenship. Aware that its principled position might scare voters away, the CCF offered cautious support to Asian voting rights. When CCF MP Angus MacInnis presented a resolution to Parliament supporting "Oriental" suffrage rights in British Columbia, it was coupled with acceptance of a cessation of all Asian immigration.

Prime Minister Mackenzie King's rather fantastic reply to this resolution – that he had never heard of any Japanese desire for the vote – did open an opportunity for the newly formed Japanese Canadian Citizens League (JCCL) to request an audience with the parliamentary committee on elections and franchise acts. The JCCL sent four highly educated, professional Nisei to Ottawa, including Hideko Hyoko. To a young Japanese Canadian Vancouverite, writer Muriel Kitagawa, the delegation to Ottawa was absolutely courageous and inspiring. In *This Is My Own*, Kitagawa recalls the "exciting aura of daring in this venture," not the least because it incited some threats of violent opposition from rather shady "gambling" interests in the Japanese community who preferred to maintain the status quo, which guaranteed their own economic power.

Hideko Hyodo's presentation to the committee opened with a brief history of the Japanese in Canada, emphasizing their strong commitment to education and their many artistic, cultural, and intellectual achievements. Her appeal rested on both a human rights argument for equality and a reassurance that Japanese Canadians would make model citizens – strategies not unlike those of earlier women suffragists. She reminded the MPs that the achievements of Japanese Canadians were evidence of their "adaptability," a word one might have thought would reassure those worried about ethnic enclaves. She also pleaded with the committee to embrace "British fair play" and justice, concepts that supposedly underwrote Canada's political system. Her liberal, universalist, anti-racist appeal asked her listeners to extend the hand of "World Brotherhood" to their fellow citizens. Other than marvelling condescendingly at her good English, the committee was unmoved by the JCCL presentations.

Hyodo's public advocacy for the vote symbolized the more visible political and social roles that Nisei women assumed during the interwar period. When Canada entered the war with Japan in 1941, Hyodo was an advocate and volunteer for Japanese families incarcerated in the Hastings Exhibition grounds cattle barns in Vancouver, and she later supervised the training of Nisei teachers to work in the Japanese detention centres in the BC Interior. She was not the only Nisei woman who placed great hope in the education of young Japanese women, believing they would play a key role in promoting Japanese Canadian citizenship rights. Her friend Muriel Kitagawa had excelled in school and attended UBC for one year before her family's economic marginality necessitated her withdrawal. She turned to journalism, writing for Japanese Canadian newspapers, the *New Age* and the *New Canadian*. Equal citizenship was one of her concerns. As a Nisei educated in Canadian schools, Kitagawa was exposed to nationalist rhetoric about the greatness of Canadian and British democracy, notions she came to see as hypocritical in the light of discrimination against her own community. Her columns also addressed gender issues, offering small rebellions against the prevailing gender norms in the Japanese community: she rejected practices of arranged marriages and endorsed enhanced opportunities for women's paid labour outside the home. Emerging from a "custom bound past" and seclusion in the home, she wrote after the Second World War, would offer more positive choices for Japanese women.

Like Hyodo, Kitagawa imagined a new hybrid, Japanese Canadian citizenship that drew on the best of two cultural worlds. Nisei women should be given "a fuller understanding of their duties as future mothers of new Canadian citizens," so that they could foster homes that would be "in harmony with the conveniences and good manners of the west" and the "respect for the older and the family interdependencies of the east." They had a responsibility to help educate the young about "good citizenship in [our] pioneering for full franchise rights so they could in turn help their younger brothers and sisters." Kitagawa's description of women's role was remarkably similar to that of earlier suffragists who stressed women's maternal citizenship. Yet she realistically saw little gender solidarity in Canada as the racist assaults on Japanese Canadians intensified during the Second World War. Japanese Canadians were incarcerated in detention camps and pressed into compulsory labour, their possessions, businesses, and homes confiscated, their loyalty disparaged.

Kitagawa found it tragically "illogical" that women were in the forefront of these assaults: How could those who were "bearers and conservers of the human race" promote such "savagery, destruction and ill-will"? Why did IODE women, "who don't know the first thing about us," create "fear and ill will by claiming we are all spies and saboteurs and that our numbers have doubled in the last ten years"? (the last claim a biological impossibility, she added). Kitagawa recognized the mutually reinforcing intersection of racism and sexism, charging that anti-Japanese rhetoric sanctioned violence against Japanese women: "We are prey for wolves in democratic clothing ... Young [Japanese] girls have faced horrors from men in uniform."

Kitagawa's wartime writing and letters to her brother are both moving indictments of racism and pleas for a true hybrid Canadian citizenship. "Who can rightfully tell me where my heart lies if I know better myself? Who can assume with omniscience that I am disloyal to Canada because I have not golden hair and blue eyes? What are these surface marks that must determine the quality of my loyalty? Nothing, nothing at all." Her conclusions were remarkably forgiving: "Hate impedes, love strengthens. It is not hate for a country one has never known but love for this familiar Canadian soil that makes me want to use my bare fists to uphold its honour, its integrity."

During the First World War, white women used their loyalty to the state and the war effort as an argument for political equality. During the Second World War, Japanese Canadians made similar declarations of loyalty – and offered to enlist – but were rebutted, and even after the advent of peace, there were attempts to deport them and prevent their return to their BC coastal homes. CCF politicians who stood up for Japanese Canadian rights paid a price in elections as other parties continued to whip up racist fears of Japanese disloyalty. Gendered images of unfair economic competition by Japanese family businesses were also dredged up. One politician opposed the Japanese return to British Columbia, warning that competing with them economically was impossible because "the Japanese woman goes into the fields with babies on her back and works all day." Protests were complicated: Aboriginal fishermen, despite their own experience of racism, opposed the return of Japanese families to the northwest coast, claiming they were a threat to Indigenous fishing rights and livelihoods.

Although some Japanese Canadians were prevented from returning to the coast, they had secured voting rights within five years. In 1947, British Columbia awarded the vote to South Asians and the Chinese; Aboriginal peoples and Japanese Canadians acquired it in 1949. Mennonites and Doukhobors, barred because they were conscientious objectors, were included in 1948 and 1952. Both federally and provincially, these changes sparked little debate. A Nisei witness to the 1948 House of Commons discussion remarked incredulously that when the franchise was finally secured, it seemed to come almost effortlessly, without the acrimonious debates of the past.

How do we explain this change of course? What appeared uncomplicated to this witness was the culmination of decades of work by Japanese Canadians to secure their rights, as well as new enlistment of white allies. After the war, the new United Nations Universal Declaration of Human Rights set out principles that were a discomforting contradiction to Canada's practices of discrimination. International embarrassment was one factor in changing the political climate, but the efforts of Japanese Canadians and their pro-democracy allies were absolutely critical. JCCL attempts to secure justice were hampered during the war by government restrictions on its activities, but after 1943, it had help from a new group, the Cooperative Committee on Japanese Canadians (CCJC). The CCJC began as an organization of white social conscience and philanthropy, aiding Japanese migrants who were pressured to move to Ontario. Concentrating on moral support, housing, and employment aid, the CCJC attracted former missionaries to Asia, such as Donalda MacMillan, and social democratic feminist Edith Fowke, who was active in the CCF Women's Council.

The CCJC did not initially challenge Ottawa's program of dispersal, but it became more militant in response to the state's coercive efforts to deport Canadians of Japanese descent at war's end. Using court cases and public mobilization, the CCJC fought the government's executive order on deportation as unworthy of any democracy committed to human rights. By 1946–47, the CCJC had developed a more direct critique of the racism underpinning the state's wartime internment policies. Reform organizations such as the National Council of Women of Canada (NCWC) now finally endorsed the CCJC's anti-deportation work, recognizing that the abrogation of citizenship rights based on race was a replication of Hitler's own policies.

The campaign against deportation paved the way for the granting of the vote, though efforts to obtain meaningful economic compensation for Japanese dispossession were less successful. Perhaps having exiled most of their Japanese Canadian citizens eastward, and with no new immigration on the horizon, BC residents could finally accept new franchise laws. A more positive interpretation should acknowledge the work of Japanese pro-democracy activists and their allies in the face of a long history of virulent racism. Women's reform and rights organizations such as the NCWC did not assume the lead, though feminists associated with the CCJC, the Women's International League for Peace and Freedom, and the CCF were involved. WIL feminist pacifist Mildred Fahrni, adamantly opposed to internment, lived her principles by volunteering to work without pay as a teacher for the New Denver Japanese detention camp. CCF feminists Laura Jamieson (a former suffragist) and Grace MacInnis pressured their own party not to waver on its unpopular platform of voting rights for the Japanese.

Women's anti-racist activism was expressed through pro-democracy political parties and pacifist and civil rights groups, rarely through women's organizations. Feminism and anti-racism were seen as parallel projects, not necessarily intertwined ones. A feminist perspective that linked gender and race oppression and took account of colonialism was never completely absent during this period: there were echoes of this analysis in the WIL. But more expansive and rigorous exploration of these connections did not emerge until decades later, with a new generation of feminists. And that too is another story.

AFTERWORD

IN MAY 1944, Francis Marion Beynon rendezvoused with historian Catherine Cleverdon in New York City to discuss the history of the Canadian suffrage movement over dinner. How I wish Cleverdon had recorded the conversation: listening in might fill the gaps in Beynon's history, since she left almost no letters for posterity. Perhaps she doubted her own historical importance. After their meeting, she urged Cleverdon to get in touch with Nellie McClung, who could provide more "interesting" stories about the Manitoba struggle. What about Beynon's story? Why did she stay in New York rather than returning home like her sister Lillian after the war? Did she remain a pacifist, socialist, feminist – or any one of those – and if not, why not? What did she think of the intense feminist struggles in Manitoba two decades before, the differences between rural and urban, working-class and middle-class, racialized and Anglo-Celtic women? What did feminism mean to her? Was Aleta Dey her true alter ego?

We will never know, but the mystery of Beynon is just one of many silences in Canadian suffrage history. Organizational records were lost, personal letters thrown out, memories never recorded. Canada's highly regional, decentralized movement meant there was no single powerful national suffrage group, busily creating its own historical importance through record preservation and self-promotion. Perhaps this is one reason that the Canadian movement has been almost completely ignored in global studies of suffrage and feminism. Canada is absent from *Women and the Vote*, Jad Adams's 2014 book on world suffrage. Nor does it appear in the list of countries that enfranchised women, with which the 2015 movie *Suffragette* concludes. Australia and New Zealand, in contrast, are often featured because they enfranchised earlier and became self-named leaders for other Commonwealth countries to emulate. Yet Antipodean feminist historians now question this celebrated leadership as a "victory with hidden costs," as they probe the racial underpinnings of women's enfranchisement, either as a means of assimilating (in New Zealand) or excluding (in Australia) Indigenous voters in land-hungry, white settler societies. The obvious parallels with Canadian history cry out for more analysis.

It is true that in some areas of Canada, the struggle for white women's enfranchisement was a one-generation battle, shorter than in the United States and Britain, where the fight spanned more than seventy years, stretching from grandmother to granddaughter and beyond. The Canadian movement is often seen, comparatively, as relatively short-lived, sedate, cautious, a model of civility. Canadian suffragists themselves contributed to this image, reassuring fellow Canadians that, especially in comparison to British suffragettes, they were reasonable, rational, law abiding, and peaceful – or "serene," as Thérèse Casgrain put it.

At the same time, suffrage is publicly commemorated far more than other historical examples of women's equality seeking in Canada. In museum displays, popular biographies, and the high school curriculum, women's history is often equated with the suffrage movement of the late nineteenth and early twentieth centuries. Understandably, the vote offers a tangible example of equality secured and a reassuring one at that. It is evidence that liberal democracies do *work* and can eventually welcome all outsiders inside. These commemorations of women's suffrage tend to stress gender differences, the arguments made, pro and con, about women's exclusion from the vote, ignoring the complicating roles that class, ethnicity, race, and religion played in the struggle.

Veronica Strong-Boag, who has reflected on suffrage writing more than any other Canadian historian, reminds us in "Taking Stock of the Suffragists" that feminist history is a constant process of re-examination. As our society, political concerns, and theoretical assumptions change, so do our interpretations of suffrage history. The intellectual standpoint of historians, the sources they can access, the audience for whom they write, and why, matter a great deal. Some of the earliest accounts of the suffrage struggle were written by participants who offered their immediate recollections but also concentrated on their own priorities and concerns. Affluent, confident campaigners such as Emily Murphy were concerned about solidifying their important place in history. Her daughter told Cleverdon that because the Persons case listed the five applicants alphabetically, Murphy did not get her proper historical due: she led the way, whereas the others "just signed their names ... That was all they ever did." The family lent Murphy's collection of press clippings (all focused on her) to Cleverdon to facilitate her research and carefully selected a sympathetic person to write Murphy's biography, to ensure her continuing importance.

Those who did *not* leave autobiographical accounts, such as Mary Ann Shadd Cary and Flora MacDonald Denison, were initially overshadowed in our histories – despite the fact that Cary pioneered a discussion about race and gender, and despite Denison's important international role. Labour and socialist suffragists were often working-class activists who had little time, resources, or ability to either travel or record their memories, and many were devoted to other causes such as unions or socialist parties, which left a less visible historical imprint. As a consequence, socialist suffragists such as May Darwin or Mary Cotton Wisdom have not received the same attention as other suffragists. Moreover, those who remained in the public eye after winning the vote tend to be better known. Thérèse Casgrain, whose post-suffrage political work with the peace group Voice of Women crossed anglophone and francophone barriers, is relatively well known in English Canada, yet Idola Saint-Jean, who died only five years after the vote was acquired, may have been just as important in Quebec. She was certainly more radical and unconventional.

Historians initially picked up on the immense pride that suffragists felt after their initial victories were won. The interwar women's reform movement that followed the 1918 extension of the federal franchise tended to portray suffrage as a victory of enlightenment and progress, an indication that women's role in nation building was recognized. They were the immediate heirs of liberal suffragist hopes, and their efforts to recreate themselves as "mothers" joining the "fathers" of Confederation were understandable, especially since they were determined to use the vote to continue their reform agenda as mother citizens. As late as the 1940s, when Catherine Cleverdon researched the first comprehensive scholarly history of the movement, this liberal, optimistic perspective, which stressed the *justice* of the cause, prevailed.

In the 1970s and 1980s, a new generation of feminist historians, professionally trained to be skeptical about causation and the motives of reformers, revisited the topic and took a more critical view of suffragists, assessing them with both sympathy and cynicism. While recognizing that earlier feminists faced denigration and patriarchal opposition, these scholars accented the class and ethnic biases, the regulatory impulses that animated the most prominent white, middle-class feminists. They also cast a critical eye on the maternalist arguments of suffragists, which seemed to limit women *only* to their reproductive essence. To this cohort of history writers influenced by second-wave feminism, these rationales seemed more like entrapment than autonomy and liberation. Quebec and English Canadian interpretations did differ. Quebec historians were highly attuned to the patriarchal power of the antis and their links to the Catholic Church, perhaps less intensely critical of their suffrage foremothers than English Canadian feminists. Moreover, the renewed socialist feminist movement in the 1970s encouraged historians to unearth new sources about working-class activists, labour, and socialism. Their curiosity opened up a previously hidden history of Canadian socialist feminists campaigning for the vote and revealed how their activism actually intensified after the First World War.

Some researchers followed up with very specific reassessments of suffragists, especially of the social reform variety, using a single analytic lens, such as region, temperance, eugenics, or race. Studies that focus only on the category of race, using very limited sources, as Mariana Valverde does, presented a rather negative view of early feminists. Yet more complex and wide-ranging histories have also emerged, complicating our understandings, suggesting new questions rather than singular certainties. They have highlighted divergent views within the suffrage struggle, and, in situating suffragists in their historical context, tried to avoid the pitfalls of both presentism (judging only by present politics) and uncritical commemorations of suffrage history. Strong-Boag's assessments have been self-reflective and critical but still sympathetic to her subjects. Though cognizant of the class and race self-interest of early-twentieth-century middle-class suffragists, she also admires their "uncommon personal politics of courage and vision." It is only too easy, she cautions, "to find in our foremothers reminders of our less worthy selves and views we have learned to hold responsible for many of the ills in the world."

I hope this book also complicates suffrage history by stretching out its chronology, introducing new players, and demonstrating its diversity of ideas, including debates within early Canadian feminism. Claims that the vote was granted to women after a short, sedate campaign and in payment for their patriotic loyalty during the First World War ignore many decades of activism, and as international historians have pointed out, the "reward for war work" theory fails the basic test of historical evidence. Debates about who deserved the franchise also spanned more than a century, from women's attempts to vote in Lower Canada during the

1840s to disputes about the Aboriginal franchise in 1960. Suffrage history does not add up to a quick and reassuring path of progress, an inexorable march toward democracy. It involved gains and losses, inclusions and exclusions, and sometimes stubborn, formidable barriers, including systemic racism. In Canada, it was also a profoundly regional and provincial story; the precipitating causes, organizational character, and ideological tenor of the struggle were shaped by local cultures and political economies. The true diversity of the movement will emerge in future volumes in this series, as suffrage is re-viewed through specific regional and thematic lenses.

The political perspectives that animated suffragists were as diverse as one can imagine, ranging from conservatism to socialism, from individualism to collectivism, from those who accepted other social inequalities to those who challenged them, and from those who equated womanhood with motherhood to those who defied taken-for-granted gender roles. Definitions of what the Canadian nation should look like lay at the heart of many suffrage struggles, and these debates were often skewed in favour of dominant groups and ideologies. Many early-twentieth-century suffragists built their arguments for gender equality around a nationalist vision of progress that extolled white frontier settlers and British institutions but ignored the dispossession of Indigenous peoples and marginalized ethnic and racialized citizens.

But there were always dissident voices, some of which gained more traction over time. Citizenship, nation, and rights were contested categories. Socialist suffragists explored the intersection of class and gender inequalities, calling for wholesale social transformation, not mere tinkering with the status quo. Pacifist feminists questioned the dominant narrative of the moral superiority of British imperialism, and women such as Indigenous elder Jane Constance Cook pointed out that the vote should not negate the recognition of Indigenous peoples as first, not "foreign," nations.

Women who fought against racist prejudice for their right to vote, such as Hideko Hyodo, don't make it into the pantheon of suffrage heroines. They should.

My own curiosity about Francis Marion Beynon's full history betrays my sympathies with her socialist and anti-war views. Helena Gutteridge's efforts to combine socialism, labour activism, and feminism in the defence of working women are also presented as highly appealing in this book. But I recognize that Gutteridge was hardly perfect: during the First World War, she did not challenge the Vancouver Trades and Labour Council's racist whites-only labour policies in the hotel industry. There are no unambiguous heroines in suffrage history, only reminders that we ourselves need to exercise both humility in the present and vigilance in our efforts to re-examine the evidence of the past, wherever it may lead us. Although we no longer debate the condition of women, as nineteenth-century liberals did, or the woman question, as twentieth-century socialists did, their intellectual curiosity and passionate commitment to understanding and ending inequality are contiguous with feminist movements today.

ACKNOWLEDGMENTS

MY FIRST DEBT is to Veronica Strong-Boag, the series editor of Women's Suffrage and the Struggle for Democracy, who asked me to write this book. Her encouragement and feedback led to my own productive rethinking of suffrage and its meaning for Canadian women's history. The other suffrage series authors – Denyse Baillargeon, Tarah Brookfield, Lara Campbell, Sarah Carter, Lianne Leddy, and Heidi MacDonald – have been a pleasure to work with. Graduate students Madeline Macnab, Julia Smith, and Sarah Jessup helped with research, Sean Antanaya with illustrations, thanks to research funds from the Social Sciences and Humanities Research Council. My deepest debt is to my students in various incarnations of women's and gender history courses over the last thirty years at Trent University. Their delight in exploring an unknown past, their questions and challenges, have sustained my own commitment to women's history. This book is dedicated to them.

SOURCES AND
FURTHER READING

THE REFERENCES for each chapter are not exhaustive but instead note useful background material and the source of direct quotations. Since the Canadian movement lacked a cohesive, long-lasting national suffrage organization with archived records, its history must be traced through other reform, women's, and political records, often of a regional and local nature. I relied heavily on print sources (such as suffrage, educational, reform, and other newspapers) in order to secure a Canadian-wide perspective, though I did consult some suffragists' collections of papers (and there are only a few such collections across the country). Writings by suffragists and anti-suffragists provide some of the best insights into their changing views and goals, but I supplement these sources with government documents, cultural artifacts, and organizational records, as well as with secondary sources and unpublished theses. The website *Women Suffrage and Beyond: Confronting the Democratic Deficit* includes a comprehensive bibliography for further reading.

INTRODUCTION
Margaret Haile's election speech was reported in the *Toronto Globe* on 17 May 1902. For commentary on the democratic deficit, visit the website *Women Suffrage and Beyond: Confronting the Democratic Deficit*. On impious civility, see Michael Dorland and Maurice René Charland, "Impious Civility: Woman's Suffrage and the Refiguration of Civic Culture, 1889–1929," in *Law, Rhetoric, and Irony in the Formation of Canadian Civil Culture*, 192–222 (Toronto: University of Toronto Press, 2002). Russell Brand's manifesto is *Revolution* (New York: Random House, 2014).

ONE: THE PRIVILEGE OF PROPERTY

The epigraph is quoted in John Garner, *The Franchise and Politics in British North America* (Toronto: University of Toronto Press, 1969), 6, as is the Papineau quote (158); quotes on the Montreal 1832 election are from Bettina Bradbury, "Widows at the Hustings: Gender, Citizenship, and the Montreal By-election of 1832," in *Women on Their Own: Interdisciplinary Perspectives on Being Single*, ed. Rudolph Bell and Virginia Yans, 82–114 (New Brunswick, NJ: Rutgers University Press, 2008). Discussion of the "remasculinization" of politics, the writing of Adelaide, and quotes from Rousseau are from Allan Greer, *Patriots and the People: The Rebellion of 1837 in Rural Lower Canada* (Toronto: University of Toronto Press, 1993), 189–218. On the gendering of politics in Upper Canada and "Mrs. Slipshod," see Cecilia Morgan, "'When Bad Men Conspire, Good Men Must Unite!': Gender and Political Discourses in Upper Canada, 1820s–1830s," in *Gendered Pasts: Historical Essays in Femininity and Masculinity in Canada*, ed. Nancy Forestall, Kathryn McPherson, and Cecilia Morgan, 12–28 (Toronto: University of Toronto Press, 2003). On paternalism and patriarchy, see Bryan Palmer, "Popular Radicalism and the Theatrics of Rebellion," in *Transatlantic Subjects: Ideas, Institutions, and Social Experience in Post-revolutionary British North America*, ed. Nancy Christie, 403–38 (Montreal and Kingston: McGill-Queen's University Press, 2008).

Women's attempts to vote in Amherst and Annapolis are discussed in Garner, *The Franchise*, and similar attempts (and subsequent challenges to their vote) in Upper Canada and New Brunswick in Jeffrey McNairn, *The Capacity to Judge: Public Opinion and Deliberative Democracy in Upper Canada, 1791–1854* (Toronto: University of Toronto Press, 2000), 228, and in Kim Klein, "A Petticoat Polity? Women Voters in New Brunswick before Confederation," *Acadiensis* 26, 1 (1996): 71–75. Colonial and nineteenth-century practices and exclusions are discussed in Gail Campbell, "'The Most Restrictive Franchise in British North America?" *Canadian Historical Review* 71, 2 (June 1990): 159–88, and in Chief Electoral Officer of Canada, *A History of the Vote in Canada* (Ottawa: Elections Canada, 2007). Quotes from the Fathers of Confederation are from Colin Gittner, "A Statesmanlike Measure with a Partisan Tail: The Development of the Nineteenth-Century Dominion Electoral Franchise" (master's thesis, Carleton University, 2009) and from Elections Canada, http://www.elections.ca/res/his/chapter1_e.pdf. The corrupt election of 1841 is outlined by Irving Abella in "The Sydenham Elections of 1841," *Canadian Historical Review* 47 (1966): 326–43; and for the controversy over Macdonald's 1874 election, see Thomas Brady, "Sinners and Publicans: Sir John A. Macdonald's Trial under the Controverted Elections Act, 1874," *Ontario History* 76, 1 (1984): 65–87.

Quotes about Isobel Macdonald are from Rusty Bitterman, "Women and the Escheat Movement: The Politics of Everyday Life on Prince Edward Island," in

Separate Spheres: Women's Worlds in the 19th-Century Maritimes, ed. Janet Guildford
and Suzanne Morton, 23–38 (Fredericton: Acadiensis Press, 1994). See also
his *Rural Protest on Prince Edward Island: From British Colonization to the Escheat
Movement* (Toronto: University of Toronto Press, 2006). On lady landlords, see
Rusty Bitterman and Margaret McCallum, *Lady Landlords of Prince Edward
Island* (Montreal and Kingston: McGill-Queen's University Press, 2008).

The exclusion of Loyalist black voters is noted in James W. St.G. Walker, *The Black
Loyalists: The Search for a Promised Land in Nova Scotia and Sierra Leone, 1783–1870*
(Toronto: University of Toronto Press, 1976), 55. The Knights of Labor, unions, and
nineteenth-century working-class ideals are discussed in Gregory Kealey and
Bryan Palmer, *Dreaming of What Might Be: The Knights of Labor in Ontario, 1880–
1900* (New York: Cambridge University Press, 1982); Gregory Kealey, *Toronto
Workers Respond to Industrial Capitalism, 1867–1892* (Toronto: University of Toronto
Press, 1980); Bryan Palmer, *Working-Class Experience: Rethinking the History of
Canadian Labour, 1800–1991* (Toronto: McClelland and Stewart, 1992); Christina
Burr, *Spreading the Light: Work and Labour Reform in Late Nineteenth-Century Toronto*
(Toronto: University of Toronto Press, 1999); and Veronica Strong-Boag, "The
Citizenship Debates: The 1885 Franchise Act," in *Contesting Canadian Citizenship:
Historical Readings,* ed. Robert Adamoski, Dorothy Chunn, and Robert Menzies,
69–94 (Toronto: University of Toronto Press, 2002). Quotes on Katie McVicar are
from Kealey and Palmer, *Dreaming of What Might Be,* 143–44, 319, and Veronica
Strong-Boag, "Only the Brave or 'Canada's Daughters Shall be Free' – Respect,
Redistribution, and Suffrage in Women's Struggle for Canadian Democracy," *Women
Suffrage and Beyond: Confronting the Democratic Deficit,* http://womensuffrage.
org/?p=22830.

TWO: RACE AND THE IDEA OF RIGHTS FOR WOMEN
On Shadd, see Jane Rhodes, *Mary Ann Shadd Cary: The Black Press and Protest in the
Nineteenth Century* (Bloomington: Indiana University Press, 1998), especially 22,
212–24, and Shirley Yee, "Finding a Place: Mary Ann Shadd Cary and the Dilemmas
of Black Migration to Canada, 1850–1870," *Frontiers: A Journal of Women's Studies*
18, 3 (1997): 1–16. On African Canadian settlements in southwestern Ontario, see
Peggy Bristow, "Whatever You Raise in the Ground You Can Sell It in Chatham:
Black Women in Buxton and Chatham, 1850–1865," and Afua Cooper, "Black
Women and Work in Nineteenth-Century Canada West: Black Woman Teacher
Mary Bibb," both in *We're Rooted Here and They Can't Pull Us Up: Essays in African
Canadian Women's History,* ed. Peggy Bristow, Dionne Brand, Linda Carty, Afua P.
Cooper, Sylvia Hamilton, and Adrienne Shadd (Toronto: University of Toronto
Press, 1994), 69–142 and 143–70. Shadd's quotes on breaking the editorial ice,
women's rights, education, and her response to Henrietta are from *The Provincial
Freeman,* 12 and 20 April, 6 May, 23 September, 4 November 1854, and 30 June 1855.

For a discussion of the links between abolitionist and feminist politics and writing, see Linda M. Grasso, *The Artistry of Anger: Black and White Women's Literature in America* (Chapel Hill: University of North Carolina Press, 2002) and Martha Jones, *All Bound Up Together: The Woman Question in African American Public Culture* (Chapel Hill: University of North Carolina Press, 2007).

Veronica Strong-Boag provides an excellent discussion of the parliamentary debates in "The Citizenship Debates: The 1885 Franchise Act," in *Contesting Canadian Citizenship: Historical Readings*, ed. Robert Adamoski, Dorothy Chunn, and Robert Menzies, 69–94 (Toronto: University of Toronto Press, 2002). For a discussion of the Six Nations and the 1885 bill, see Malcolm Montgomery, "The Six Nations Indians and the Macdonald Franchise," *Ontario History* 57 (1965): 13–25, and on the history of Six Nations efforts to maintain their own forms of governance, see Andrea Lucille Catapano, "The Rising of the Ongwehònwe: Sovereignty, Identity, and Representation on the Six Nations Reserve" (PhD diss., Stoney Brook University, 2007). "Indian Murderers to Vote – Patriot Volunteers Not to Vote" is from *The Globe*, 2 May 1885. Quotes from MPs during the 1885 debate are from Canada, *House of Commons Debates*, Fifth Parl., Third Sess., 16–17 April, 1133–1204; 21–24 April, 1227–1385; and 27 April to 27 May, 1388–2157.

The Garneau quote is from Bruce Trigger, *Natives and Newcomers: Canada's Heroic Age Reconsidered* (Montreal and Kingston: McGill-Queen's University Press, 1986), 30, and on the nineteenth-century treatment of Indigenous peoples in Canada, see Julie Evans, Patricia Grimshaw, David Philips, and Shurlee Swain, *Equal Subjects, Unequal Rights: Indigenous Peoples in British Settler Colonies, 1830–1910* (Manchester: Manchester University Press, 2003); Daniel Francis, *The Imaginary Indian: The Image of the Indian in Canadian Culture* (Vancouver: Arsenal Pulp Press, 1992); and James Miller, *Skyscrapers Hide the Heavens* (Toronto: University of Toronto Press, 1989). Sarah Carter discusses the racist aftermath of the 1885 Rebellion in *Capturing Women: The Manipulation of Cultural Imagery in the Prairie West* (Kingston and Montreal: McGill-Queen's University Press, 1997) and the history of white women, landownership, and dispossession in *Imperial Plots: Women, Land, and the Spadework of British Colonialism on the Canadian Prairies* (Winnipeg: University of Manitoba Press, 2016).

Matilda Gage's writing on patriarchy, matriarchy, and Indigenous society are taken from her *Women, Church and State* (New York: Truth Seeker, 1893), with quotes also from Sally Roesch Wagner, *Sisters in Spirit: Haudenosaunee (Iroquois) Influence on Early American Feminists* (Summerton, TN: Native Voices, 2001), 39, 49, 65. For Pauline Johnson's words, see "The Iroquois Women of Canada, by One of Their Own," in National Council of Women of Canada, *Women of Canada: Their Life and Work* (Ottawa, 1900), 440–42. For academic studies of Indigenous influences on the suffrage movement, see Gail Landsman, "The 'Other' as Political Symbol:

Images of Indians in the Woman Suffrage Movement," *Ethnohistory* 39, 3 (1992): 251–75. Marlene Brant Castellano discusses women in Indigenous societies in "Women in Huron and Ojibwa Societies," *Canadian Women's Studies* 10, 2–3 (1989): 45–48. The account of the clan mothers and the revolt at the St. Regis/Akwesasne Reserve is told in Rarihokwats, *How Democracy Came to St. Regis and the Thunderwater Movement* (Rooseveltown, NY: Akwesasne Notes, 1974).

THREE: SUFFRAGE AS A SOCIALIST ISSUE

T. Phillips Thompson's (usually known as Phillips Thompson) opening quotes are from Enjolras [his pseudonym], "Woman's Rights," *Palladium of Labor*, 20 March 1886. On the late nineteenth-century Canadian reform movement, see Ramsay Cook, *The Regenerators: Social Criticism in Late Victorian English Canada* (Toronto: University of Toronto Press, 1985) and T. Phillips Thompson, *The Politics of Labor* (Toronto: University of Toronto Press, 1975). On utopian socialism in England, see Barbara Taylor, *Eve and the New Jerusalem: Socialism and Feminism in the Nineteenth Century* (London: Virago Press, 1984), and on Sointula and Kurikka, see Donald Wilson, "Matti Kurikka and A.B. Makela: Socialist Thought among Finns in Canada, 1900–1932," *Canadian Ethnic Studies* 10, 2 (1978): 9–21, and "Matti Kurikka: Finnish-Canadian Intellectual," *BC Studies* 20 (1973): 50–65. On the international mobilization of socialists and feminists, including the 1907 SI conference, see Mary Jo Buhle, *Women and American Socialism, 1870–1920* (Urbana: University of Illinois Press, 1983); Ellen Carol Dubois, "Woman Suffrage and the Left: An International Socialist-Feminist Perspective," *New Left Review* 1, 186 (1991): 20–45; and June Hannam, *Feminism* (London: Pearson Education, 2007).

The quote on Sarah Wrigley is from Linda Kealey, *Enlisting Women for the Cause: Women, Labour and the Left in Canada, 1880–1920* (Toronto: University of Toronto Press, 1998), 95; the quote by Edith Wrigley is from *Cotton's Weekly*, 5 September 1908. For Ruth Lestor's quote and a treatment of both the SPC and SDCP, see Janice Newton, *The Feminist Challenge to the Canadian Left, 1900–1918* (Montreal and Kingston: McGill-Queen's University Press, 1995), 140, 136–49, and for the words of Finnish socialists, see Varpu Lindström, *Defiant Sisters: A Social History of Finnish Immigrant Women in Canada* (Toronto: Multicultural History Society, 1992). On the left, see also Ian McKay, *Reasoning Otherwise: Leftists and People's Enlightenment in Canada, 1890–1920* (Toronto: Between the Lines, 2008), 281–344. Different views within the SPC, including those of Ruth Lestor, are found in the *Western Clarion*: see, for example, 15 September 1908, 26 June 1909, and July 1911. On the non-sneering SDPC, see *Cotton's Weekly*, 9 January 1913. Mary Cotton's columns appear in *Cotton's Weekly* from 1909 to 1913: see, for example, 20 May 1909, 4 May 1911, and 27 March 1913. Dora Foster Kerr's comments on the vote is from *Cotton's Weekly*, 22 April 1909, and her letter to Denison (4 March 1914) resides at the University of Toronto, Thomas Fisher Rare Books Room, Flora MacDonald Denison fonds, box 2.

On the early labour-oriented Winnipeg suffrage group, see Anne Molgat, "*The Voice* and the Women of Winnipeg, 1894–1918" (master's thesis, University of Ottawa, 1988). The Equal Suffrage Club speeches are covered in a series starting 12 March 1895 in the *Winnipeg Voice*, and for Charles Hislop's defence of suffrage and better "human relationships," see Molgat, "*The Voice* and the Women of Winnipeg," 64. On Helena Gutteridge, see Linda Kealey, *Enlisting Women for the Cause*, 148; Irene Howard, *The Struggle for Social Justice in British Columbia: Helena Gutteridge, the Unknown Reformer* (Vancouver: UBC Press, 1992), and the *B.C. Federationist*, 21 November 1913. On the BC and Vancouver movement, see Elsie Gregory MacGill, *My Mother the Judge* (Toronto: Ryerson Press, 1955), and on the Nanaimo resolution, see Doreen Madge Keppler, "Early Forms of Political Activity among White Women in British Columbia, 1880–1925" (master's thesis, University of British Columbia, 1971), 106.

Margaret Haile is fictionalized in CBC TV's *Murdoch Mysteries*, Season 8, Episode 17, "Election Day," aired 23 March 2015.

FOUR: MAKING SUFFRAGISTS
Emily Stowe's 1889 address is quoted online in the *Dictionary of Unitarian and Universalist Biography*. Stowe and Stowe-Gullen's comments come from Victoria College, E.J. Pratt Library Special Collections, Augusta Stowe-Gullen fonds, box 1, scrapbooks. See also Heather Murray, "Great Works and Good Works: The Toronto Women's Literary Club, 1877–1883," *Historical Studies in Education* 11, 1 (1999): 75–95.

The Newfoundland manifesto is reprinted in Margo Iris Duley, "The Radius of Her Influence for Good: The Rise and Triumph of the Women's Suffrage Movement in Newfoundland, 1909–25," in *Pursuing Equality: Historical Perspectives on Women in Newfoundland and Labrador*, ed. Linda Kealey (St. John's: Institute of Social and Economic Research, 1993), Appendix A, 225. Margret Benedictsson's quotes are from Mary Kinnear, "The Icelandic Connection: *Freyja* and the Manitoba Woman Suffrage Movement," in *Canadian Woman Studies: An Introductory Reader*, ed. Nuzhat Amin, 79–85 (Toronto: Inanna, 1997) and Ryan Eyford, "Lucifer Comes to New Iceland: Margret and Sigfus Benedictsson's Radical Critique of Marriage and the Family" (paper presented at the Canadian Historical Association, Saskatoon, May 2007).

New Brunswick suffragists, including Elle Hatheway (and her quote), are discussed in Mary Eileen Clarke, "The Saint John Women's Enfranchisement Association, 1894–1919" (master's thesis, University of New Brunswick, 1979). On the Maritimes, see also Judith Fingard, "The Ritchie Sisters and Social Improvement in Early 20th-Century Halifax," *Journal of the Royal Nova Scotia Historical Society* 13 (2010): 1–22; Duley, "The Radius of Her Influence for Good"; and Michael Joan Smith, "Female Reformers in Victorian Nova Scotia" (master's thesis, St. Mary's University, 1987).

On Dandurand, see Sophie Doucet, "Joséphine Marchand-Dandurand ou 'Le Laurier féminin': Une journaliste féministe, modern, libérale and nationaliste (1861–1925)" (master's thesis, Université de Montréal, 2003) and, on Robertine Barry, see *The Canadian Encyclopedia* online. The FNSJB and Quebec reform and suffrage women are covered by Micheline Dumont in *Feminism à la Québécoise* (Ottawa: Feminist History Society, 2012); Micheline Dumont and Louise Toupin, eds., *La pensée féministe au Québec* (Montreal: Les éditions du remue-ménage, 2003); Karine Hébert, "Une organisation maternaliste au Québec: La Fédération nationale Saint-Jean-Baptiste et la bataille pour le vote des femmes," *Revue d'histoire de l'Amérique française* 52, 3 (1999): 315–44; Marie Lavigne, Yoland Pinard, and Jennifer Stoddart, "The FNSJB and the Women's Movement in Quebec," in *A Not Unreasonable Claim: Women and Reform in Canada, 1880s–1920s*, ed. Linda Kealey, 71–88 (Toronto: Women's Educational Press, 1979). Quotes from Marie Gérin-Lajoie are from *La bonne parole*, 1915–18; for her views on suffrage, see "Entre Nous," *La bonne parole*, December 1917.

Western Canadian issues, including those related to land, dower rights, and reform, are covered in Sarah Carter, *Capturing Women: The Manipulation of Cultural Imagery in Canada's Prairie West* (Montreal and Kingston: McGill-Queen's University Press, 1997); Sarah Carter, *Imperial Plots: Women, Land, and the Spadework of British Colonialism in the Canadian Prairies* (Winnipeg: University of Manitoba Press, 2016); Patricia Roome, "From One Whose Home Is among the Indians: Henrietta Muir Edwards and Aboriginal Peoples," in *Unsettled Pasts: Reconceiving the West through Women's History*, ed. Sarah Carter, Lesley Erickson, Patricia Roome, and Char Smith, 47–78 (Calgary: University of Calgary Press, 2005); Catherine Cavanaugh, "Irene Marryat Parlby: An Imperial 'Daughter' in the Canadian West, 1896–1934," in *Telling Tales: Essays in Western Women's History*, ed. Catherine Cavanaugh and Randi Warne, 100–22 (Vancouver: UBC Press, 2000); and Catherine Cavanaugh, "The Limitations of the Pioneering Partnership: The Alberta Campaign for Homestead Dower, 1909–25," *Canadian Historical Review* 74, 2 (1993): 198–225.

Violet McNaughton quotes are from Georgina Taylor, "Ground for Common Action: Violet McNaughton's Agrarian Feminism and the Origins of the Farm Women's Movement in Canada" (PhD diss., Carleton University, 1997) and James Hughes's quote from *Equal Suffrage* (Toronto: William Briggs, 1895). Quotes on missionary views of Indigenous women are from Sarah Carter, "Categories and Terrains of Exclusion: Constructing the 'Indian Woman' in the Early Settlement Era of Western Canada," *Great Plains Quarterly* 13 (Summer 1993): 147–61, and Kirsten Burnett, "Aboriginal and White Women in the Publications of John Maclean, Egerton Ryerson Young, and John McDougall," in *Unsettled Pasts*. W.H. Alexander is quoted in Sarah Carter, "Geneva Misener, W.H. Alexander, University of Alberta Classics Professors and Women's Suffrage Activists, 1914–1918," *Women Suffrage and Beyond:*

Confronting the Democratic Deficit (online). On British Columbia, see Melanie Ihmels, "The Mischiefmakers: Woman's Movement Development in Victoria, British Columbia, 1850–1910" (master's thesis, University of Victoria, 2013); Michael Cramer, "Public and Political: Documents of the Woman's Suffrage Campaign in British Columbia, 1871–1917: The View from Victoria," in *British Columbia Reconsidered: Essays on Women*, ed. Gillian Creese and Veronica Strong-Boag, 55–72 (Vancouver: Press Gang, 1992).

On nation building and quotes about South Asian immigration, see Enakshi Dua, "The Hindu Woman's Question," *Canadian Woman Studies* 20, 2 (2000): 108–16; Enakshi Dua, "Racialising Imperial Canada: Indian Women and the Making of Ethnic Communities," in *Gender, Sexuality and Colonial Modernities*, ed. Antoinette Burton, 119–33 (London: Routledge, 1999); and *Women's Century*, December 1915. On race, imperialism, and the colour line, see Philip N. Cohen, "Nationalism and Suffrage: Gender Struggle in Nation-Building America," *Signs* 21, 3 (1996): 707–27, and Marilyn Lake and Henry Reynolds, *Drawing the Global Colour Line: White Men's Countries and the International Challenge of Racial Equality* (Cambridge: Cambridge University Press, 2008). Writing on Indigenous women in the early twentieth century includes Henriette Forget, "The Indian Women of Western Provinces," in National Council of Women of Canada, *Women of Canada: Their Life and Work* (Ottawa, 1900), 435–37, and Pauline Johnson, "The Iroquois Women of Canada, by One of Their Own," also in *Women of Canada*, 440–42.

Social reform, eugenics, temperance, and maternalism are discussed in Veronica Strong-Boag, "Introduction" to Nellie McClung, *In Times Like These* (Toronto: University of Toronto Press, 1972), Chris Clarkson, *Domestic Reforms: Political Visions and Family Regulation in British Columbia, 1862–1940* (Vancouver: UBC Press, 2007); Cecily Devereux, *Growing a Race: Nellie L. McClung and the Fiction of Eugenic Feminism* (Montreal and Kingston: McGill-Queen's University Press, 2005); Linda Kealey, ed., *A Not Unreasonable Claim*; and Ian Tyrell, *Woman's World/Woman's Empire: The Woman's Christian Temperance Union in International Perspective, 1880–1930* (Chapel Hill: University of North Carolina Press, 1991). On the National Council of Women of Canada, see Veronica Strong-Boag, *Liberal Hearts and Coronets: The Lives and Times of Ishbel Marjoribanks Gordon and John Campbell Gordon, the Aberdeens* (Toronto: University of Toronto Press, 2015); on the WCTU, see Sharon Cook, *Through Sunshine and Shadow: The Woman's Christian Temperance Union, Evangelicalism, and Reform in Ontario, 1874–1930* (Montreal and Kingston: McGill-Queen's University Press, 1995). Quotes on temperance and eugenics are from *Western Woman's Weekly*, 1918, 1920, and 1922; on the "Eskimo," see *The Champion*, July 1913. The *Calgary Sun* is quoted in Carter et al., eds., *Unsettled Pasts*, 50.

Jean Blewett's quotes are from her pamphlet *The Canadian Woman and Her Work* (Toronto: Canadian Suffrage Association, 1912).

FIVE: THE ANTI-SUFFRAGISTS

The ideas of the elite men against suffrage are discussed in S.E.D. Shortt, *Search for an Ideal: Six Intellectuals and Their Convictions in an Age of Transition* (Toronto: University of Toronto Press, 1979) and in Veronica Strong-Boag, "Independent Women, Problematic Men: First- and Second-Wave Anti-feminism in Canada from Goldwin Smith to Betty Steele," *Histoire sociale/Social History* 29, 57 (1996): 1–22.

The quote that opens the chapter is from Stephen Leacock's "The Woman Question," reprinted in Alan Bowker, ed., *The Social Criticism of Stephen Leacock: The Unsolved Riddle of Social Justice and Other Essays* (Toronto: University of Toronto Press, 1973), and Smith's anti-Semitic comments are quoted in Gerald Tulchinsky, *Taking Root: The Origins of the Canadian Jewish Community* (Toronto: Lester Publishing, 1992), Chap. 12. The quote by Andrew Macphail is from "Votes for Women: An Argument Against, 1914," reprinted in Ramsay Cook and Wendy Mitchinson, eds., *The Proper Sphere: Woman's Place in Canadian Society* (Toronto: Oxford University Press), 300–9; the quote by Goldwin Smith is from his *Essays on Questions of the Day, Political and Social* (New York: Macmillan, 1893). The anti view is presented in the pamphlet by James McGrigor Allan, *Woman Suffrage Wrong in Principle and Practice: An Essay* (London: Remington, 1890), and a counter view appears in R.J. Hutcheon, *Man's World* (Toronto: Canadian Suffrage Association, 1911). The words of French Canadian antis are found in Susan Mann Trofimenkoff, "Henri Bourassa and the 'Woman Question,'" in *The Neglected Majority: Essays in Canadian Women's History,* ed. Susan Trofimenkoff and Alison Prentice, 104–15 (Toronto: McClelland and Stewart, 1977), and in Marie-Aimée Cliche, "Droits égaux ou influence accrue? Nature et rôle de la femme d'après les féministes chrétiennes et les antiféministes au Québec 1896–1930," *Recherches féministes* 2, 2 (1989): 101–19. The *Champion* quotations are from November 1912, November 1913, and April 1914.

Clementina Fessenden and the Toronto AOWSC are quoted in Sheila Eileen Powell, "The Opposition to Woman Suffrage in Ontario, 1872–1917" (master's thesis, Carleton University, 1987). The AOWSC is also discussed by Wayne Roberts in "Rocking the Cradle for the World: The New Woman and Maternal Feminism, Toronto 1877–1914" in *A Not Unreasonable Claim: Women and Reform in Canada, 1880s–1920s,* ed. Linda Kealey, 15–46 (Toronto: The Women's Press, 1979). The quotes by New Brunswick anti-suffragists are from Shannon M. Risk, "Against Women's Suffrage: The Case of Maine and New Brunswick," *American Review of Canadian Studies* 42, 3 (2012): 384–400; the quote by James Wilberforce Longley is from Michael J. Smith, "Female Reformers in Victorian Nova Scotia: Architects of a New Womanhood" (master's thesis, Saint Mary's University, 1986). Newfoundland examples are taken from Margo Duley, *Where Once Our Mothers Stood We Stand: Women's Suffrage in Newfoundland, 1890–1925* (Charlottetown: Gynergy Books, 1993), 32, 89.

The American antis are analyzed in Susan E. Marshall, *Splintered Sisterhood: Gender and Class in the Campaign against Woman Suffrage* (Madison: University of Wisconsin Press, 1997); cartoons are discussed in Alice Sheppard, *Cartooning for Suffrage* (Albuquerque: University of New Mexico Press, 1994) and in Katharina Hundhammer, *American Women in Cartoons, 1890–1920* (Frankfurt: Peter Land, 2012).

SIX: FEMINIST COUNTERCULTURES

Nellie McClung's fictional account of the Winnipeg Mock Parliament is in *Purple Springs* (Toronto: The Ryerson Press, 1921), 273–89. On Mock Parliaments, see Kym Bird, "Performing Politics: Propaganda, Parody and a Women's Parliament," *Theatre Research in Canada/Recherches théâtrales au Canada* 13, 1–2 (1992): https://journals.lib.unb.ca/index.php/TRIC/article/view/7253/8312.

For first-hand descriptions of the 1896 Toronto Mock Parliament, see *Evening Star*, 17 February 1896, and *The Globe*, 18 February 1896. Nellie McClung's quotes from the Winnipeg Mock Parliament of 1914 are from the *Winnipeg Free Press*, 29 January 1914, and reprinted in Nellie McClung, *The Stream Runs Fast* (Toronto: Thomas Allen and Son, 1965), 120–22.

For a discussion of emotion and affect in feminist organizing, see Rosemary Hennessy, "Open Secrets: The Affective Cultures of Organizing on Mexico's Northern Border," *Feminist Theory* 10, 3 (2009): 309–22, and on later feminist journalism and the "public sphere," see Barbara Marshall, "Communications as Politics: Feminist Print Media in English Canada," *Women's Studies International Forum* 18, 4 (1995): 463–74. Feminist journalism in the suffrage era is discussed in Ramsay Cook, "Francis Marion Beynon and the Crisis of Christian Reformism," in *The West and the Nation: Essays in Honour of W.L. Morton*, ed. Carl Berger and Ramsay Cook, 187–209 (Toronto: McClelland and Stewart, 1976); Janice Fiamengo, *The Woman's Page: Journalism and Rhetoric in Early Canada* (Toronto: University of Toronto Press, 2008); Sophie Doucet, "Joséphine Marchand-Durand ou 'Le Laurier féminin': Une journaliste féministe, modern, libérale and nationaliste (1861–1925)" (master's thesis, Université de Montréal, 2003); Deborah Gorham, "Flora MacDonald Denison: Canadian Feminist," in *A Not Unreasonable Claim: Women and Reform in Canada, 1880s–1920s*, ed. Linda Kealey, 47–70 (Toronto: Women's Press, 1979); Tracy Kulba and Victoria Lamont, "The Periodical Press and Western Woman's Suffrage Movements in Canada and the United States: A Comparative Study," *Women's Studies International Forum* 29, 3 (2006): 265–78; and Michele Lacombe, "Songs of the Open Road: Bon Echo, Urban Utopians and the Cult of Nature," *Journal of Canadian Studies* 33, 2 (1998): 152–67.

Quotes from women's columns and articles appeared in *La bonne parole*, 1919, and *The Champion*, 1912 to 1914. Those from the *Grain Growers' Guide* are reproduced in

Barbara Kelcey and Angela Davis, eds., *A Great Movement Underway: Women and the Grain Growers' Guide, 1908–1928* (Winnipeg: Manitoba Record Society, 1997). Denison's columns from *The World* and other journalism are collected in her papers, as is the private letter quoted. The collection is located at the University of Toronto, Thomas Fisher Rare Books Room, Flora MacDonald Denison fonds, box 2. Quotes about Denison are from Fiamengo, *The Woman's Page*, 166. International coverage is from *Votes for Women,* including Pethick-Lawrence's article, 11 October 1912. All comments written to Catherine Cleverdon, including those of Lillian Thomas, are from Library and Archives Canada (LAC), Catherine Cleverdon Fonds, MG 30 D160, box 1.

For responses to the suffragettes, see June Hannam, *Feminism* (Edinburgh: Pearson Longman, 2007); Gretchen Wilson, *With All Her Might: The Life of Gertrude Harding, Militant Suffragette* (Fredericton: Goose Lane, 1996); Kulba and Lamont, "The Periodical Press"; and Deborah Gorham, "English Militancy and the Canadian Suffrage Movement," *Atlantis* 1, 1 (1975): 83–112. Laura McCully's comments and those of Helen Cunningham are from Sophia Sperdakos, "'For the Joy of the Working': Laura Elizabeth McCully, First-Wave Feminist," *Ontario History* 84, 4 (1992): 283–314. Pageants and parades are described in *The Champion;* the Washington parade in *The Toronto Daily Star,* 1, 3, 4 7, 25, 27 March 1913, and in *The Globe,* 3, 12, 14, 15 March 1913.

On consumer culture, cartoons, and film, see Margaret Finnegan, *Selling Suffrage: Consumer Culture and Votes for Women* (New York: Columbia University Press, 1999); Katharina Hundhammer, *American Women in Cartoons, 1890–1920* (Frankfurt: Peter Lang, 2012); Alice Sheppard, *Cartooning for Suffrage* (Albuquerque: University of New Mexico Press, 1994); Kay Sloan, "Sexual Warfare in the Silent Cinema: Comedies and Melodramas of Woman Suffragism," *American Quarterly* 33, 4 (1981): 412–36; Shelley Stamp, *Movie Struck Girls: Women and Motion Picture Culture after the Nickelodeon* (Princeton: Princeton University Press, 2000); and the screenings in Montreal in Laura Carlson, "A Demonstration of Citizenship: The Response of Canadian Suffragists to the Emergence of Film" (master's thesis, Carleton University, 2012).

For an introduction to New Woman short stories and those quoted, see Lorraine McMullen and Sandra Campbell, eds., *New Women: Short Stories by Canadian Women, 1900–1920* (Ottawa: University of Ottawa Press, 1997). McClung's stories also appear in Marilyn Davis, ed., *Stories Subversive: Through the Field with Gloves Off – Short Fiction by Nellie McClung* (Ottawa: University of Ottawa Press, 1996). For two different views on McClung, see Randi Warne, *Literature as Pulpit: The Christian Social Activism of Nellie L. McClung* (Waterloo: Wilfrid Laurier University Press, 1993) and Cecily Devereux, *Growing a Race: Nellie L. McClung and the Fiction of Eugenic Feminism* (Montreal and Kingston: McGill-Queen's University Press, 2005). Writing about working-class women, including Marie Joussaye's "Only a Working Girl," is discussed in Lindsey McMaster, *Working Girls in the West: Representations of Wage-Earning Women* (Vancouver: UBC Press, 2008).

Pauline Johnson is discussed in Veronica Strong-Boag, "A Red Girl's Reasoning," in *Painting the Maple: Essays on Race, Gender, and the Construction of Canada*, ed. Veronica Strong-Boag, Joan Anderson, Sherrill Grace, and Avigail Eisenberg, 130–54 (Vancouver: UBC Press, 1998); Veronica Strong-Boag and Carole Gerson, *Paddling Her Own Canoe: The Times and Texts of E. Pauline Johnson, Tekahionwake* (Toronto: University of Toronto Press, 2000); Edith Eaton (Sui Sin Far) in Jinhua Emma Teng, "Miscegenation and the Critique of Patriarchy in Turn-of-the-Century Fiction," *Asian American Studies: A Reader*, ed. Jean Yu-wen Shen Wu and Min Song, 95–110 (Piscataway, NJ: Rutgers University Press, 2000); and Mary Chapman, *Becoming "Sui Sin Far": Early Fiction, Journalism, and Travel Writing by Edith Maude Eaton* (Kingston and Montreal: McGill-Queen's University Press, 2016). Other short stories quoted include Francis Marion Beynon (Ginty Beynon), "Noonie: A Story of Thirty Years Ago in the New Canadian Northwest," *Munsey's Magazine*, November 1925, 253–55; Margret Benedictsson, "The Widow," in *Writings by Western Icelandic Women*, ed. and trans. Kirsten Wolf, 74–79 (Winnipeg: University of Manitoba Press, 1996); and Laura Goodman Salverson, "Hidden Fire," *Maclean's*, 15 February 1923, 14, 50–51. Flora MacDonald Denison's unpublished "Pateeka" is in her papers, cited above. Jean Blewett's nonfiction article from *Colliers* was reprinted as *The Canadian Woman and Her Work* (Toronto: Canadian Suffrage Association, 1912).

SEVEN: DEBATING WAR AND PEACE

J.G. Sime, "Munitions," is reprinted in *New Women: Short Stories by Canadian Women, 1900–1920*, ed. Sandra Campbell and Lorraine McMullen (Ottawa: University of Ottawa Press, 1997), 326–33. On women's war experience, see Sarah Glassford and Amy Shaw, *A Sisterhood of Suffering and Service: Women and Girls of Canada and Newfoundland during the First World War* (Vancouver: UBC Press, 2012); Joan Sangster, "Mobilizing Canadian Women for World War I," in *Canada and the Great War*, ed. David Mackenzie, 157–93 (Toronto: University of Toronto Press, 2005); Linda Kealey, *Enlisting Women for the Cause: Women, Labour and the Left in Canada, 1890–1920* (Toronto: University of Toronto Press, 1998), Chaps. 5 and 6; and Linda Kealey, "Women and Labour during World War I: Women Workers and the Minimum Wage in Manitoba," in *First Days, Fighting Days: Women in Manitoba History*, ed. Mary Kinnear, 76–99 (Regina: Canadian Plains Research Center, 1987).

Jean Blewett's quote is from *Canadian Women and Their Work* (Toronto: Canadian Suffrage Association, 1912); Augusta Stowe-Gullen and Denison are quoted in *Report of the Proceedings of the Deputation of the Canadian Suffrage Association* (c. 1912); and the Borden interview with the WSPU ran in *The Champion* in September 1912. For quotes on the war, see *La bonne parole*, March 1918; *Women's Century*, August 1916; and *Western Woman's Weekly*, June 1924.

Francis Beynon's comment on the Manitoba victory is from the *Grain Growers' Guide,* 9 February 1916. To learn more about temperance and suffrage victories on the Prairies, see John Thompson, *The Harvests of War: The Prairie West, 1914–1918* (Toronto: McClelland and Stewart, 1978) and Elizabeth Ann Kalmakoff, "Woman Suffrage in Saskatchewan" (master's thesis, University of Regina, 1993). Billy Bowser's quote appears in Irene Howard, *The Struggle for Social Justice in British Columbia: Helena Gutteridge, the Unknown Reformer* (Vancouver: UBC Press, 1992), 85. For developments in Ontario, see Bryan Tennyson, "Premier Hearst, the War, and Votes for Women," *Ontario History* 57, 3 (1965): 115–22; for the Maritimes, see Janet Guildford, "Edith Jessie Archibald: Ardent Feminist and Conservative Reformer," *Journal of the Royal Nova Scotia Historical Society* 11 (2008): 110–33, and Ernest Forbes, "The Ideas of Carol Bacchi and the Suffragists of Halifax: A Review Essay on *Liberation Deferred: The Ideas of the English Canadian Suffragists, 1877–1918,*" *Atlantis* 10, 2 (1985): 119–26. Comments made to Cleverdon are from her letters, box 1, Cleverdon fonds, Library and Archives Canada.

Denison's pamphlet *War and Women* is reproduced in Nancy Forestall and Maureen Moynagh, eds., *Documenting First Wave Feminisms,* Vol. 2, *Canada – National and Transnational Contexts* (Toronto: University of Toronto Press, 2014), 293–97; McClung's comments are from *In Times Like These* (Toronto: University of Toronto Press, 1972); Constance Boulton's are from *Women's Century,* January 1918. Letters about Denison's New York state organizing are from Thomas Fisher Rare Books Room, Denison Fonds, box 2.

Laura Hughes is discussed in Barbara Roberts, "Why Do Women Do Nothing to End the War?," *Canadian Feminist-Pacifists and the Great War* (Ottawa: CRIAW, 1985), and quotes by Gertrude Richardson are taken from Barbara Roberts, *A Reconstructed World: A Feminist Biography of Gertrude Richardson* (Montreal and Kingston: McGill-Queen's University Press, 1996) and her columns in the socialist paper the *Canadian Forward,* 24 November 1917. Helena Gutteridge's views on war are from the *B.C. Federationist,* September and October 1914 and discussed in Howard, *The Struggle for Social Justice.* Biographical information on Wales is in Lorna McLean, "The Necessity of Going: Julia Grace Wales's Transnational Life as a Peace Activist and a Scholar," in *Feminist History in Canada: New Essays on Women, Gender, Work and Nation,* ed. Catherine Carstairs and Nancy Janovicek, 77–95 (Vancouver: UBC Press, 2013).

Quotes on conscription appear in *La bonne parole,* June 1917, and *Women's Century,* September and November 1917. The FNSJB's opposition to the WEA is quoted in *La bonne parole,* October 1917, and Harriet Prenter is quoted in Kealey, *Enlisting Women for the Cause,* 216. Constance Boulton's support for the WEA is recorded in *Women's Century,* January 1918. On the 1917 election, see Tarah Brookfield, "Divided by the Ballot Box: The Montreal Council of Women and the 1917 Election," *Canadian*

Historical Review 89, 4 (2008): 473–502; Ramsay Cook, "Francis Marion Beynon and the Crisis of Christian Reformism," in *The West and the Nation: Essays in Honour of W.L. Morton,* ed. Carol Berger and Ramsay Cook, 187–209 (Toronto: McClelland and Stewart, 1976); and Deborah Gorham, "Flora MacDonald Denison: Canadian Feminist," in *A Not Unreasonable Claim: Women and Reform in Canada, 1880s–1920s,* ed. Linda Kealey, 47–70 (Toronto: Women's Press, 1979), 47–70.

Francis Marion Beynon's parting critique appeared in *Canadian Forward,* 10 December 1917. The conflict between McClung and Beynon is captured in Wendy Lill's play *The Fighting Days* (Vancouver: Talonbooks, 1985) and with Winnipeg socialist and labour women in Paul Kelly, prod., *The Notorious Mrs. Armstrong* (Buffalo Gal Pictures, 2001).

EIGHT: OLD AND NEW AGENDAS IN PEACETIME
The excerpt from a newspaper clipping that opens this chapter comes from the Leon Ladner Fonds, MS 641, "Voters, Women," clippings file, Vancouver City Archives. The Idola Saint-Jean quote comes from *La Sphère féminine,* 1934. The *Chatelaine* articles discussed are as follows: Grattan O'Leary, "Is Women's Suffrage a Success?," *Chatelaine,* September 1930, 12, 52; Helen Gregory MacGill, "Are Women Wanted in Public Life?," September 1928, 2–4; and Mrs. George Holis, Miss Mildred Low, Miss Beatrice Brigden, Miss F.S. Greenwood, and Mrs. Donald Macdonald, "Why I Failed to Be Elected," October 1930, 17, 37. On the sputtering of the movement, see Robert Clarke and Patricia McMahon, *The Persons Case: The Origins and Legacy of the Fight for Legal Personhood* (Toronto: University of Toronto Press, 2008), 7.

On New Brunswick, see Elspeth Tulloch, *We, the Undersigned: A Historical Overview of New Brunswick Women's Political and Legal Status, 1784–1984* (Moncton: New Brunswick Advisory Council on the Status of Women, 1985); on PEI, see Catherine Cleverdon, *The Women's Suffrage Movement in Canada* (Toronto: University of Toronto Press, 1974 [1950]), 200–8. For quotes on the Newfoundland struggle, see Margo Duley, *Where Once Our Mothers Stood We Stand: Women's Suffrage in Newfoundland, 1890–1925* (Charlottetown: Gynergy Books, 1993), 75–76; on the early 1920s, see Sean Cadigan, *Death on Two Fronts: National Tragedies and the Fate of Democracy in Newfoundland, 1914–34* (Toronto: Penguin, 2013).

For the Quebec struggle, see Thérèse Casgrain, *A Woman in a Man's World,* trans. Joyce Marshall (Toronto: McClelland and Stewart, 1972); Karine Hébert, "Une organisation maternaliste au Québec: La Fédération nationale Saint-Jean-Baptiste et la bataille pour le vote des femmes," *Revue d'histoire de l'Amérique française* 52, 3 (1999): 315–44; Gabrielle Roy, *The Tin Flute* (Toronto: McClelland and Stewart, 1989); Louise Toupin, "Des 'usages' de la maternité en histoire du feminism," *Recherches féministes* 9, 2 (1996): 113–35; Micheline Dumont, *Feminism à la Québécoise* (Ottawa: Feminist History Society, 2012); Andrée Lévesque, *Making and Breaking the Rules:*

Women in Quebec, 1919–1939 (Toronto: Oxford University Press, 1994). Tachereau's "Latin mentality" and Scott's responses are from *Jus Suffragii*, March and December 1922; for Quebec women's resolutions to the British Dominion Women Citizens Union conferences, see London School of Economics, Women's Library, British Commonwealth League Papers, BDWCU Annual Reports, 1925–39. Quebec suffragist writings appear in *La bonne parole*, December 1917 and February and May 1918, including Casgrain's call for "serene" suffragists, January 1928. Quotes by Idola Saint-Jean's are from Diane Lamoureux, "Idola Saint-Jean et le radicalism féministe de l'entre-deux-guerres," *Recherches féministes* 4, 2 (1991): 45–60; *La Sphére féminine*, 1935; and her radio address, "Discours d'Idola Saint-Jean: Radio diffusé sous les auspices de l'alliance Canadienne pour le Vote des Femmes du Québec," in Biblioteque de la Ville de Montreal, Collection Gagnon. Quotes by Éva Circé-Côté are from "Le suffrage féminine," in Andrée Lévesque, *Chroniques d'Éva Circé-Côté: Lumière sur la société québécoise, 1900–1942* (Montreal: Les éditions du remue-ménage, 2011), 176–79.

On the gender divide during the 1919 General strike, see Todd McCallum, "'Not a Sex Question'? The One Big Union and the Politics of Radical Manhood," *Labour/ Le Travail* 42 (Fall 1998): 15–54; on US postwar conservative tendencies, see Kirsten Marie Delegard, *Battling Miss Bolsheviki: The Origins of Female Conservatism in the United States* (Philadelphia: University of Pennsylvania Press, 2012), esp. 47–51; June Purvis, *Emmeline Pankhurst: A Biography* (London: Routledge, 2002), 318–39; and on the waitress and race issue in Vancouver, see Lilynn Wan, "Out of Many Kindreds and Tongues: Racial Identity and Rights Activism in Vancouver, 1919–1939" (PhD diss., Dalhousie University, 2011). The Vancouver Women's Party quote comes from *Western Woman's Weekly*, 28 March 1918, and the portrait of Emily Murphy is from Clarke and McMahon, *The Persons Case*.

On peace and imperialism, see Peter Campbell, *Rose Henderson: A Woman for the People* (Montreal and Kingston: McGill-Queen's University Press, 2010). On Henderson, see her *Woman and War* (Vancouver: Federated Labour Party, 1925) and her testimony for the 1919 Mathers committee, quoted in Joan Sangster, "Mobilizing Canadian Women for World War I," in *Canada and the Great War*, ed. David Mackenzie, 157–93 (Toronto: University of Toronto Press, 2005). The Six Nations are discussed in *Jus Suffragii*, December 1923, and Jamieson's speech at the Pan Pacific conference appeared in the *Vancouver Sun*, 26 July 1937.

On education, see the 1930 report in *Jus Suffragii*, including Montreal feminists lobbying McGill and the Agnes Macphail quote appear in Thomas Socknat, "For Peace and Freedom: Canadian Feminists in the Interwar Peace Campaign," in *Up and Doing: Canadian Women and Peace*, ed. Janice Williamson and Deborah Gorham, 66–90 (Toronto: Women's Press, 1989). On women and school boards, see Patricia Roome, "Amelia Turner and Calgary Labour Women, 1919–35," in *Beyond the Vote:*

Canadian Women and Politics, ed. Linda Kealey and Joan Sangster, 89–117 (Toronto: University of Toronto Press, 1989). Regarding labour, ethnicity, and the left, the UWEFO is quoted in James Naylor, *The New Democracy: Challenging the Social Order in Industrial Ontario, 1914–1925* (Toronto: University of Toronto Press, 1991), 140–41, and the quote by Beatrice Brigden is from Joan Sangster, "The Making of a Socialist Feminist: The Early Career of Beatrice Brigden," *Atlantis* 13, 1 (1987): 13–28. The quote by Sanna Kannasto comes from Varpu Lindström, *Defiant Sisters: A Social History of Finnish Immigrant Women in Canada* (Toronto: Multicultural History Society, 1992), 151. On African Canadian women, see Peggy Bristow, "The Hour-a-Day Study Club," in *And Still We Rise: Feminist Political Mobilizing in Contemporary Canada,* ed. Linda Carty, 145–72 (Toronto: Women's Press, 1997) and Jennifer Mills, "A Critical Examination of the Early Years of the Hour-a-Day Study Club, 1935–1955" (master's thesis, University of Windsor, 1995).

On international comparisons and connections, see Maria DiCenzo, "Our Freedom and Its Results: Measuring Progress in the Aftermath of Suffrage," *Women's History Review* 23, 3 (2014): 421–40; Angela Woolacott, *To Try Her Fortune in London: Australian Women, Colonialism, and Modernity* (London: Oxford University Press, 2001); and Fiona Paisley, *Glamour in the Pacific: Cultural Internationalism and Race Politics in the Women's Pan-Pacific* (Honolulu: University of Hawai'i Press, 2009).

NINE: VOTES FOR ALL WOMEN

Muriel Kitagawa's quotes in the epigraph come from *This Is My Own: Letters to Wes and Other Writing on Japanese Canadians, 1941–1948* (Vancouver: Talonbooks, 1985). Hideko Hyodo's testimony appears in Canada, House of Commons Special Committee on Elections Acts, 22 May 1936.

On race and the early suffragists, see Janice Fiamengo, "Rediscovering Our Foremothers Again: The Racial Ideas of Canada's Early Feminists, 1885–1945," *Essays on Canadian Writing* 75 (2002): 85–117; Janice Fiamengo, "The Death of the New Woman in Sara Jeannette Duncan's *A Daughter of Today," Studies in Canadian Literature* 34, 1 (2009): 5–21; Sara Jeannette Duncan, *The Imperialist* (Toronto: McClelland and Stewart, 1971 [1904]); Linda Ambrose, "Our Last Frontier: Imperialism and Northern Canadian Rural Women's Organization," *Canadian Historical Review* 86, 2 (June 2005): 257–84; Katie Pickles, *Female Imperialism and National Identity: The Imperial Order Daughters of the Empire* (Manchester: Manchester University Press, 2002); and Melinda Plastas, *A Band of Noble Women: Racial Politics in the Women's Peace Movement* (Syracuse: Syracuse University Press, 2011). On Violet McNaughton, see Georgina Taylor, "Ground for Common Action: Violet McNaughton's Agrarian Feminism and the Origins of the Farm Women's Movement in Canada" (PhD diss., Carleton University, 1997), and McNaughton's *Western Producer* column reprinted in *The Native Voice,* October 1947. Helen Gregory MacGill's study "The Oriental Delinquent in the Vancouver Juvenile Court," 1935, can be located at Library and Archives Canada, Japanese Canadian Citizen's Collection, MG 28, V 8, vol. 17, file 14.

On the context for Aboriginal enfranchisement, see Robin Brownlie, "'Living the Same as the White People': Mohawk and Anishinabe Women's Labour in Southern Ontario, 1920–1940," *Labour/Le travail* 61 (2008): 41–68; Alan Cairns, *Citizens Plus: Aboriginal Peoples and the Canadian State* (Vancouver: UBC Press, 2000); H.B. Hawthorne, C.S. Belshaw, and S.M. Jamieson, *The Indians of British Columbia: A Study of Contemporary Social Adjustment* (Toronto: University of Toronto Press, 1958); Aroha Harris and Mary Jane Logan McCallum, "'Assaulting the Ears of the Government': The Indian Homemaker Clubs and Maori Women's Welfare League," in *Indigenous Women and Work: From Labor to Activism*, ed. Carol Williams, 225–39 (Urbana: University of Illinois Press, 2012); R. Scott Sheffield, *The Red Man's on the Warpath: The Image of the "Indian" and the Second World War* (Vancouver: UBC Press, 2004); and Paul Tennant, *Aboriginal People and Politics: The Indian Land Question in British Columbia, 1849–1989* (Vancouver: UBC Press, 1989).

For more on Constance Cook and the quote from Andrew Paull, see Leslie Robertson with the Kwagu'l Gixsam Clan, *Standing Up with Ga'axsta'las: Jane Constance Cook and the Politics of Memory, Church, and Custom* (Vancouver: UBC Press, 2014), 381. Quotes on the vote appear in the following issues of the *Native Voice*: July 1948, February 1960, April 1960, November 1947 [Constance Cook]; and May 1947 [Peter Kelley]. Federal documents quoted include the Senate and House of Commons Joint Committee on the Indian Act, *Minutes and Proceedings of Evidence*, March 1947, and the Senate and House of Commons Joint Committee on Indian Affairs, *Minutes and Proceedings of Evidence*, June 1959. See also *House of Commons Debates*, Twentieth Parl., Fourth Sess., 15 June 1948, and Twenty-Forth Parl., Third Sess., 8–10 March 1960. For newspaper coverage, see *Globe and Mail*, 16 June 1948, and 10, 11, 12 March 1960; *Vancouver Sun*, 1 March 1947.

On the treatment of Japanese Canadians and the fight against discrimination, see Ken Adachi, *The Enemy That Never Was: A History of the Japanese in Canada* (Toronto: McClelland and Stewart, 1976); Edith Fowke, *They Made Democracy Work: The Story of the Co-operative Committee on Japanese Canadians* (Toronto: Japanese Canadian Citizens Association, 1951); Patricia Roy, *The Oriental Question: Consolidating a White Man's Province, 1914–41* (Vancouver: UBC Press, 2004); Roy Miki, *Redress: Inside the Japanese Canadian Call for Justice* (Vancouver: Raincoast Books, 2004); Patricia Roy, *The Triumph of Citizenship: The Japanese and Chinese in Canada, 1941–67* (Vancouver: UBC Press, 2007); Jean Barman, *The West beyond the West: A History of British Columbia* (Toronto: University of Toronto Press, 2007); Ann Gomer Sunahara, *The Politics of Racism: The Uprooting of Japanese Canadians during the Second World War* (Toronto: James Lorimer, 1981); and Stephanie Bangarth, *Voices Raised in Protest: Defending North American Citizens of Japanese Ancestry, 1942–1949* (Vancouver: UBC Press, 2008).

Racist quotes are from *Western Woman's Weekly,* 18 April 1918, 8 June 1918, and 11 October 1922, and from Roy, *The Oriental Question,* 157. On the Native Sons, see Lilynn Wan, "Out of Many Kindreds and Tongues: Racial Identity and Rights Activism in Vancouver, 1919–1939" (PhD diss., Dalhousie University, 2011), 65–71. All quotes by Muriel Kitagawa are from *This Is My Own,* and newspaper coverage is taken from the *Vancouver Sun,* 1, 2, 8, 18, 22, 25, 31 March 1949.

AFTERWORD

The first full-length study of suffrage was Catherine Cleverdon's *The Woman Suffrage Movement in Canada* (Toronto: University of Toronto Press, 1950), followed over thirty years later by more critical views such as those presented in Carol Bacchi, *Liberation Deferred? The Ideas of the English-Canadian Suffragists, 1877–1918* (Toronto: University of Toronto Press, 1983) and Mariana Valverde, "'When the Mother of the Race Is Free': Race, Reproduction and Sexuality in First Wave Feminism," in *Gender Conflicts: New Essays in Women's History,* ed. Franca Iacovetta and Mariana Valverde, 3–26 (Toronto: University of Toronto Press, 1992). For a more contemporary reflection, see Veronica Strong-Boag, "Taking Stock of Suffragists: Personal Reflections on Feminist Appraisals," *Journal of the Canadian Historical Association/Revue de la Société historique du Canada* 24, 2 (2010): 76–89.

On "hidden costs," see Patricia Grimshaw and Katherine Ellinghaus, "White Women, Aboriginal Women and the Vote in Western Australia," *Studies in Western Australian History* 19 (1999): 1–19. For international comparisons, see Caroline Daley and Melanie Nolan, eds., *Suffrage and Beyond: International Feminist Perspectives* (New York: NYU Press, 1994); June Hannam, "International Dimensions of Women's Suffrage: 'At the Crossroads of Several Interlocking Identities,'" *Women's History Review* 14, 3–4 (2005): 543–60; and Jad Adams, *Women and the Vote: A World History* (Oxford: Oxford University Press, 2014).

PHOTO CREDITS

Page 13: Antoine Plamondon, *Julie Papineau (née Bruneau) and her daughter Ézilda,* 1836, oil on canvas, 121.8 x 107 cm, National Gallery of Canada, Ottawa.

Page 24: *Potash Boiling,* from Charles W. Jefferys, *The Picture Gallery of Canadian History* (Toronto: Ryerson, 1945), 2:222.

Page 33: From a photograph published in a newspaper, c. 1845, photographer unknown, Library and Archives Canada, C-029977.

Page 55: Major Matthews Collection, Vancouver City Archives, AM54-S4-2 CVA 371-2693-HG.

Page 65: Political cartoons, *Prostitution, Western Clarion,* 2 August 1913; *A Reminder, Vancouver Sun,* 2 December 1913.

Page 70: J. Newton Fonds, York University, 2014-034/006 (23).

Page 79: Victoria College Archives, University of Toronto.

Page 88: *Freyja* cover courtesy of the Icelandic Collection, Elizabeth Dafoe Library, University of Manitoba; photo of Benedictsson courtesy of Sigrid Johnson.

Page 93: Library and Archives Canada, Catherine Cleverdon fonds, C-068507.

Page 95: University of Saskatoon Archives, S-B2048.

Page 146: Photograph by E. Lyont, Library of Congress, Manuscript Division, National Woman's Party Records, group 1, container I:149.

Page 161: Flora MacDonald Denison Fonds, University of Toronto Thomas Fisher Rare Books Room, vol. 2.

Page 162: Thunder Bay Finnish Canadian Historical Society Collection, Lakehead University Archives, series D, category H, item 478.

Page 195: War Records Survey Posters, Library and Archives Canada, R 1185-67-0-E, no. 3667273.

Page 200: Archives of Manitoba, N13687.

Page 205: Library and Archives Canada, C-009482.

INDEX

Note: "(f)" after a page number indicates an illustration.